Collaboration with Cloud Computing

Collaboration with Cloud Computing

Security, Social Media, and Unified Communications

Ric Messier

Allan Konar, Technical Editor

AMSTERDAM • BOSTON • HEIDELBERG • LONDON
NEW YORK • OXFORD • PARIS • SAN DIEGO
SAN FRANCISCO • SINGAPORE • SYDNEY • TOKYO
Syngress is an imprint of Elsevier

SYNGRESS.

Acquiring Editor: *Steve Elliot*
Editorial Project Manager: *Benjamin Rearick*
Project Manager: *Malathi Samayan*
Designer: *Matthew Limbert*

Syngress is an imprint of Elsevier
225 Wyman Street, Waltham, MA 02451, USA

Library of Congress Cataloging-in-Publication Data
Application Submitted

British Library Cataloguing-in-Publication Data
A catalogue record for this book is available from the British Library

ISBN: 978-0-12-417040-7

For information on all Syngress publications,
visit our website at www.syngress.com

Working together
to grow libraries in
developing countries

www.elsevier.com • www.bookaid.org

This book is dedicated to my sister, Cheryl, for the strength she has demonstrated over the last couple of years. It's also dedicated to Zoey, who was always an inspiration to me.

Contents

Preface

This book began in a conference room with the realization that cloud services are exploding, and the open nature of them as well as the ease of their use means anyone can sign up for a service. This may be completely outside of the context and control of the company's security organization as well as its traditional information technology group. Storing business data with another provider could put the company at risk, and there is a potential liability that exposes the company to. It seemed like a good idea to think about and talk about how to make use of cloud services in a way that encourages businesses to think about how they could benefit from them while also educating their people to the risks as well as the rewards of cloud computing.

Eventually, I had an opportunity to give a talk at Interop New York in the fall of 2012 and talking about cloud computing and social media seemed like a good buzzword laden topic but since I'm still a security guy at my core, I wanted to make sure I had a security spin on it. I can't say the talk was a huge success. However, it did provide me with an idea to pitch the whole thing as a book, which eventually led me here with the completed manuscript off in production, writing the preface. The process of writing the book and the experiences I had playing around with different services and looking at different providers got me rethinking the whole project a little.

As I was writing, it became clear that there is one thing that ties everything we'll be talking about in this book together. That idea is collaboration. Businesses really need their employees to be able to work together effectively—to collaborate. Without that collaboration, businesses are far less productive. When businesses can find ways to foster collaboration and productivity, they have a far better chance of succeeding. It is clear that cloud computing can be a vehicle for businesses to save costs and enable collaboration and productivity.

Additionally, cloud computing in its many forms can free businesses from geographic constraints. While some businesses may be tied to the work force in their area, knowledge-based businesses can reach out beyond the region they are in and hire anywhere they can find the talent they need to make their business thrive. This is even easier if the business is putting their infrastructure with service providers, rather than relying on the more traditional virtual private network (VPN) model to support employees.

Cloud computing does have a number of forms and even though it's become something of a catch-all name, almost on the brink of losing all meaning, it is a useful umbrella term to describe outsourcing a wide range of information technology (IT) services to service providers. Companies have been doing this on and off for decades, but with network access coming down in price and service providers building out extensive and robust infrastructure, a variety of services can be very cost effective. This may include storage, a number of applications like customer relationship management, and even simply offering virtual servers for companies to use any way they see fit.

Being a security guy, I'm especially interested in ensuring that businesses understand the risks associated with deploying cloud services, and there are certainly plenty of risks. This doesn't mean that businesses should avoid these services. After all, nearly every activity comes with a measure of risks. However, making an informed decision requires understanding the risk so it can be weighed against benefit and costs. My hope is that this book will provide some ideas on how businesses can make use of cloud services to improve their businesses processes or save costs while also ensuring they are looking out for the security of the company.

Intended audience

This book is intended for anyone who may have an interest in learning more about cloud services, including how businesses can make effective use of them. I hope that business executives will find the content of the book helpful so they can understand the technical challenges, as well as the security considerations related to the adoption of cloud computing. Finally, I hope technical staff responsible for implementing and deploying cloud services would find the book of some help, in part to understand the business needs that could lead to the implementation of services in the cloud.

Organization of this book

This book consists of 12 chapters following this preface. The chapters are as follows.

Chapter 1: The Evolving Nature of Information Security

This chapter is intended to set the stage for the security-related requirements in subsequent chapters. Information security is a mobile animal and not everyone views it the same. Your idea of risk may be different from mine. However, there are some things that should be a concern for most businesses and people, and Internet access is now available to a substantial proportion of people around the world. This means that there are a lot of people with systems that could be exposed to malicious software. The malicious software could be used to give others access to those systems leading to what we call botnets of computers engaged in illegal activity, including attacks against business systems.

Chapter 2: Cloud Computing

After some historical context with respect to the early days of managed services in the 1960s, we discuss the protocols that have evolved to support the network services being offered today. This includes platform as a service (PaaS), software as a service (SaaS), storage as a service, and unified communications as a service (UCaaS). This will provide an understanding of the types of offerings that make up the general term cloud computing before we get into the specifics of each type and how they may be beneficial.

Chapter 3: Software as a Service

Software as a service (SaaS) may be the oldest form of cloud computing, going back to the days of service bureaus that used mainframes to provide functionality to businesses. This was especially helpful for smaller businesses that couldn't afford the enormous cost of a mainframe. There are a number of types of software that can be easily supplied over a network connection. We discuss a number of functional areas for SaaS providers.

Chapter 4: Storage in the Cloud

We, collectively, are storing an enormous amount of data. Storage has become cheap enough that everyone can easily have multiple terabytes storing pictures, videos, e-mail, and a variety of other documents. Storage providers are offering multiple gigabytes for almost nothing, if not actually nothing, to users to store data in their infrastructure. The advantage to that is the provider becomes responsible for the infrastructure, the upkeep, the resilience, and reliability. Another advantage to storage in the cloud is your data is available everywhere you go, as long as you have an Internet connection. No matter what device you are on, you can get access to your data. This can be very useful.

Chapter 5: Virtual Servers and Platform as a Service

Again, just as with other cloud services, virtualization has been around since the mainframe and the 1960s. Virtualization on the personal computer (PC) is very cost effective and provides a lot of features that are beneficial, including snapshots and quick backups, not to mention quick reconfiguration of systems. This virtualization in the hands of a service provider gives companies quick access to a lot of computing resources. Rather than going out and buying hardware, or even deploying virtualized servers yourself, a service provider might have the ability for you to quickly provision dozens of servers, speeding the deployment of an application.

Chapter 6: Social Media

Social networking has become a primary means of communication for a lot of people, and it provides a lot of capability for businesses to interact with their customers. Social media can also be useful for human resources, for both hiring and screening. It's worth being cautious on social media, though.

Chapter 7: Mobile Computing

Today, the majority of people are carrying around a computer that is several orders of magnitude more powerful than the very first computer system I ever worked on, a Digital Equipment Corporation PDP 11. They also have several orders of magnitude more memory than that system did since I think it may have had somewhere around 64 kB. People are carrying around very powerful computing devices and using them not only to communicate but also to access corporate data. This can cause issues for the company, especially when it's management who wants to get access remotely from their smartphone or tablet. Companies can choose to provide devices they can lock down or they can, more probably, find ways to give access to the devices people already have.

Chapter 8: Unified Communications

While Voice over IP has been around for the better part of a couple of decades, newer technologies have helped its adoption rate in recent years. In part, the ability to check whether someone is actually there before placing a call using a presence feature has been considered important. Making use of other features like instant messaging, desktop sharing, and videoconferencing have helped unified communications (UC) a big hit with businesses. The fact that they can save money by making using of their existing data infrastructure has also been a big plus.

Chapter 9: Remote Workers

Remote workers can be an enormous benefit for companies, allowing employees to be flexible with their time, which boosts productivity while simultaneously increasing worker health and well-being through a better work/life balance. Remote workers can also open the potential hiring pool for some positions to a wider area than your local region. There are challenges with remote workers, however, and some of those can be more easily solved by making use of cloud computing solutions and providers.

Chapter 10: Risk Management and Policy Considerations

In order to make better decisions, including whether to move to a cloud-based model for your infrastructure, it's helpful to have a risk assessment. This should be something you do for your organization on a regular basis anyway, constantly revisiting the results. This chapter covers a variety of techniques to manage risk and make better decisions for the company. This includes covering qualitative and quantitative assessment strategies as well as return on investment. We will also cover a social return on investment, which is a newer tactic.

Chapter 11: Future Technology

If you haven't seen someone with Google Glass or a smart watch like the Samsung Galaxy Gear or Pebble, you will soon. Wearable computing is already here. In fact, In addition to wearable computing, we are becoming more intimately connected to our computing devices. Think about the newer interfaces to Microsoft's Xbox that allow you to make gestures. Other devices are also moving to the gesture model, including smartphones like the Samsung Galaxy S4. Some Android devices can determine whether you are looking at the device and shut off or perform another task based on that. The days of simply typing into a keyboard while sitting at a desk are numbered when it comes to productivity.

Chapter 12: Pulling It All Together

After spending the book talking about a number of different providers for cloud-based services, we pull it all together by imagining a new company. This new company will make use of cloud services to minimize the amount of money that needs to be spent on computing infrastructure. We have a set of requirements, and we will go looking for providers that will be able to meet those requirements in a secure and cost-effective manner.

Acknowledgements

I'd like to thank Allan Konar, my technical reviewer for his support and invaluable input into this book. I'd also like to thank my family (Kathleen, Izzy, Atticus and Zoey) for their support and encouragement.

The Evolving Nature of Information Security

INFORMATION INCLUDED IN THIS CHAPTER

- Internet history
- Significant security events
- Evolution of services
- Today's risks (in a Nutshell)

INTRODUCTION

It may seem a strange place to start, but a good beginning here is the Boston Marathon bombings in April, 2013 and the days that followed. In particular, the Friday when officials shut down the city of Boston and neighboring communities. Businesses all over the city were forced to shut down while the manhunt took place over the course of the day on Friday. While retail establishments were really out of luck because no one on the streets meant no one in the stores, other businesses were able to continue to operate because of a number of technologies that allowed remote workers to get access to their files, the systems they needed, and their phone systems. Any business that implemented a full unified communications (UC) solution could have employees also communicating with instant messaging and know who was online because of the presence capabilities. Additionally, news of the events spread quickly and less because of news outlets who were, quite rightly, not allowed to provide specifics about many of the activities.

I had friends who lived within a couple of blocks of the final standoff with one of the suspects and so were restricted to their houses throughout the day on Friday. Using social media outlets like Facebook and Twitter, we were all able to stay in touch with friends and family in the city. Additionally, we were able to spread the news by retweeting or passing along Facebook statuses as well as pictures. Without being in that situation, it's hard to know for sure, but it had to be comforting to be in touch with a lot of friends and family on a regular basis. One of the downsides to social media, however, is the risk of inaccurate information getting out. The speed of social media allows even wrong information to get around quickly and in cases where there is a crisis, often people will latch onto any piece of information, no matter what it is. Services like Twitter and Reddit both misidentified the Boston bombing suspects, as an example. Fortunately, there are sites like snopes.com that will debunk inaccurate stories, but it takes time to gather the right information in order to debunk the inaccurate story and in the mean time, the bad story is getting pushed out all over the place. When you think about it, social networking sites are like the old Faberge shampoo commercials where you tell two friends and they tell two friends and so on and so on. It's an exponential growth curve and that's how social networking works, whether it's true or not. If I share a story and two of my friends share the story then it quickly gets into the tens or hundreds of thousands of people who have seen the story.

If you are wondering at this point what exactly the point of all of that was, you'll begin to see over the course of the next several chapters. In short, though, the world is shrinking while communities get larger. In the world we live in today, I can perform any number of jobs from anywhere in the world and still remain in close touch with those I work with as well as my friends and family. Our ability to quickly communicate has been improved by both social media outlets, like Facebook, Twitter, and LinkedIn, and UC implementations that allow cheap phone calls around the world and also allow for voice, text, and video communication from your computer through Google Talk, Skype, and Microsoft Lync. What is it that has made all of this possible?

History of the Internet

The story begins in the 1960s, which is as good a starting point as any. Computers had been around for a while and many industries were starting to see the advantages of using computers to perform very tedious and repetitive tasks. There was also a lot of research taking place at this time to extend the uses of computers and make their use more efficient. One of the efforts was led or at least funded by a government organization called the Advanced Research Projects Agency.

Significant security events

There's not much point in pretending that the Internet hasn't had serious security events. However, it's important to note that this hasn't prevented people from soldiering on, finding ways to protect their services and keep providing newer and better services to their constituents and clientele.

By the late 1980s, there were a lot of networks that were connected together, but it was still a very small network by comparison to what we have today. It was still primarily a research network connecting universities and government institutions, and it was primarily mainframes and other larger computing systems that were connected. There were a lot of well-known vulnerabilities but it wasn't considered to be a big deal to ensure software was up to date and to say there weren't as many people searching for vulnerabilities then would be understating it by several orders of magnitude. There were certainly people interested in security and poking around to see what they could do and whether things might break in interesting ways, but it was still a very trusting environment. That all changed on November 2, 1988. Robert T. Morris was a graduate student at Cornell University and he had written a piece of software to exploit a few vulnerabilities in UNIX systems. Once it had penetrated the system, it would work on finding other systems that it might similarly exploit and penetrate. He released this worm, so-called because it was capable of moving from system to system on its own, from a system at MIT. No one was prepared for the damage this small piece of software caused on the fledgling Internet. Malicious software was very rarely heard of. It was, after all, a very cooperative community.

At the time, there were about 60,000 systems connected to the Internet, and it was assumed that roughly 10% of those systems or 6000 systems had been infected. A number of estimates have been made about the cost of responding to this worm and they generally fall into the $100,000–10,000,000 range. Morris claimed to be trying to gauge the size of the Internet and there were limiting factors to keep the spread of the worm to a minimum; however, the limiting factors didn't work as expected.

While it was a major catastrophe, causing several nodes to be pulled off the network completely or even shut down, it caused the Defense Advanced Research Projects Agency to fund the creation of an incident response program, based at Carnegie Mellon University. Previously, all response to events was *ad hoc* resulting from node operators generally knowing other node operators and communicating informally. After the creation of the Computer Emergency Response Team (CERT), there was a central place to go to coordinate efforts necessary to combat attacks like the Morris Worm.

Less than a dozen years later, the Internet had become completely commercialized and the Web had been created, helping to fuel the growth. Large companies had substantial presences on the Web and there was a lot of business being transacted there. There was a lot of money on the line. Enter another young man, this one from Montreal, Quebec. His name was Michael Calce, though he called himself MafiaBoy, and he unleashed much larger attacks against several big names on the Internet at the time including eBay, E*Trade, CNN, Amazon, and Buy.Com. The story here actually begins even earlier since he didn't create the software that was used. A programmer who goes by the name Mixter wrote a piece of software called Tribe Flood Network (TFN).

The idea behind TFN was new at the time, though it has become very well known over time. At a time when many users didn't have a lot of bandwidth and certainly not enough to compare with the enormous pipes used by the biggest companies with a Web presence, it wasn't feasible for one or even a handful of users to launch attacks against such companies. You may be able to knock a friend or a rival off of an Internet Relay Chat server for fun or to cause annoyance but to take on a large company was just not possible. This sort of attack would take a coordinated effort by a large number of systems. Since getting that many willing participants together in a coordinated way would be difficult, it became easier to just go with infected systems. You infect a system, install a small piece of software that you can control remotely, and you have yourself a robot or a zombie, waiting to do your bidding. TFN was just the starting point, though. Mixter then wrote a piece of software called TFN2K to replace TFN. Trin00 and Stacheldraht, created by other developers, then followed. Dave Dittrich of the University of Washington did some of the early analysis of these programs.

Controlling such a large number of hosts individually would be too challenging so eventually, these programs began using a master/slave model. The attacker could communicate with a controller that would then send messages out to the bots/zombies who would then carry out the deeds. The attacks by MafiaBoy were carried out by TFN/TFN2K and were a number of flooding attacks, including a SYN flood that takes advantage of how TCP works. A number of good things ended up coming out of those attacks, including a handful of strategies for preventing or at least mitigating SYN floods against targets. Additionally, there were challenges associated with tracking down the sources of these attacks since they were primarily spoofed, or fake, sources. With faked source addresses, it's hard to determine where they are coming from without tracking the flow back through several networks. Since the targets can't determine that the sources are bogus, they respond to them, generating what's known as backscatter with their responses. This backscatter has been used to provide information regarding these denial-of-service (DoS) attacks. The attack also provided some practice for different network service providers to work together since many of these businesses use multiple providers and as a result, the targets had multiple vendors for their network and Web hosting. It was beneficial for all of them to work together to get the attacks under control.

While there were a number of notorious worms in the 2000s like Blaster and Code Red, attacks got a lot more serious in the 2010s with state-sponsored malware like Stuxnet and Duqu. It's the state-sponsored nature that makes it troubling. It's one thing when a handful of young people are unleashing attacks, but when a government decides to employ their military or intelligence personnel to create attacks against organizations in other countries the stakes get higher.

Various groups have been involved in hacktivism, performing malicious digital acts in order to make a point or protest other actions. One of the most troubling, potentially, is the attacks against a number of US banks in 2012. While attacks have become commonplace over the years and businesses have to expect them, it's the duration and the scale of the attacks that are the most troubling. A group of Muslim hacktivists has claimed ownership of these attacks that have been continuing periodically over a period well over 6 months. Some of the attacks have lasted several days at a time and has caused a great deal of difficulty for customers of the bank who have become accustomed to doing a lot of their banking online. According to the group responsible, it costs the banks $30,000 per minute while the Distributed Denial of Service (DDoS) attack is happening.

Evolution of services

One of the big things that has evolved over time is not only the nature of services and their complexity but also the level of trust that is involved with those services. When the network was young, it was a research network full of people with more or less the same purpose. When you have a close community like that where many of the members in the community know one another, are working together, and share many of the same goals, you may be able to have a decent level of trust with one another. At a minimum, there is a certain camaraderie and unified sense of purpose that happens in that situation. It's not surprising that given those circumstances that many of the fundamental protocols that evolved to run the network didn't have a lot of security in mind.

ARP, for instance, is the Address Resolution Protocol and it exists to translate IP addresses to MAC addresses so systems can communicate with one another on the same network. When you are communicating on a local network, you use local addresses like the MAC address not long-distance addresses like the IP address. However, there is nothing in the protocol to ensure that the MAC address you are being given really belongs to the system you are trying to communicate with. It's trivial to send out a message to everyone on the network indicating that your MAC address should be associated with every IP address on the network. Not only is it trivial but all of the systems will happily take the address you provide and store it away in case they need to communicate with that IP address at some point in the near future. It doesn't occur to any system that it would be unusual for one system with one MAC address to have a large number of IP addresses. Of course, it's entirely possible that this is legitimate because you can have multiple IP addresses on a system and, in fact, before virtual hosts became possible, that's what you needed to do to have multiple Web sites on a single server—you had to load it up with IP addresses.

However, it's still a bit out of the ordinary and not only is it out of the ordinary but why would that system just advertise itself like that across the network when no one asked. ARP is very Socratic in nature. Questions are asked, questions are answered. If I want to know what your MAC address is, I'll ask for it. Of course, I'll ask the entire network for it but that's the nature of the protocol. Since I don't know how to communicate with you directly on the local network, I have to ask everyone how to get to you just to get you to respond. It's a bit like a small town in that regard, where everyone knows everyone else's business—I send out a request to talk to you and everyone gets to know that it's happening. But back to the point about these gratuitous messages I'm sending. If you don't ask, what's the point of me giving you the answer? I'm answering a question that hasn't been posed. It's a bit like Jeopardy in that regard. As it turns out, of course, there are legitimate purposes for doing those sorts of announcements including sharing an IP address across multiple systems which helps with high-availability solutions and redundancy.

You may be wondering by this point why I've been going on and on about this little protocol called ARP since, as nearly as you can tell, it has nothing at all to do with clouds or security or social networking or any other topic that was provided as a pretext for you to acquire and read this book. The point is that ARP is a very trusting protocol by nature and it's very much a poster child for the way that the basic protocols of the Internet were created. It's a helping hand spirit. ARP works by you answering present when your name is called but if I announce to you which seat someone else is located in, you are quite happy to take me at my word on that because we're all in the same neighborhood, working together.

The problem is that's very much not the way the world today works. Today's network is very adversarial in nature, even if the network doesn't work in a particularly adversarial manner. This isn't to say that the Internet isn't being used for serious collaboration and productivity. If it weren't, you wouldn't be reading this book. Doing business on the Internet may be like owning a jewelry store with gang hangouts on both sides of you and organized crime businesses across the street. Your customers may get hassled, you may get hassled. If something were to happen, it's hard to know where to start investigating. Just because you have some good prospects around you, there are a lot of them and it may not even be them.

In spite of all of this, we have evolved the services that are offered. Where many of the services offered decades ago had to do with the care and feeding of the systems themselves as well as transmitting basic information from one system to another (e-mail, file transfer services, network management protocols), services that are offered today have built on the foundations that have existed for decades and now provide a rich user experience. A lot of this has to do with the introduction of the HyperText Transfer Protocol (HTTP) and the HyperText Markup Language (HTML) in the late 1980s and early 1990s. Even those protocols, though, were targeted at simple information sharing among what was basically a research community.

Services built on top of HTTP have really exploded, which seems naively understated to say in that way. It has turned into a terrific way to deliver services to end users as well as between businesses. HTTP, however, has a number of flaws since it was really designed to deliver pretty static pages and users, particularly less sophisticated users, prefer a graphically rich experience. It was necessary to add some additional components in with HTML and HTTP to help create those graphically rich services that would help users more easily consume the services. Of course, the front-end isn't enough if there aren't back-end changes as well, allowing not only for programmatic access but also a way to allow for persistent data.

In addition to database connections and programming languages to be able to handle the processing of form data, there are a number of other technologies like Java; JavaScript; Microsoft's .NET Framework; Web application servers like Tomcat, JBoss, WebSphere, Ruby on Rails and many others; SOAP; XML; Flash and now HTML5 that have become part of the mix. Some have called the combination of all of these technologies in order to create a rich user experience Web 2.0, simply indicating that the first version of the World Wide Web has been more or less superseded by a new model and that model is interactivity, both with the Web pages themselves and with the companies and organizations providing the service, not to mention more and more interacting with one another through many of these services in ways many were never able to dream of previously. Web 2.0 was made possible by introducing Asynchronous JavaScript and XML (AJAX) because it allowed the server to update the Web page without any interaction on the part of the user. Static pages require the user to click on a link or enter a different URL into the address bar to initiate communication with a server. With AJAX, the server can push updates to the Web page. One example is in the notification badges on Facebook indicating how many comments, messages, and friend requests you have. Something the server sent to my Web browser while I had the Facebook page open triggered the badge to get displayed. Underneath the notification area is a rolling list of activity from people on my friends list. I can quickly see what people are saying and where they are saying it so I can go directly there to interact myself. This would not be possible without AJAX.

Beyond what's happening on the Web, our world is changing around us with networked technology becoming ubiquitous. For many years now, Apple has had the ability for the employees at its stores to "ring out" any customer anywhere in the store using a handheld device. They could print a receipt to a networked printer or simply e-mail you the receipt and save the paper and the hassle. It was meant to be fast and efficient. Now, companies like JC Penney are picking up the same model by introducing handheld devices based on older iPhones that are used as the basis for portable scanners that could be used anywhere in the store to ring out customers. AT&T Wireless is moving its agents out from behind their older terminals, using tablets to interface with Web applications in helping customers. These are just a couple of examples of companies using technology to be more direct and interactive with their customers.

These technologies are not only good for businesses because they have the ability to significantly cut costs but they also have the ability to create a more customer-centric experience. There isn't a counter between the customer service person and the customer anymore. The appearance is they are working together, on the same side. This has the potential to create a lot of positive customer experience and, as a result, potentially a lot of customer loyalty.

We consume media in a significantly different way than we have in the past. Print media companies, whose deaths have long been hailed as being imminent, have found new ways to become relevant in a technology-centric world by moving their operations onto the Web, providing a better and more personal experience for their readers. It also opens the door for more personalized newspapers culled from a number of different sources. I can't help but remember reading a book by Stewart Brand back in the 1980s about MIT's Media Lab and the visionary and inventive things they were doing. He wrote about an idea Nicholas Negroponte had about intelligent agents, capable of pulling together information from a large number of sources into a personalized newspaper that Negroponte called the *Daily Me*. Not surprisingly, this has happened through a number of apps on Android phones and tablets as well as iPhones and iPads, though it had been going on for a while before that through various Web sites. There have been news aggregators now for a number of years.

The Web and ubiquitous Internet has allowed us to be far more mobile, allowing the services that are offered to follow that model. Where you may have offered a service through a Web interface previously, that same service can be consumed using a mobile device like a phone or a tablet and it can be consumed anywhere without the constraint of sitting at home or at work in front of a computer screen. The mobility allows services to be far more immediate and available than they ever were before.

Mobility is also providing the ability for many people to perform duties from locations other than their offices. Offering a way to access e-mail remotely is commonplace, and more and more people are using their own phones to access their e-mail at any hour of the day. This makes them more accessible to their employers, which cannot only be helpful but also has the potential to get more productivity out of their employees for very little cost. Beyond e-mail, businesses have been moving to converged services for a number of years. Converged services means merging data and voice services using voice over IP (VoIP) since VoIP pushes voice services onto the same infrastructure as the existing data. You can also add instant messaging services as well as the ability to track presence to make sure someone is actually at their desk or even just online before placing a phone call to them or sending them a message. When you add voice services plus instant messaging capabilities and the ability to see whether someone is online or at their phone, you have what's called UC. UC has the ability to enable how and when we communicate, and the rich platforms being developed are also allowing communication everywhere.

Today we have highly mobile employees. UC, for example, may provide a find me feature where you give one phone number out and that one phone number can find the device or location where you actually are and get the call or message to you there. We also offer highly mobile, highly interactive services that are often consumed using some sort of Web-based technology. This move toward highly interactive changes the way businesses behave, and it also has the potential to introduce a lot of risk.

Today's risks (in a Nutshell)

While the state-sponsored DoS attacks mentioned earlier are bad, there are a number of other threat vectors to be concerned with. One of these risks is corporate espionage. Recently, it has become public knowledge that China has an organization that has been systematically infiltrating companies and stealing terabytes of data including intellectual property and information about how they do business. Basically, whatever they can get their hands on. When this stolen data gets passed on to Chinese companies, it creates a playing field that is significantly skewed toward the Chinese company since they know how their competitors are doing business as well as details about how their products are created.

One of those companies, Huawei has long been suspected of making use of such data in the creation of their products. In fact, Cisco Systems accused Huawei in 2003 of using Cisco source code in their products. While Cisco eventually withdrew their lawsuit, based on an agreement with Huawei, there was evidence that Huawei had access to the Cisco source code, though it's not entirely clear how they may have gotten access to that. This is not to smear Huawei or accuse them of anything but the reality is that Chinese operatives have been removing enormous quantities of data from businesses around the world, and a Chinese business has been accused of making use of the intellectual property of at least one other business in the past. This would constitute a significant risk to a large number of businesses.

That's not to suggest that the Chinese are the only ones engaging in this activity. Corporate espionage is nothing new and digital avenues have done little to make that espionage harder. The risk is not even technical or architectural in nature from an IT perspective. The Chinese attackers were using social techniques, primarily, to get into systems. They send e-mail to their victims and get backdoors installed on the victim's system from which they can get in and begin removing data. Because of the techniques they are using, it can be very difficult to spot their activities unless you know exactly what to look for and, of course, that can change from one incident to another. Anyone else can use the same techniques to get into systems and extract data.

Because of this, your users put the business at significant risk simply because of the way they operate. They don't mean to put the business at risk. It's not malicious in nature. It's just the way people are. On top of that, often there are vulnerabilities in e-mail clients or in Web browsers that help get the malware installed on the target systems. Because of this, users often have no idea that their system has been attacked. There was no popup box with any warning that they ignored and clicked through. There was no setting somewhere that they turned off that allowed their system to be compromised. Software and systems have become so complex that it gets harder and harder to find all of the vulnerabilities. Software companies don't have nearly the same motivation to find the vulnerabilities as other entities do.

In addition to other entities, Russian-organized crime has set up shop on the Internet, though they aren't selling trinkets to the tourists. They are buying exploits from talented programmers who understand security. They use these exploits to infest the systems of normal users, creating large botnets much like the botnets created in the late 1990s and early 2000s that were used in the attacks led by MafiaBoy. The difference now is the scope of these botnets. Once again, users are the target here because the more bots you can have under your control, the more you can do from contributing in DDoS attacks to sending out spam around the Internet.

A number of organizations will pay big money to programmers who are willing to create exploits that can be used to attack end-user systems. This is a source of significant risk since these are vulnerabilities that the vendors aren't aware of so there is no fix coming to prevent the vulnerability from being exploited. In addition, there is likely no antivirus signature or intrusion detection signature for these attacks, at

FIGURE 1.1 Anonymous' Twitter Feed

least not initially but it doesn't take long for a large number of systems to be infected before any sort of signature can be released to detect or locate the malware.

Is it bad enough that organized crime and governments are getting involved in the activities that make the Internet such a dangerous place without having social protest as well? One protest organization, known as Anonymous, has been involved in a number of actions of hacktivism, which is performing malicious digital acts in the name of protesting something. Anonymous launched a DDoS attack against the International Federation of the Phonographic Industry in 2009 after members of The Pirate Bay, a large torrenting site, were found guilty of copyright infringement. They have taken down government Web sites and attempted to stop child pornography sites. They also launched attacks against companies who opposed the Web site Wikileaks. Figure 1.1 is a capture of a few tweets as shown on their Web site. If you try to take on Anonymous, either they or an affiliated organization will come after you and your organization.

Moving services off of a fixed line model onto a shared network like a local area network or even the Internet can be risky since you're no longer dealing with a dedicated line from a sales terminal to a large system in the back room that keeps track of everything. In the case of using mobile devices to ring up sales on the floor, using wireless technology to transmit information like credit card data, this brings up some risk, primarily to the customer, though some to the retailer as well since a large number of stolen credit cards from a breached wireless network will surely make the news and might cause sales to drop off for a while.

Mobility also comes at a price. The more services we open up to our employees from the outside world, even if it's simply through a virtual private network connection, is an exposure to our infrastructure and while attackers will generally take the easiest route, which has long been exploiting user behavior, it's not worth gambling that our infrastructure isn't in play because e-mail and Web services are more likely to be exploited.

More and more of life takes place on the Web and this introduces risk as well, both personally and from a business perspective. Imagine that you have an employee who is holding a big grudge because their poor performance kept them from getting an average bonus, not to mention the promotion they had been hoping for the last 3 years. Previously, they would tell their friends who may tell their friends and so on and so on but word of mouth like that tends to fall off pretty sharply the further away from the source it gets unless there is a truly spectacular story to go along with it. Today, they will take to Twitter and Facebook, thinking that only their friends can see it. The thing about Facebook and Twitter that people often forget is that it's incredibly easy to retweet a message or share a status update. Now we're beyond the realm of your own friends. We're into their friends and the potential for viewing it grows exponentially. Out of 100 friends, maybe one shares it. That one share has now increased the number of people who have seen it by adding in their friend count. It grows pretty quickly, and it's such an easy thing to do that people simply forget that the Library of Congress is archiving every tweet that is sent out over Twitter.

Even beyond the unexpected reach through status sharing or repeating is simply the privacy settings you may have for your posts without even realizing it in Facebook. Many people post fully public status updates without, apparently, realizing that anyone can read their posts without even being their friends. Facebook has an application programming interface that allows anyone to programmatically pull information from them. It's through this interface that the Web site www.weknowwhatyouredoing.com gets its data—all public posts to Facebook. Figure 1.2 shows a couple of posts that the posters probably didn't mean to be public since they make unflattering references to their bosses.

Social networking is great for reconnecting with friends you haven't seen in the 30 years since you graduated high school and it can be beneficial for you socially as well as professionally to reconnect with all of those people. It can also be terrific for businesses that want to more actively engage with their customers and clients. Have you ever had a lousy experience with a product or service and jumped straight on Twitter to complain about it, expecting that the company would see it and maybe do something about it? Would you have ever done that if it required a phone call and talking to someone or even simply leaving a voice message? Twitter and Facebook are just so simple to toss something out and forget about it that it has changed our behavior as consumers and businesses are reacting to that. However,

Who wants to get fired?

Angel V.
i hate my boss he is a total
asshole ...." to me n others .
sorry to say but we need an
AMERICAN BOSS!
about 35 minutes ago, no people
like this, posted from Facebook
for Every Phone, report

Rosa M.
Good morning ppls getting
ready for work hope it goes
by fast hate working with
my boss lol
about 36 minutes ago, no people
like this, posted from Facebook
for Android, report

FIGURE 1.2 Facebook Posts from www.weknowwhatyouredoing.com

there is a risk to that, of course. Those complaints are broadcast to anyone who wants to go looking for them, typically. This isn't good for your business if a small number of disgruntled users want to complain about what you are doing.

Collaboration

Over the course of researching, thinking about and writing this book, the one concept that kept coming up over and over is that of collaboration. Communication and a feeling of closeness or proximity are important to collaboration. The different technologies we will be talking about all provide some aspect of these requirements for collaboration. Social networking sites and UC provide ways to quickly and easily communicate as well as know whether someone is available or not. This knowing about availability gives a sense of proximity. It's the virtual version of poking your head in the door of a coworker to see if they are there or not.

Between communication and information sharing, we have the unprecedented capability of collaborating quickly and easily with anyone, anywhere. Not only can they be anywhere but with mobile devices, you can be nearly anywhere yourself and get instant access to information like presence, phone calls, voice mail, e-mail, document sharing, and a large number of cloud-based services. Remote access and a central place for information to be stored pull it all together. With cloud-based services, either storage or software, you don't have to remember to take that document with you or remember to sync with the central repository to ensure you have the latest copy of something. If it's stored "in the cloud" you can get access to it from anywhere you have access to the Internet.

CONCLUSION

Certainly the Internet can be a scary and dangerous place but then so can your house if your drunken neighbor shows up at 3 a.m. waving a knife around complaining about what his wife supposedly did to him. It's all about context and what you can do to protect yourself and at least be aware of the risks. The Internet holds an enormous amount of potential for business to improve their positions, and it also holds an enormous potential for people to improve their lives in a number of different ways, not least of which simply having the access to a lot of information quickly and easily. Certainly there is a lot of incorrect, inaccurate, or malicious information out there, and it's because of that there are a number of Web sites dedicated to rooting out inaccurate and misleading information and setting the record straight. In spite of that, there is still enormous potential for making life better for people.

As I mentioned, it also has the potential to improve the position for businesses as well as their employees. The world is shrinking and people can be fully connected and engaged anywhere they are. Cloud computing, social networking, and UC are helping with that as well as the drive toward mobile platforms like tablet computers, ultrabooks, and powerful smartphones. Our goal over the next few chapters is not to scare you away from any of these technologies but to provide you with information about how to implement them in a way that makes sense for you, for your business, for your family while keeping your interests as safe as possible. These technologies that are evolving and growing now can be great, as long as you are aware of the potential for risk and do what you need to do to mitigate that risk. So, let's go exploring this new world together.

Summary

Here are some concepts to take away from this chapter:

- The Internet has existed in one form or another for over 40 years.
- As the Internet has grown, the risks associated with being on it have increased.
- Our current needs have changed the services that are offered—including more interactive services like social media.
- New services have required new protocols to be created like HTTP and AJAX.
- The Morris worm, while devastating, had a positive outcome by forcing the creation of the CERT.

Cloud Computing

INFORMATION INCLUDED IN THIS CHAPTER

- Protocols used
- Defining the cloud
- Software as a service
- Infrastructure as a service
- Platform as a service

INTRODUCTION

It's nothing new to suggest that more and more of life is revolving around our interactions with computers and more specifically with other computers and people over the Internet. We are finding more and more ways to get things done making use of the Internet connections that have become more and more ubiquitous. Coffee shops, fast-food places, more traditional restaurants, health professionals. What do they all have in common? Often, they have complimentary wireless access, providing us with a way to get online. Additionally, people are getting so-called smartphones which also provide them with a way to stay online from nearly anywhere they might be. We can complain about texting and driving but it's not just SMS. How many people do you know who Facebook and drive?

So, what does all this have to do with the cloud? Well, we are more and more connected, and many of the ways we are connected these days is through some sort of "in the cloud" technology. Businesses are also finding ways to streamline their operations and reduce infrastructure, operations footprint, and overall cost. They are doing this in a number of ways because "the cloud" (and I'll stop putting it in quotes soon) has a number of facets. It's not simply a way to stick all of your iTunes library or a bunch of documents you want to share with someone else. It has become a lot more, and there are a number of technologies that have allowed all of this to happen, finally.

What makes me say finally? Well, the reality is that technology has been going back and forth between local and remote for a while now. Life started with everything centralized since all we had was very large systems. There was no way to have local storage so it had to be centralized. In the 1980s, the arrival of PCs allowed for local storage and a movement away from the exclusively centralized, mainframe approach, although it took some time for the local storage to get big enough and cheap enough to really be effective. Applications were a mix of local and centralized, though.

In the 1990s, there was again a movement toward centralized, remote applications as the Web took off. There was a lot of talk about thin clients and dumb terminals making use of applications living on remote servers using Web interfaces or even remote procedures or methods. The thin client and dumb terminal approach never really took off, and there was still a preponderance of local storage and local applications. The mix of financials and functionality was never really able to make the push to using remote applications over local applications. In the late 1990s and early 2000s, I was working at a large network service provider and we started talking about offering services "in the cloud" which made it the first time I had heard that term. When the dotcom collapse really started taking everyone down, the potential clients and the resources necessary to create those services and applications were just no longer available. Again, services and applications remained local.

Now, we're into the 2010s and you'll hear "in the cloud" everywhere you go. There is an enormous movement of applications, functionality to a remote model with remote functionality and remote storage. What is it that has made that possible? Some of it has been the rise in virtual technology, some has been an improvement in the protocols, and there is also the economies of scale that come with enormous storage and processing power. On top of that, last mile network services like cable modem, Digital Subscriber Line, and cellular data networking have provided the ability to have Internet services nearly everywhere you go. All of that storage and processing can be shared across a large number of clients, and it makes sense as a business opportunity as well as a way to cut costs and reduce internal risk to the organization, especially when you consider the large number of potential customers and their ability to consume services from anywhere.

The protocols that made it possible

Cloud services didn't just happen overnight, of course, and there are a number of incremental advances that have taken place in how we offer services and applications over networks that have made cloud services possible. While the origins of many of these concepts go back decades in at least their conceptual stages, the concrete introduction of some of the really important ones began in the late 1980s, just as the Internet itself was really starting to come together with all of the disparate research and educational networks being pulled together into a larger, single network that was being called the Internet.

HTTP and HTML

Hypertext has been a concept since at least the 1960s, and it was made possible in the late 1980s with the introduction of a protocol, a language, and a set of applications that brought it all together. Initially, this was done to simply share information between scientists and researchers around the world. Eventually, the rest of the world started to figure out all of the cool and interesting things that could be done using a couple of very simple protocols. The implementation of hypertext in language form is HyperText Markup Language (HTML). A basic example of HTML would be something like

```
<html>
<head> <title> My page </title> </head>
<body text = "steelblue" bgcolor = "white">
<h1> Hello, everybody! </h1>
</body>
</html>
```

You can see HTML is a reasonably easy to read, structured formatting language. It uses tags to indicate elements, and each tag could potentially have parameters that would alter the behavior of the tag. An example is the body tag, which has two parameters. The first, text, sets the color of the text, while the second parameter, bgcolor, sets the color of the background of the page. It's not challenging to learn basic HTML, but basic HTML wasn't enough so that evolved into Dynamic HTML (DHTML) because static text wasn't particularly interesting and it was thought that people wanted movement and interaction in their Web pages. DHTML is a combination of HTML with a client-side scripting language like JavaScript providing a more interactive experience with what was previously a static page.

It's important to note here that HTML continues to go through a lot of evolution and the latest, HTML5, is completely different from previous versions. The parameters mentioned above are no longer supported in HTML5. HTML5 is part of the continued evolution toward more interactive Web pages. HTML5 has not yet stabilized as a standard at the time of this writing, though they are releasing candidate recommendations. The expectation is that a final, stable standard will be available in 2014. In addition to markup, HTML5 has support for application programming interfaces (APIs), which previous versions of HTML did not have.

The HTML is the visual representation but we still need a way to get the HTML to us. Certainly existing protocols like FTP could have been used but the existing protocols didn't offer the right level of information necessary to provide functions like detailed errors or redirection. When you are interacting with a Web server, you may generate errors on the server for a number of reasons including the page not being found or a more serious error with the server itself. You might also generate a server-side error if the programmatic components had an error in them on the server side. These types of interactions would be impossible with previous document retrieval protocols like FTP. Additionally, FTP was designed in a way that might cause problems on the application side. As a result of all of this, Tim Berners-Lee and his team at the European Organization for Nuclear Research (CERN), developed a new protocol called the HyperText Transfer Protocol (HTTP), designed to transfer HTML documents from a server to a client. The initial version of HTTP was very simple, providing a way to make a request to the server and get a response back. Later, the protocol was altered to include more information like metadata, extended negotiation, and extended operations.

```
Accept: text/html,application/xhtml + xml,application/xml;q =
0.9,*/*;q = 0.8
Accept-Encoding:
gzip,deflate,sdch
Accept-Language:
en-US,en;q = 0.8
Connection:
keep-alive
Host:
www.washere.com
User-Agent:
Mozilla/5.0 (Macintosh; Intel Mac OS X 10_8_3) AppleWebKit/537.36
(KHTML, like Gecko) Chrome/27.0.1453.93 Safari/537.36
```

The listing shows a sample HTTP request using a current version of the protocol. The original published version was 0.9. 1.0 was published in 1996 followed by 1.1 in 1997 where we are today after some modifications in 1999. HTTP is one of the fundamental building blocks of the way applications are delivered today. The methods that HTTP allows in addition to the data the can be conveyed using HTTP makes it a very flexible protocol for the delivery of information and functionality in interacting with users. Reasonably simple and extensible has made it very useful.

XML

At this point, we have a way of describing what a page of information should look like and a way of delivering the pages to clients so they can be displayed. There are even programming languages that can be used. One thing missing from what we've been talking about so far is a way of transmitting complex data from the client to the server and vice versa. The HTTP allows for passing parameters but, while you can provide a variable name for each parameter, you can't describe the data at all. The even bigger problem with just using plain HTTP and being stuck with form parameters is that you need user action in order to trigger the content to be sent off to the Web server in order to get data back.

In 1999, Microsoft came up with a way to handle interaction behind the scenes and send data to the server while loading the data back into the script rather than having the browser handle it and render as it saw fit. The script could update components in the page based on the Document Object Model (DOM), which provided programmatic access to different parts of the page. You may have a frame on your page that you want to update with data you've received from the server. You could access the frame and elements within it using the DOM. The data being sent back and forth is formatted using the eXtensible Markup Language (XML), which descends from the Structured Generalized Markup Language (SGML), as does HTML. By way of a historical note of interest, SGML was preceded by the Generalized Markup Language developed in the late 1960s by researchers at IBM.

XML is written in such a way that you can present data while also describing it in a detailed and structured way. Data can be sent back and forth with either side not needing to know what comes next as long as they both sides understand the language used to describe the data. Let's take a look at some XML and then we can pull it apart from there.

```
<?xml version = "1.0" encoding = "UTF-8"?>
<!-- the first person starts here -->
<person>
<name> Zoey Messier </name>
<address> Somewhere Street </address>
<town> Wubble </town>
<state > WV </state>
<zip> 33992 </zip>
</person>
```

You can see from the code that each piece of data has the type of data associated with it. Also, the beginning and end are clearly marked with a beginning tag and an ending tag. XML also provides a way to describe the version of XML in use and comments, which you can see in the first and second lines of the listing. One advantage of using XML is the fact that each of the entries is described, meaning that it doesn't matter which order the data is presented in. It's not a question of getting a stream of data and needing it to be in the correct order so that it can be parsed correctly. With XML, it doesn't matter what order the data is presented in. XML can provide something of a rudimentary database where data can be stored in a way that it can be retrieved by data field, and you can store a number of records in a single file with all of the records fully described.

The way XML is sent back and forth is through JavaScript. Google took the approach that Microsoft was using with XML and HTTP and changed it slightly. Rather than using an ActiveX control to send the data back and forth, Google opted to use JavaScript in order to implement their Gmail and Maps services. Microsoft had been using XML and HTTP to implement Outlook Web Access among other things for several years by that point, but since they were using ActiveX controls, it wasn't as standards compliant as the approach Google used since not all browsers or operating systems supported ActiveX controls.

RESTful services

One of the challenges with HTTP has always been that it was an entirely stateless protocol, meaning that it didn't have any internal mechanisms to keep track of whether a particular endpoint had previously requested anything from the server or not and who that endpoint actually was and whether they were trusted or not. All of those factors had to be sorted out outside of the HTTP. One of the early mechanisms for maintaining that sort of data was something called a cookie, which is a small piece of data that is stored on the client at the request of the server. When necessary, the client will transmit the data in the cookie to the server so that information about the client can be retrieved, including the list of items in a shopping cart, for example.

There was a need for an architectural model that allowed clients and servers to share state information, meaning they needed to both be aware of the current transactional state of their connection. In 2000, Roy Fielding defined the term representational state transfer in his doctor dissertation, and it became the specification for an architecture called REST. REST specifies a way of developing an application in a general way by outlining some core concepts that are critical including scalability of interactions, generalization of interfaces, and independent deployment of components. A system using a RESTful architecture has the following constraints but allows the remainder of the system to be developed and deployed as needed.

- **Client server**—Clients and servers are defined, providing a clear delineation between responsibilities. Clients are responsible for the interface and servers are responsible for data storage.
- **Stateless**—The server isn't to be responsible for storing any context information about the client. The client would be responsible for storing state information and providing the context to the server when it generated and transmitted a request.
- **Cacheable**—The client should be able to cache responses. This requires that any response from the server needs to be tagged as either cacheable or not cacheable.
- **Layered system**—This allows that the service could be broken up into separate components so that the client wouldn't know whether they were communicating to the actual server or an intermediary.
- **Uniform interface**—Interfaces between each component should use standards so the exchanges between them would be easily understood so that the internals of each component could be developed as necessary without having to worry about what they could or should expect or thinking that the interface might change. With a uniform interface, that's one part of the design that doesn't need to be worked on.

Of course, this is the specification of an architecture, and there are many different frameworks that implement this type of architecture. It also doesn't specify any protocols or specific implementations, but it does outline the need for an agreed-upon manner of exchanging information as well as a clearly defined set of functions for the client side and the server side. What we haven't talked about are all the different ways of implementing the architecture including SOAP, RPC, RMI, WSDL, and so on. These are all important to specific implementations of an application, but those are higher level implementation protocols rather than fundamental building blocks that are common to all or at least most of the types of applications and implementations we will be talking about going forward.

With all the right protocols, architectures, and implementations in place, the stage was set for a far richer user experience than had been seen previously. Web 2.0, such as it was, was a result of implementations of these different protocols, and Web 2.0, subsequently, really led to what we now refer to as cloud-based services or services "in the cloud."

The cloud

With the protocols in use firmly in place, we can start talking about what exactly the cloud is. In fact, the cloud has been around longer than the services we have been talking about as cloud-based computing has been. The origin of the term "cloud" or "cloud computing" is unclear, though I can tell you from my own experience I first heard it in roughly the year 2000. I was working at Genuity (formerly GTE Internetworking, formerly BBN, the company that was hired to build the ARPANET and a pioneer in Internet protocols and network services) at the time, leading a team responsible for developing managed security services. Product management at Genuity was beginning to talk about Virtual Private Network (VPN) and firewall services "in the cloud" rather than at the customer premise. The idea being that we could handle all of the work within our network so that the customer wouldn't have to have anything on their premise.

This is the same premise with what we consider to be cloud-based computing today—services that may be handled somewhere other than the customer premise, in the case of public cloud services. Whether it's data stored off-site or whether it's an entire application that's stored off-site, the idea is to off-load the work of managing systems or applications and reap the benefits of getting some of that workload off your plate. What exactly do we mean when we talk about cloud computing then? The cloud itself is a bit of a generic term that might mean a number of things but we can talk about what may be offered in a cloud-computing service.

- **Location agnostic**—A cloud-computing service doesn't generally care where you are located or where the consumers of the service may be located. In general, you may not even have an idea where the cloud-computing service is as long as you get good performance when trying to access the service.
- **Provisioning speed**—Generally, you are paying for a service that you can either activate or expand quickly, allowing you to get up and running significantly faster than if you were to be working from a physical server model in your own location.
- **Scalability**—The service should be scalable. This is partly a result of the speed of provisioning. You should be able to quickly move to a larger platform if necessary. It also has to do with bandwidth and ensuring that you can access the service with adequate performance, as you need.

- **Geodiversity**—This may not always be the case but often cloud-computing vendors will offer a measure of geodiversity by either giving you some control over where you want your service being provisioned or offering a way to replicate or distribute the service or at least the data offered by the service. This may be done using a caching service like the one offered by companies like Akamai. It may also be done simply by the cloud-computing vendor having redundant systems that are replicated without you needing to be in the middle.
- **Availability**—One advantage that a cloud-computing vendor may have that companies may not have themselves, particularly if they fall into the small- or medium-sized category is being to offer better availability for the service offering. Where a smaller company may not be able to offer things like multiple network connections from multiple locations as well as redundant power sources and large-scale generators to ensure constant power, a cloud-computing vendor might typically have those facilities to ensure near-constant availability for their customers.
- **Multitenancy**—While it may look and feel as though you are the only company making use of the resource, be assured that many other companies are using the same resources, whether it's the physical servers through virtualization technology or whether it's the network connection or a mixture of all of it, this is a shared hosting model.
- **Multiple OS support**—Often, cloud-computing vendors will support access from a number of OS platforms, including iOS and Android for mobile devices.
- **Virtualization**—Virtualization is typically part of a cloud-based solution because it helps provide the segmentation necessary to provide adequate security for clients. However, just because a solution is virtualized doesn't necessarily make it a cloud-computing solution. I could easily have a VMWare or a Parallels virtual machine and install either Windows or Linux and stick a Web server on it. That doesn't make it a cloud service. The cloud portion is the idea that it's this amorphous thing "out there" somewhere.

While those are some of the primary differentiators of cloud-computing services, it really comes down to changes to the hosting model that has been in use to varying degrees for years. The big difference now is that the services are more differentiated and sophisticated than they have been previously. Web hosting has been available for a couple of decades now, from both an infrastructure perspective as well as from Web server instance perspective. This is really an enhancement on that model, offering a broader range of services with more flexibility and a number of other benefits.

Speaking of benefits, there are a number of reasons to move to a cloud-computing platform. Just as a starting point, we can take a look at this list.

- **Reduced infrastructure**—There is much more to this than the two words in bold-faced type. Reduced infrastructure means fewer hardware purchases for the systems to support the application, whatever the application may be. Reduced hardware, both in terms of systems and network equipment required to connect the system to the network, translates to reduced floor space need and also reduced air conditioning requirements.

- **Reduced staff**—With fewer systems, you should need fewer people on staff to support all of those systems. You may still need people to deal with whomever you choose as a vendor as well as an expert to handle the particular application you are outsourcing. This isn't always the case since some cloud services still require staff to support completely, if you want the service to be effective. This may include bringing in development staff, though this moves the responsibility higher up in the stack and away from supporting physical equipment.
- **Disaster recovery**—When you send your systems and applications off to another vendor, that vendor takes on the need to have a disaster recovery plan. You will need to add their plan to your own, but it's a set of systems and data you don't have to worry as much about, assuming you trust your vendor to do the right thing and protect their systems and the data that resides on them.
- **Support costs**—You may reduce costs in support as well as licensing, depending on the service you have chosen and the cost model the vendor uses.
- **Incident response**—This is almost the same scenario as with disaster recovery, though you aren't completely outsourcing the response since it's your data and you will be responsible for notifications if customer data has been lost. You will need to have people who are capable of working with your vendor in an appropriate way to ensure that whatever incident may have happened has been handled appropriately.
- **Backups**—This is again a reduced cost. Having the data stored with a cloud-computing vendor also puts the data at a site other than yours in case something catastrophic happens at your facility. You may also have to use backups for legal or compliance reasons. This does not, however, mean you don't have to ensure that your cloud-computing vendor is backing up any data you may be storing so it can be retrieved later. If they are not or don't have a service where they can provide that facility for you, you may want to consider either getting a third party to handle that, pulling the data back yourself if you aren't already replicating it, or finding another vendor who will ensure your data is protected through backups.
- **Improved vulnerability control**—Your cloud-computing vendor should have a way of keeping their systems up-to-date; reducing the risk to the system you are making use of, whether it's strictly for storage, as a general-purpose computing device or as an application host.
- **Reduced costs**—This may be obvious from the items above, but if you are able to reduce staff and infrastructure as well as complexity, reduced costs should follow as a matter of course.

This is not to say that there aren't risks associated with cloud computing as well and some of them have been hinted at above. Any time you let data out of your hands, you are taking on a risk. You have off-loaded the control over the data without off-loading any of the responsibility. If your customer data is put at risk, you are still responsible. If critical company information is lost or stolen from where it was being stored, the company is at risk.

Before talking any more about risks that may be associated with cloud computing, we should get into more detail about the different types of cloud-computing platforms there are and make some sense of the buzzwords that seem to clutter the landscape making it harder to decipher exactly what it is you are getting for your money and what you can do with it.

Infrastructure as a service

According to Gartner, infrastructure as a service (IaaS) is defined as a service that provides customers the ability to self-provision computing resources. This would include processing power, disk space, and network capacity. In the case of IaaS, there is nothing on top of it. What you are renting is simply raw computing power. You get a virtual instance of a system where the service provider owns all of the resources. If you want anything on top of IaaS, you would provide it yourself, including an operating system image or any applications. Once you have the operating system installed and the applications up and running, you are responsible for keeping it all up to date.

Typically, management and provisioning of these resources would be done through a Web interface and may also have an API that a customer may get access to. Billing for this sort of service would be based on a very old model—computing time. The more CPU time you use, the more you will be billed. You may also be charged for other resources like disk space or network bandwidth used.

A number of vendors offer IaaS as an offering. Figure 2.1 shows the provisioning wizard for an Amazon Elastic Compute Cloud (EC2) instance. The tab selected here shows where you would create your own image that could be deployed on a computing instance. If you want to use other images, you can do that. Amazon offers several operating system images that could be used as well as their own system image including their toolset. Microsoft offers not only services but also offers software that would allow you to create your own cloud hosting service through the Windows Server and Systems Center. You could become your own service provider using Microsoft's software solution, and they will provide guidance on service-level agreements, among other topics that are important to becoming a service provider.

Often, we think about cloud-based services as being Web oriented so they involve Web servers and HTTP and so on. If you have IaaS, you could make use of the system to do anything you didn't want on your network. You could, for example, install a Jabber server to have an instant messaging system that anyone in your organization as well as all of your customers could get access to. This moves the server off your network meaning you don't have to poke holes through your firewall and potentially expose your network to vulnerabilities in the server, should they exist. It gives you some capabilities without all of the risk.

You might also use it for a VoIP solution, again without introducing the risk to your network. You could install an Asterisk server and connect the server to an SIP

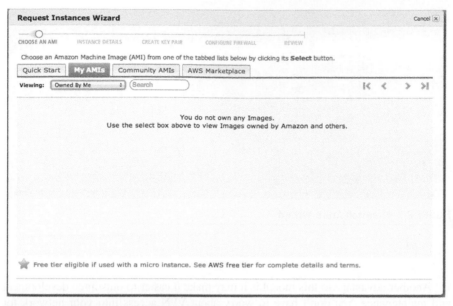

FIGURE 2.1 Creating Instances With Amazon

trunking service and then let all of your road warriors connect to that server and potentially allow customers to connect to it as well to support voice and video calling between your people and your customers. Having the ability to have infrastructure outside of your internal network can open a lot of possibilities without all of the potential risk.

Platform as a service

Platform as a service (PaaS) takes IaaS a step further and has been around for a long time as a hosting model. It's really the classic Web hosting setup where you rent a system hosted on someone else's network and in their data center. It's also likely to be much cheaper today than it was several years ago because it's far more likely to be a virtual host on a very powerful multi-CPU system. In addition to the system as well as the operating system of your choice, with PaaS you would typically get a Web server and an application development environment as well as a database server. You may also get a content management server like Wordpress or Joomla. This gives you the ability to develop your own Web applications with a server-side language and the ability to connect to your database. At that point, you have a system just as you would in your own environment, except that it's not in your environment so it may be more accessible and also, as mentioned previously, removes the risk of having that system on your own network and exposing the services through your firewall into your network.

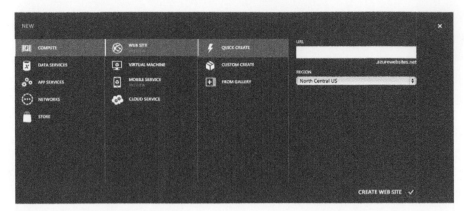

FIGURE 2.2 Microsoft Azure Wizard

Used with permission from Microsoft.

Another advantage to this model is it may make it easier to outsource development and maintenance. You don't have to worry about VPN access into your network for your partners or vendors who might be performing this work. You provide them access to your PaaS from your cloud-services provider and segment access to the appropriate component on that system. Again, you can keep your internal network safer by not needing to give access to someone who doesn't work directly for you. This is not to say that you shouldn't trust your vendors or can't trust your vendors. When it comes to vendors, though, they aren't directly under your control and it's a different type of risk.

When you get a PaaS solution, your vendor may provide a Web interface where they make it easier to develop your solution. Google Sites gives you a Web interface to develop your site and pages without needing to learn any HTML. Microsoft Azure also provides a Web interface and also provides wizards to assist with creation of your application. Figure 2.2 is a capture of a wizard used to create a Web site. As mentioned previously, you may have a need for a database and you can create a database with Microsoft Azure. Again, you'll find a wizard, as shown in Figure 2.3 to create the database you may use. You can also see from these figures that there are a number of other components you can create including a virtual network or application services like a notification hub or a service bus queue. The wizard will walk you through doing quick creation of any component you need. Making use of these wizards helps in getting services up and running quickly.

PaaS will also typically offer a lot of automation to eliminate common tasks from the administration of a system. They will also offer a lot of instrumentation so you can keep a close eye on the performance of the platform. This level of management and ease of use can make PaaS a very appealing way to go in order to develop an application or a service. PaaS providers also commonly use Web-based administration, alleviating the need to know arcane command-line administration. Making use of a well-known application like CPanel can make it much easier for anyone to

FIGURE 2.3 Microsoft Azure Data Sources

Used with permission from Microsoft.

administer the platform, reducing the need for support staff with specific technical skills.

Software as a service

Under the "everything old is new" category, software as a service (SaaS), is basically what we used to call application service providers (ASPs). The ASP model goes back a number of years. The idea of ASP or SaaS goes back several decades, however, to John McCarthy of MIT in 1961who saw computing services as a utility like electricity or phone service. Following that idea, an ASP provides access to a specific application or set of applications on a remote system, again providing an interface to those applications, often through a Web interface. You may also get a thin client for remote access that connects to the service using some of the protocols discussed earlier. It actually took a long time for ASPs to really catch on, though. A small software company I worked at in the late 1990s tried an ASP model for one of their products, but coming up with a model that worked was difficult and most customers wanted to have their data in-house. Slowly, though, ASPs have caught on and you're probably run across an ASP or two.

SaaS shares the same characteristics as the other cloud services where the application is hosted at a remote location and you gain access to it from wherever you are. All of the data would be stored with the service provider, not locally. This means that you can access it from any system or device and not have to worry about carrying it around with you. You also get the advantage of having the latest, up-to-date software without having to worry about managing updates yourself. All of the management of the application and deployment, such as it is, can be taken care of by the service provider.

One of the most common ones today is the suite of Google Apps including Google Docs, though they are far from the only ones. Microsoft has actually deployed their Office suite as a cloud service. Figure 2.4 shows the management

information among a number of people crossing multiple organizations but you don't want it all to be public. This could be a collection of cloud services like storage plus project management, using a service like SmartSheet.

When you begin blending cloud models together, like using a private and a public cloud for the same application, you end up with a hybrid cloud model. You might use a hybrid model if you had a need to be able to take periodic bursts of large amounts of traffic that a private cloud may not be able to handle. In that case, you would be employing cloudbursting to push an application to a public cloud that was better able to handle the short-term volume.

CONCLUSION

Cloud services and everything to do with them have become a hot set of buzzwords. There is still, however, a lot of misunderstanding over what they are and what they can offer. Primarily, cloud services are those that are offered in a way that they can be easily accessed from anywhere using standard protocols. These services are extensions on the hosting model that has been around for years and are really natural extensions on ideas that have been around since the 1960s. We have long tried to find ways to use computing resources more economically including time-sharing services going back to the 1960s on mainframes.

The feasibility of virtual systems really came with the ability to have a large amount of memory and disk space as well as multiple processors. The introduction of 64-bit processors brought in the ability to have more than 4G of physical memory which provides a platform to host multiple virtual servers without significant impact to their performance since memory can be more or less dedicated to each virtual machine meaning less swapping of physical memory for virtual memory. All of these factors made it cost effective to be able to partition a single system into multiple virtual systems, allowing customers to create their own server that they could then manage and use as they please.

Once this door was open, all of the other possibilities came flying through. ASPs could better segment their offerings to protect their customers and offer SaaS. Other companies began to see how complex solutions could be handled in the cloud and began to offer easier solutions like word processing and spreadsheets. Of course, the fact that all of this is potentially more cost effective than hosting systems and applications in-house hasn't hurt at all. There are a number of advantages to going with a cloud-based solution. This isn't to say that everything is sweetness and light. There are downsides and risks to moving to a cloud-based model as well but we'll begin talking about some of the risks and how to better mitigate them over the next few chapters.

CASE STUDY 2.1

The first case study will be my own because it's indicative of many common needs but it's not a very complicated scenario so it's a good place to start. I have a small consulting business, in addition to the various other things I do. Like most businesses, I have a need for e-mail, a Web server for presence. Additionally, a calendaring service where I can store all of my appointments and access them from any device I am using, whether it's one of two laptops I use, my tablet, or my phone. They all use different software and operating systems so I need something that's standards based.

Additionally, having a way to store data at a remote server so I can access it anywhere from any devices as necessary as well as share with people I need to. As an example, when I finish a chapter in this book and transmit it to my publisher, adding the document to all of the figures for the chapter can make it too large to easily send by way of e-mail, not to mention taking up a lot of space in my e-mail account. Because of that, I sometimes need to upload the collection of files for each chapter and put it somewhere that I can give my editor access to it.

Just to recap, I had the following needs:

1. E-mail with enough storage that I could use IMAP and keep my messages on the server rather than local.
2. Web server to have a presence for my business.
3. Calendaring with the ability to store appointments with the service provider and gain access to them from any of my devices.
4. Remote, sharable storage.
5. Web conferencing is a nice to have.

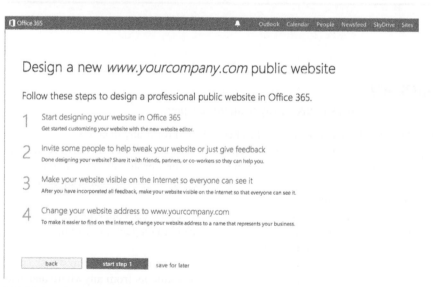

FIGURE 2.5 Creating a Web Site with Office 365

Used with permission from Microsoft.

Previously, I had been using a Web hosting provider that offered me e-mail, but I kept bumping up against the storage limit for each mailbox because I receive a lot of e-mail and often send messages with attachments and those attachments add up pretty quickly and take up a lot of space. I was making use of Google for calendaring, but I couldn't send invites from my own e-mail address. I was also using Web conferencing from a free Web conferencing vendor because it was easy and reliable, and I didn't have enough of a regular need for it to sign up for a service. All of these solutions together were more or less working, but they didn't send a solid message to those I was working with that I had my complete act together. As a result, I needed to move to one platform for everything.

I ended up choosing Microsoft Office 365. In addition to resolving all of my needs as outlined above, they provided me with far more storage than I currently have need for as well as the Web conferencing that was a nice to have. Additionally, I get a number of licenses for all of their Office software products. In the end, I pay a little more per year for the service than I was with all of the services cobbled together, but I get a single place to host all of my communications needs and they provide a very functional interface for me to manage my site, including the Web server and e-mail addresses. Figure 2.5 shows the wizard they use to walk people through creating a Web site for their business. The service I am using is targeted at small- to medium-sized businesses, though they also have plans and pricing for larger businesses as well. The one feature that would be nice to have and it's strange that it's offered to enterprise customers but not the smaller business who would likely have more need for it, is hosted voice mail. Again, I am making use of a central phone number that gets pointed to a couple of lines that can take care of voice mail for me but having it integrated into my e-mail and other communications systems would be far more convenient.

Summary

Here are some ideas to take away from this chapter:

- "The cloud" is a concept that has been around for many decades.
- Currently, an implementation of cloud services uses HTTP, HTML, JavaScript, AJAX, database support, XML, and other related protocols and languages.
- PaaS is making use of someone else's hardware to quickly stand up servers that you can use for anything.
- SaaS is where you let someone else host your data for you, and you access the business application like customer relationship management or human resources functions through a Web interface.
- Storage as a service is where you use a cloud provider as structured disk space, which can offer access to critical business documents from anywhere and also make them easier to share with partners or vendors as necessary.
- UCaaS is where you would outsource your PBX to a vendor and you would access it through a data connection to the Internet.
- There are a lot of advantages to making use of cloud services, including cost savings and speed to completion.

Software as a Service

INFORMATION INCLUDED IN THIS CHAPTER

- Definition
- Models
- Security implications
- Policy considerations

INTRODUCTION

While we are using the term software as a service (SaaS) today, the reality is that the concept has been around for decades. The earliest application providers offered services on mainframes. If you had computing needs, you probably didn't have your own computer and it may simply have been easier to purchase time from a provider, considering the costs involved in purchasing, setting up, caring, feeding, and maintaining one of the large computers that were available in the 1960s and early 1970s. A company might decide to get into the service bureau business by either making use of an existing system that was underutilized or acquiring a new system altogether expressly for the purpose of offering a time-sharing service for users.

This was made possible because of the push into time-sharing operating systems in the early 1960s. Once time-shared operating systems became feasible so multiple users could be on the system at the same time, the door was opened to selling the computer resources. One of the earliest successful commercial ventures into the time-sharing space was the Dartmouth Time-Sharing System (DTSS). DTSS was finally decommissioned in 1999 after 35 years of use, coming online first in 1964.

Time sharing was really just the beginning, though. There had to be services that would be available for a user to take advantage of as well as a way to access those services. The access was typically by means of a Teletype device, and the method for connecting the Teletype to the mainframe was typically through the use of a modem. You might make use of it in order to do your payroll, for example. Calculating pay, taxes, and deductions could be a very time-consuming activity, particularly if you have a large number of employees. The problem, of course, is that acquiring a computer to perform that payroll, particularly if that's the only task it has, was very expensive.

To give you a sense of it, when the IBM/370 was released in 1972, IBM was charging $9,870 per month to rent one. That was for a low-end version of the IBM/370 without much memory or disk and that was the value in 1972. Today's value would be $55,135.99 per month. The IBM/370 was one of the best computers of its time and introduced virtualization so it was also a very powerful system. Outright purchase was somewhere between half a million and a million and a half, again in 1972 dollars. This is not to say that this is what all computers cost but they were still into well over a hundred thousand dollars to purchase a computer. Paying that much money to run payroll and maybe a few other time-consuming and computationally challenging tasks was very cost-prohibitive. You could hire several people to do the work, if you had to.

The cost of the computers in that time was part of what made service bureaus a viable concern. It made sense to pay someone else to take care of time-consuming and computationally challenging tasks or other things that were a lot easier using computers. In 1985–1986, I worked at what was essentially a small service bureau in Vermont as a computer operator on IBM mainframes and several Pr1me minicomputers. Of course, by minicomputer, I'm talking about something at least the size of a large refrigerator. One of the big things this company did was print delivery labels for catalogs for mail-order houses. They would sort and merge mailing lists then print the labels once all the duplicates had been removed and everything put into the right order.

Excuse the lengthy reminiscence but I wanted to make sure to put a little context around the idea of shared infrastructure and going to another company to handle your data and tasks for you. Of course, we are talking about slow, text-based access and text-based services. It's not what we expect today, of course. Today, services are delivered over the Web and the interface is primarily through a browser, though mobile is making it easier to consume Web services through a handheld device without directly involving a browser.

Contact lists

It's not really accurate to label this section contact lists because it's so much more than that, though at its heart is a list of contacts. One of the earliest beginnings of this was the ACT! contact manager in the late 1980s. ACT! was a great contact manager but when it came to using a single contact manager across an enterprise where notes, leads, and other information about customers could be stored and accessed by anyone in the organization. I was at a small software company in the mid-1990s, and we used ACT! not only for the salespeople to store their contacts but also for the company to really maintain all of the information in the case that a salesperson were to move on or be moved on as a result of lack of adequate performance. Salespeople were mostly not in an office but were on the road or in a home office and since the primary data store was at the corporate office, salespeople had to have a way of synchronizing their information with the corporate data store. ACT! had a way of performing that sync but since it was often over dial-up, there were challenges and sometimes even on the local network, syncing the installation on the laptop of a salesperson could cause problems.

On top of the problems of having a large number of people with their own local database expected to synch on a regular basis with a central repository, salespeople have more needs than simply keeping track of contacts and when they contacted them. In fact, beyond a contact database is a customer relationship manager (CRM) that encompasses the contact database aspect while providing a richer experience to help service the customer and also provide capabilities of doing effective marketing and communication in general. All of this is something of a long-winded way of introducing you to a company founded in 1999—Salesforce.com.

Salesforce.com solves several problems that contact managers can have from the perspective of businesses. A contact manager like ACT! relied on a database on the individual computer for each salesperson. Even with regular synchronization, the data is still stored on a laptop until it is synchronized. If the laptop were to experience a failure or get stolen or lost before the data could be synchronized, all of the data would be gone. On top of that, with information stored locally, if the laptop were lost or stolen, the contact information there could be of some value.

Certainly companies could have gone the route of having a database stored at the company and provided access through an interface but that would require the development of an interface, whether it's a Web interface or some more traditional application interface. On top of that, you have to provide a way for your users to get access to the data all the time. This may require a virtual private network (VPN), which means that the only way to access is from a system that had the VPN software on it. While VPNs can be deployed through a Web interface, it still often requires client software to be installed and that doesn't always work from mobile devices. The company could provide access to the data through a Web interface that's exposed to the outside world via the Internet, but there are significant security risks associated with exposing services and data like that. A Web application may have vulnerabilities that could put not only the information in the database at risk but potentially other parts of the organization.

Fortunately, Salesforce.com already has infrastructure that is protected against attack. Where you would have to worry about things like firewalls and attacks against your Web server plus the application itself, Salesforce.com has taken care of that. One way that attackers end up finding ways into your site is by footprinting it. This is a process that takes in a lot of information about not only the platform (i.e., the Web server and anything from the operating system that may be exposed) but also the application itself and any frameworks that may be in use. An attacker may do this because the system software or the frameworks may have known vulnerabilities, whether they are published or unpublished, that could be exploited to get access to either the system itself or the application and its data. It's commonly considered good practice to hide as much data about what you are doing as possible

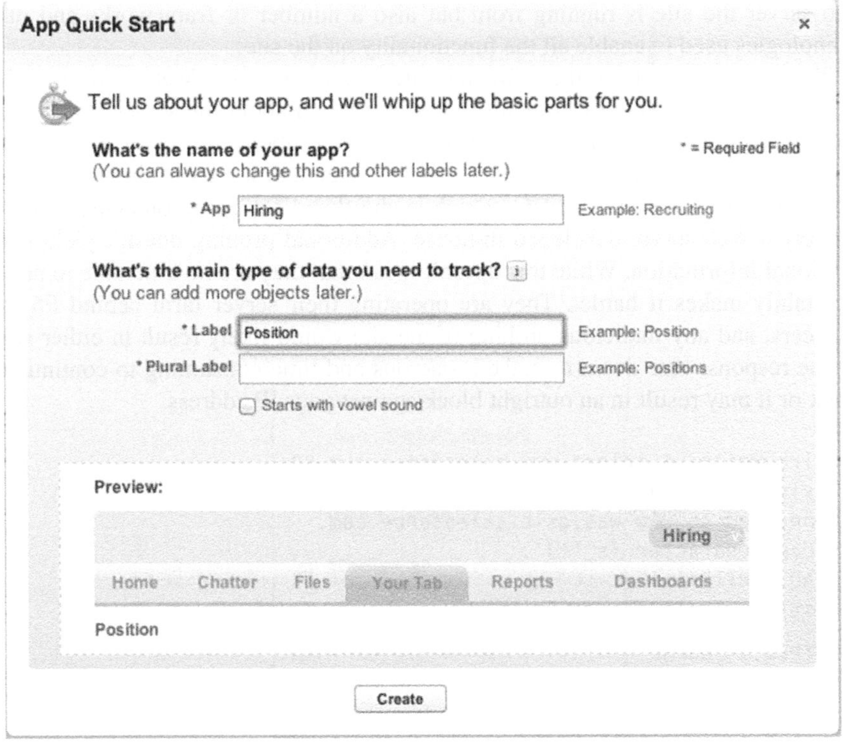

FIGURE 3.3 Creating a Salesforce.com App

your trust into that company and assuming that they will do all the right things with respect to testing and code auditing to make sure the application is solid and secure. This doesn't completely remove the risk associated with putting your data into someone's hands, but it does make it much easier to vet because you are vetting only one company rather than not even being sure who you are vetting because you don't know who you are on a shared server with.

Speaking of applications, though, there are other advantages to going to a SaaS model. In the case of Salesforce.com, they have exposed functionality that their customers can put together in particular ways and create their own applications. This allows them to display and manage their own data in ways that make sense to them. You can see the process of creating an application in Figure 3.3.

This isn't writing an application in a programming language but instead, it's more like pulling together a specific set of data and organizing it in a particular way that makes sense. You may create a marketing application, for example, from the data you are storing with them. Another application you may create, as shown in Figure 3.4, is a contracts application where you have a way to quickly store and organize all of the contracts you are working on. With salesforce.com, there is also a

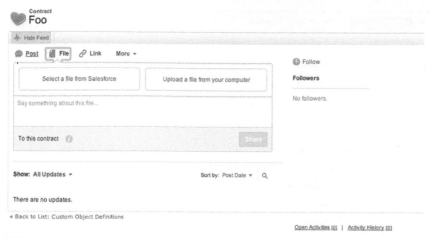

FIGURE 3.4 Salesforce.com Contracts Application

social and collaborative component. You can see on the right-hand side of the image a list of people who are following a particular piece of information. This allows for you to quickly and easily determine the status of a contract if you want to track it.

You could certainly develop applications that do all of this in-house but that requires development resources and a lot of time to get everything you want. You could also buy a CRM solution and deploy it. The problem with both of these situations is you have a list of considerations including access by remote staff, data security, platform security, location of data, and network security. On top of that, you have all the care and feeding considerations like rack space, power, air conditioning, and sparing and replacement costs. There is a lot to consider when you deploy an application in-house as well as a lot of potential cost to it in terms of both capital for the hardware and the expense of the people who will be required to support all of the aspects of the deployment. Making it someone else's problem can be a very enticing answer.

CASE STUDY 3.1

It shouldn't be much of a surprise that school systems have a need to use computers, both to manage the school and to allow teachers to instruct more effectively. Students also need access to computers. Grades have moved on from the traditional paper grade book that you may remember from your school days. Now not only grading is done using computers but also assignments, tests, and interaction with students are done using a computer. I have been working with a small school in the town I live in, providing some outside guidance on their technology. They had several needs that could use SaaS. The first was a grading system. Fortunately, there are a number of advantages of to using cloud computing, and there are sites offering a grade book as a service.

Initially, there weren't a lot of requirements. Kathleen Nichols of the Lyndon Town School in Vermont asked me to help find a solution that would make the grading process easier for the math team. One of the basic requirements was a grade book that could

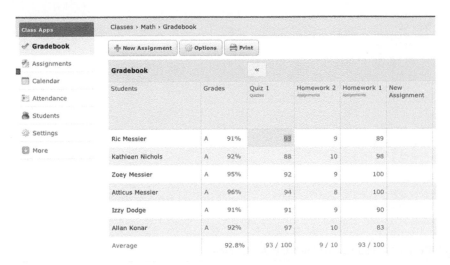

Class Apps	Classes › Math › Gradebook					
✓ **Gradebook**	✛ New Assignment	⚙ Options	🖶 Print			
📋 Assignments	**Gradebook**		«			
🖼 Calendar	Students	Grades	Quiz 1	Homework 2	Homework 1	New
📊 Attendance			Quizzes	Assignments	Assignments	Assignment
👥 Students						
⚙ Settings	Ric Messier	A 91%	93	9	89	
📄 More	Kathleen Nichols	A 92%	88	10	98	
	Zoey Messier	A 95%	92	9	100	
	Atticus Messier	A 96%	94	8	100	
	Izzy Dodge	A 91%	91	9	90	
	Allan Konar	A 92%	97	10	83	
	Average	92.8%	93 / 100	9 / 10	93 / 100	

FIGURE 3.5 Using an Online Gradebook

Name	ID	Access Code
Messier, Ric	5	ricmessier-5-4958

Name	ID	Access Code
Nichols, Kathleen	6	ricmessier-6-1105

Name	ID	Access Code
Messier, Zoey	7	ricmessier-7-5978

Name	ID	Access Code
Messier, Atticus	8	ricmessier-8-8719

Name	ID	Access Code
Dodge, Izzy	9	ricmessier-9-8822

FIGURE 3.6 Online Gradebook Students

handle categories to allow a weighted average. Previously, she had been doing this using Excel spreadsheets but some of it was a manual process. The other requirement was a way for multiple teachers to share the same system, allowing students to be moved from teacher to teacher, as necessary, based on what group they were in each quarter.

Engrade offered a free service that could be used to store grades and calculate averages. Everything a typical grade book offers plus performing all the calculations for you. Figure 3.5 shows an example of the grade book functionality with multiple categories and automatic weighting and averaging. Since you could group teachers according to the school they were in, there was a single roster of students to pick from for each class and the students could be put into different classes by subject area. Since it was initially just the math teachers using the service, the other subject matter areas didn't provide any value.

While initially this was just to make life easier on the teachers, it did have a lot of potential value for the students and the parents as well. In addition to being an online grade book, Engrade also provided the ability to give both students and parents access to the grades in a real-time fashion rather than waiting until the middle of the grading period to get a progress report or the end for the actual grade. This, though, is where we run into some legislative concerns. The Family Educational Rights and Privacy Act (FERPA) was passed in 1974 to give students and families some control over the student's records. FERPA requires that records, both grading and behavioral, be private unless the parent or student gives consent. Because of this, any online grade book has to be concerned with the security and privacy of the grades being kept for the student. One way to handle this is to ensure that there are special codes for each student so only the parents of the student or the student themselves can get access to their grades. Figure 3.6 shows a fragment of a report Engrade generated with slips that could be cut up and distributed to parents. When they use that particular code, they get access to the grades for the student the code belongs to and only that student. This separation of information is critical and mandated by law.

Documents on the go

You're probably quite familiar with this and you may be using it already. As of the moment this is being written, Apple is trying to jumpstart interest in their cloud storage service as well as their office suite by recreating them both. While we'll discuss iCloud and what came before it in a subsequent chapter, Apple is marrying a relaunch of iCloud with their iWork document creation software. Currently, it's in beta and based on the screen captures available on Apple's Web site, it looks an awful lot like the existing iWork software, just rendered in a browser window. Apple is racing to catch up to the other big players. Google introduced Google Apps in 2006, providing SaaS features to users including Google Calendar, Google Talk, and Google Page Creator. Google Docs was added in 2007. The interface to Google Docs is currently Google Drive, which you can see in Figure 3.7.

When you go to the Google Docs Web site, you'll drop into your drive where all of your documents are stored and we'll get into that in a subsequent chapter. Selecting any of the documents in your drive or even creating a new one will drop you into one of the Google document applications. Figure 3.8 shows a spreadsheet in Google Docs. Google Docs, using asynchronous communication with the server

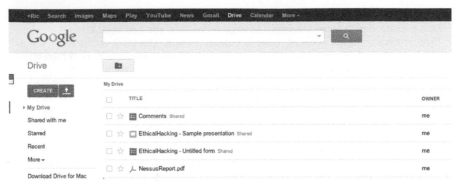

FIGURE 3.7 Google Drive

Google and the Google logo are registered trademarks of Google Inc., used with permission.

Name Path	Method	Status Text	Type	Initiator	Size Content	Time Latency
bind?id=16CSE0X_Y0yBmDZHsTtr49bKFg... 0.docs.google.com/document/d/16CSE0X_Y	GET	200 OK	text/plain	3782954654-bc_man... Script	0 B 1.4 KB	57.63 s 70 ms
save?id=16CSE0X_Y0yBmDZHsTtr49bKFgY... /document/d/16CSE0X_Y0yBmDZHsTtr49bK	POST	200 OK	application/...	1980645551-kix_mai... Script	0 B 55 B	506 ms 504 ms
save?id=16CSE0X_Y0yBmDZHsTtr49bKFgY... /document/d/16CSE0X_Y0yBmDZHsTtr49bK	POST	200 OK	application/...	1980645551-kix_mai... Script	0 B 55 B	81 ms 78 ms
save?id=16CSE0X_Y0yBmDZHsTtr49bKFgY... /document/d/16CSE0X_Y0yBmDZHsTtr49bK	POST	200 OK	application/...	1980645551-kix_mai... Script	0 B 55 B	85 ms 83 ms
csi?v=3&s=kix&action=edit&it=cursorMov... csi.gstatic.com	GET	204 No Content	image/gif	[VM] edit?usp=drive... Script	336 B 0 B	41 ms 39 ms

FIGURE 3.8 Browser Plugin Firebug

where the document is stored opens the doors to true, real-time collaboration since everything is stored somewhere other than on your hard drive. Rather than needing to share a screen or check in and check out documents from a revision control system, Google Docs gives you the ability for multiple users who a document is shared with to make simultaneous changes to a document.

Google Docs has a significant advantage because of the way it works. Let me explain this with an anecdote that many people can relate to. A few weeks ago, I was working on writing a number of questions for another book. I had added 15–20 over the course of a couple of hours, but I'd opened another Word document to refer to and tried to close it. Rather than closing the window I had intended to close—the one I had opened to refer to—I accidentally hit the little red circle on the wrong window and without thinking about it, answered Don't Save when the question came up. It was only after the wrong window closed that I realized I had lost the questions I had been working on. Word does auto-save in order to protect you against system or application failure. If you specifically indicate that you don't want to save a document that has been changed, there is no recovery.

Google Docs uses Asynchronous JavaScript and XML (AJAX) to provide an interactive feeling to what is really a Web page. Where you would normally have to submit a form to get data from the client/browser to the Web server, AJAX provides the ability for the page to trigger a message to be sent from the browser to the server without any other involvement from the user. Using Firebug, you can get a listing of all of the interactions with the server that would otherwise happen under the hood. You can see a fraction of the interaction in Figure 3.8 followed by the full URL indicating the method that was called on the server and the parameters that were provided. This URL shows that the server was asked to save the document.

```
https://docs.google.com/document/d/16CSEOX_
YOyBmDZHsTtr49bKFgYAzoW8Z3kXs3cSWrQc/save?id=16CSEOX_YOyBmD
ZHsTtr49bKFgYAzoW8Z3kXs3cSWrQc&token=AC4w5VjsCeIQPUA3P5bgQ
ptn-C52zJUHeA%3A1376344316046
```

With AJAX, the document will automatically save itself periodically ensuring that all changes to the document are stored. Since the document is stored outside of your local control and any access to it requires network access, it's important to keep storing it whenever possible just in case of a network outage or even a system failure on your side. Any time you return to the document, it is up-to-date without the user actually needing to perform a save function.

Having the document save itself when the browser initiates it also makes real-time collaboration possible. Let's say you were using a traditional approach with a word processor opening a file on some shared storage. Forget for the moment the access issues and let's just assume for the purposes of this example that two people both have access to a file share somewhere and both people have opened the document and are trying to edit it. The first person, who we will call Atticus, makes some changes in the document then the second person, who we will call Zoey, also makes some changes. If they both go to save at the same time, whose changes win and actually get stored to the file on the disk? Let's say that Atticus saves his changes and Zoey wants to pick up those changes. Atticus would have to save and Zoey would have to reload the document in the application. If Zoey made changes, Atticus would have to reload his document. This cycle of saving and reloading doesn't even take into account how the two would communicate when changes were made and what each needed to do.

While applications could be written, and some have been, to be in sync with a server-storage model, Google Docs works exactly this way because of the technology used. While the existing paradigm of load, write, save, close could have been implemented, the fact that there was no state for the browser to be able to share with the server its communicating with meant that some different assumptions should be made for the Web-based model to work well. In a traditional model, the application always knows what the state of the document is in. The operating system that handles the actual storage also knows the state of the document. It's either open or closed. With

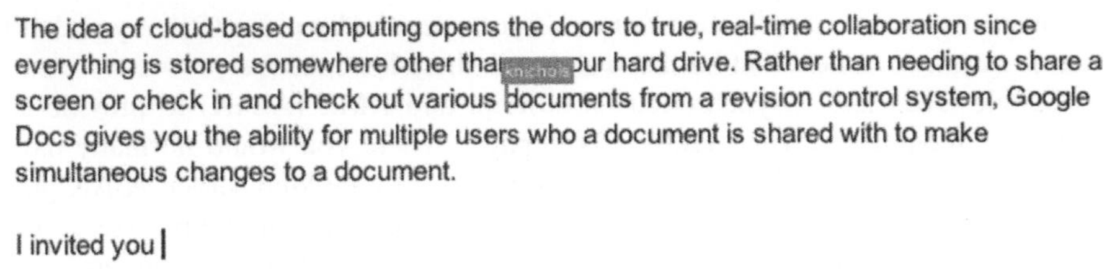

The idea of cloud-based computing opens the doors to true, real-time collaboration since everything is stored somewhere other than your hard drive. Rather than needing to share a screen or check in and check out various documents from a revision control system, Google Docs gives you the ability for multiple users who a document is shared with to make simultaneous changes to a document.

I invited you|

FIGURE 3.9 Using Google Docs

the Google Docs, Web-based model, the server doesn't have a native way to know what the state of the document is. As a result, there is no "file open" state or "file closed" state. The application needed to manage whatever the state of the application is and that state could change on a moment-to-moment basis.

At this particular moment, in my browser that's in the background because I'm working in Word, I have a document that's sitting dormant. Since nothing is going on, the document is in a constant state of flux. While I haven't touched the document in nearly an hour, there has been a steady stream of data passing between my browser and the Google servers. The reason for that is because there is every possibility that the document could be open somewhere else. Again, I have no way of knowing because the application lives inside the browser, not on the server itself. The storage is somewhere else but the functionality, just as with a traditional application, is primarily local. Since the application is local, the server can't indicate to the client that someone else has the document open. In part, this is because there is no sense of open or closed. If someone who I have shared the document with clicks on the document in their Google Drive and they display it in their browser. Until they actually do anything in the document, there is no particular reason to let any other user who is also "in" the document know about the presence of other users. Once a change has happened, all the other users who are displaying the document in their browser need to get the update so they have the most current version. Unless any changes have been made, none of the requests are particularly large. Looking back at the document I have open, Firebug indicates to me that I have 95 requests totaling 3.0 kilobytes transferred.

There are challenges to collaboration, of course. With Google Docs, in order to collaborate with someone, you have to share the document with them. Once you have shared the document, you can select different levels of permissions but let's assume that you have given them permission to make changes. They can now come in and start editing everything that you have done. You can see in Figure 3.9 a screen capture of a Google Doc that someone else is in making changes to. You can see the user-name in a small pink box above the cursor indicating where they are making changes.

Let's say, though, that they go in and either make a lot of changes that you didn't want in your document or they accidentally remove a large chunk of the document. Of course, with the Web-based approach, changes are saved regularly

FIGURE 3.10 Google Docs Revision History

so the accidental deletion has been saved back out to your Google Drive where the document is stored. With the possibility of a number of people in a document, all making changes, what does undo mean? Do you just undo something that you have done, which would require storing that information somewhere, or do you undo the last changes to the document as a whole? Google solves this problem by providing an automatic revision history that not only provides you the ability to revert to a particular version of the document but also gives you a clear audit trail of who edited the document and what they changed. You can see the revision history for a Google Doc in Figure 3.10. This level of accountability and auditing for a document may be much better than you would get from a more traditional document. The audit trail is not a new concept, of course, since there have been document management solutions around for decades now, though a traditional document management solution required software and infrastructure in order to provide a repository and a way to access it.

Google, of course, isn't the only one playing the SaaS game with office documents. Microsoft got into the game themselves with Office Web Apps in 2008. It wasn't until 2 years later, though, that they released them to the public. Since then, Microsoft has also released SkyDrive as a cloud storage offering to collect Office Web Apps documents as well as anything else you want to store. They have also released Office 365 to provide cloud-based communication tools like Exchange e-mail and Lync for instant messaging and voice communication. As you may expect, the Office applications on the Web look a lot like their traditional application

FIGURE 3.11 Microsoft Word Online

Used with permission from Microsoft.

analogs. You can see the Word Web App in Figure 3.11, and it looks quite a bit like the current version of Word, except that it's running inside of a Web browser.

Now that we've gone under the hood a bit, we can get back to the idea of collaboration. SaaS added to data storage in a remote and easily accessible location provides a lot of freedom and possibilities for productivity. We've discussed, at a basic level, the idea of collaboration and the technology and functional concepts that made it possible. However, let's talk about some specific examples around collaboration.

Real-time editing

You've just spent the last 2 months with the members of your team each providing a section of a document that will become a deliverable for the team. Imagine that it's a marketing plan or an engineering design or some other critical business document. At some point, all of the pieces need to be pulled together into a coherent whole with all of the formatting the same and a consistent style and tone. How do you accomplish this? In an older technology manner, this may mean people are sitting around a table where a laptop is displaying a document and one person is in control of the keyboard. You have to walk through the document one chunk at a time and someone has to facilitate the conversation while the person at the keyboard has to take dictation essentially.

Now, why was this model even necessary to begin with? Because with a traditional model and file locking, you can end up making it harder for people to all work at essentially the same time. The application opens a file for writing or reading. If it's for writing, no one else can open it for writing. If it's for reading, you can see what has been done but not make any changes. As a result, you can use a scheduled approach or you can just let everyone go about writing their own document and then merge everything at the end.

Using a cloud-based SaaS model, everyone can jump in and make changes to different sections of the same document. You may construct an outline ahead of time and assign different people to different sections. This means that someone at the end doesn't have to cobble something together from a bunch of different documents, leading to the consistency meeting described above. The consistency meeting may still need to happen but instead of one person making changes at the keyboard, you can have a few people cleaning up different sections. This can lead to some confusion, however, where you may have two people trying to make changes to the same section at the same time. This is always a concern when it comes to real-time document editing, and you may resort to using the version control feature.

Geo-diverse teams

One situation that helps SaaS really shine is when you have people trying to work together from all over the country or world. Anyone can get into a cloud-based document from anywhere and make changes to it. In this case, you may have a situation where you have a technology partner who doesn't have access to any of your company storage, whether through a permanent connection between offices or through a VPN. If you wanted to collaborate on a document, whether a spreadsheet or a presentation or just a word processing document, you might have to resort to saving and e-mailing or, as above, multiple documents that need to be combined or merged after all of the separate work has been completed.

One situation we haven't discussed so far is where you launch a screen sharing session either through an instant messaging exchange or through a commercial provider. This allows you to share your screen with someone who you may want to work with but that can get clunky and difficult to manage, as you have to keep ceding control to the other person in order to allow them to make changes then take control back so you can make changes. While this does work, it's not an ideal situation because of the lack of efficiency and the time it takes to keep switching back and forth and changing the location of the document.

In the case of cloud-based documents, you and your collaborator can work in the same document, as long as it's been shared between the two of you and you can be in completely different time zones without worrying whether each person has the correct version of the document. In the cloud model, there is only one version of the document. This is another huge advantage of using a SaaS model where the data is housed remotely and everyone works from the same set of data. You don't have version control issues.

Agendas

This is a very specific example, but it applies just as well to a number of similar situations. You are trying to pull together an agenda for a large meeting, and you want to make sure that all of the items that need to be discussed are pulled together.

You can send out e-mail and get all of the ideas but then you have to put all of them into one document and then send it out once it's done. You'll also invariably get a lot of duplicate ideas. If you were to use a cloud-based document, everyone could get in and edit the agenda directly and you'd avoid duplicates. On top of that, everyone could see what others have said it and it may spur an idea that wouldn't have made it otherwise. This is one of the advantages of this sort of collaboration—people have a tendency to take an idea someone else has and use it to trigger an idea of their own. We feed off one another and take ideas in our own unique directions. Using cloud-based documents for collaboration allows this sort of creative inspiration and feedback.

Document sharing

This isn't collaboration so much as it is simply avoiding printing out copies of documents for people or e-mailing them around. You write the document, share it with the people you want to see it with appropriate permissions and then they automatically have a copy of it. It also allows you to keep updating it after sharing the link, which wouldn't be the case if you were to e-mail the document around. Again, once you get into e-mailing documents, you end up with version control issues unless you save every change to the document as a new name, which can end up cluttering your storage device with a lot of differently named versions of the same document

While you don't have version issues with cloud-based documents, you can inadvertently end up with an organizational challenge that's similar to the multiple version issue. If everyone starts distributing documents via a cloud-share, these documents start to show up in your shared folder on the cloud storage. This can end up cluttering your own folders making it difficult to find anything. There do need to be some reasonable limits on distribution of data via cloud-shares.

Advantages

You've been driving home, utterly oblivious to the traffic around you as you are consumed with a mixture of the days events and looking forward to spending an evening doing not much of anything on the couch in front of the television. You pull into your driveway on autopilot and as you are putting the car into park, you realize that you have a document due today that you needed to make some final changes to before sending it in. The problem is that you have left your laptop at the office and your company doesn't allow for remote access from anything other than a company-owned device. If you expect to get the document done, you'll need to actually drive into the office and get your laptop. That will take a large chunk out of your evening and once you've done with the drive to get your laptop just to make a few minor changes for submission, your relaxation time will essentially be gone.

The ability to work from anywhere is a significant advantage to SaaS that we haven't spent much time focusing on. You don't have to have a company-controlled computer to get access to critical business functionality because of the concern over transmission of malware from your home system to the corporate network. With SaaS solutions, all of the access control becomes the problem of the service provider and as long as you have vetted them carefully, you can spend your time worrying about whether the work is getting done and not worrying about whether it's safe.

We've talked about cost savings, previously, and it's true that there are cost savings to take into consideration when you are evaluating a SaaS solution. You factor in rack and floor space, power, HVAC, and the support costs, not just from the vendor but also for the care and feeding of the system and the application within your organization and those softer costs can add up quickly. With SaaS, you often end up in a situation where there is a large group of users that can end up supporting one another, as in the case of salesforce.com and their application exchange where an application developed by one company can be put up for use by other companies. Each company's experiences end up building on another's experiences to make the solution more powerful. Again, we come up against the collaboration situation. You may see an opportunity for an application on salesforce.com because you saw something similar but not quite what you need. This enhances the experience for everyone if you end up sharing it.

You can also end up with a consolidated platform for a lot of functionality. In the case of Google Apps or Office 365, you have e-mail, voice, instant messaging, office documents, and more inside a single platform. This has the potential to not only reduce cost but also complexity and productivity. With one vendor for all of those functions, you get a consistency across all of the applications so there is less learning curve. You also get better integration, hopefully, between all of the applications. Finally, you minimize your vendor management by just having one place to go in case you have issues.

CASE STUDY 3.2

In addition to existing companies adding cloud services to their legacy offerings, a number of companies have been created for the purpose of offering cloud services. One of those companies, SmartSheet, offers project management, collaboration, and file sharing in the cloud to its clients. This set of services has allowed companies to be more productive. Since 2006, over 20,000 organizations have made use of SmartSheet services. While SmartSheet provides a way to do project management without buying a complete software solution and the infrastructure to support it, it also offers more collaboration features than some project management solutions. Figure 3.12 shows one of the features SmartSheet offers to allow discussion around a project and its plan.

SmartSheet works well with companies of different sizes as well as local and distributed work forces. It's also a good step up for any organization that doesn't have a project management infrastructure. Behr Paint, for example, was managing by spreadsheets in their marketing organization, but it required shipping spreadsheets around by way of e-mail. In Behr's case, it also meant a number of different formats for the spreadsheets they were using, all of which needed to be reconciled into a single document. Behr needed a project management solution that could work for all of its people, allowing updates from anywhere since one of the major projects was organizing the Behr

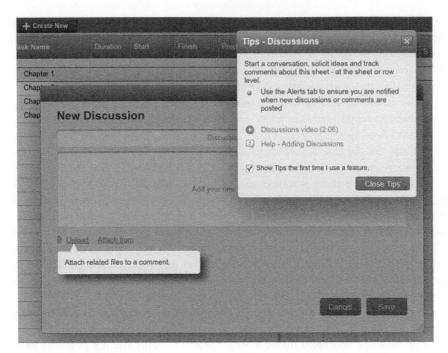

FIGURE 3.12 Using SmartSheet

Used with permission from Smartsheet.com.

FIGURE 3.13 Setting a Reminder in SmartSheet

Used with permission from Smartsheet.com.

Pro Experience Tour in 75 markets over 34 states with five separate teams. This level of organization required an easy to use solution for project management that would also allow attachments for the different events being tracked.

Enterasys also uses SmartSheet to manage their New Product Introduction, which was previously handled using Microsoft's SharePoint. Enterasys manufactures network equipment using vendors from all over the world to create those products. Enterasys needed to have strong control over their project management since delays and errors could be very costly to the company. Enterasys was looking for accessibility from anywhere since their vendors were located all over the world. They also needed flexibility and ease of use. SmartSheet offered the company all of those things. Setting up projects in SmartSheet is very easy, and there are also extensive project management tools available. You can see in Figure 3.13 a new project that was created by clicking a single button as well as a new alert in the project, which could be used to trigger reminders for pending events that may cause a delay to the schedule.

Of course, companies entrusting critical project information to an external organization will have security concerns. When Enterasys puts their product development plans on a Web site, they want to make sure that competitors can't see them. SmartSheet recognizes these needs and implements a multitier application model with a traditional firewall out in front. They also make use of partners like Google to implement services like single sign on rather than trying to implement a lesser service on their own. SmartSheet also implements TLS to ensure communication with the end user is performed over an encrypted link. Additionally, they implement role-based access control to ensure that users can only perform functions they are authorized to, based on their role.

Security considerations

You didn't think you'd get away that easily, did you? We've spent a lot of time talking about all of the functionality you get as well as the freedom you get from deploying SaaS solutions. Actually, security can be an advantage just as collaboration, cost savings and ease of access can be advantages. One example is, again, the advantages you get from putting a lot of resources into one place. When you are trying to go about securing your applications, you may end up with a lot of challenges because you lack the resources to deploy sophisticated solutions that provide multifactor authentication, enhanced identity management, and strong encryption.

Google is offering multifactor authentication making use of something most people already have and use on a regular basis. You can add a mobile phone number to your Google account and you can get a second authentication factor by letting Google send verification codes to your phone. When you get the text message with the code in it, you have proven that you have the phone that has been linked to your account. Of course, this is not perfect, since someone could break into your account and add their own phone to it, locking you out and making the account theirs.

However, thinking positively, the multifactor is an example of a technology that you may have difficulty deploying or implementing on your own, but Google is spreading this technology across a large number of their platforms so in the bigger

▶ Watch the video on application-specific passwords

┌─ **Step 1 of 2: Generate new application-specific password** ─────────────────
│
│ Enter a name to help you remember what application this is for:
│
│ **Name:** [   ] [Generate password]
│
│   ex: "Bob's Android", "Gmail on my iPhone", "GoogleTalk", "Outlook - home computer", "Thunderbird"
│

FIGURE 3.14 Using Google Multi-Factor Authentication

picture, this isn't costing them much on a case by case basis and it reduces their liability while increasing the satisfaction and security of their customers. Not all applications, though, can support this multifactor authentication. As a result, you can create application-specific passwords, as seen in Figure 3.14. These passwords would be generated randomly by Google and apply to specific applications on specific devices. As you can see in the screen capture, you might create a specific password for e-mail on your iPad so you can continue getting e-mail on your tablet. You may also need an application-specific password for Outlook on your PC.

Having specific account and device passwords also gives you a lot of control. You can see a list of the application-specific passwords I have created on one of my Google accounts. I have a couple of laptops I use and I check my Google mail through Outlook so I have two separate passwords for those two applications. I also have a separate password for my phone. Using this little dashboard, I can check the last time each application accessed my account. If this doesn't fit with what I expect, I can then revoke the password meaning the application–device combination will no longer get access to my Google account.

This doesn't mean that all is sunshine and happiness when it comes to security and SaaS solutions. There are a lot of considerations and often it's not an easy decision. As nice as the advantages are, there are also a number of risks with letting the information out of your hands. An easy one, of course, is just the fact that if the provider were breached your data would be gone and your provider may or may not have transparency when it comes to their security policies or how they protect the information entrusted to them by their customers. It's easy to go right to a breach scenario but in reality, you may be just as likely to be breached and your data will be just as gone if that were to be the case. The one difference is that you may be less of a target than a service provider since with you, the attacker would only get your data. If a service provider were breached, all the customer data may be at stake, making the service provider a very enticing target.

Another situation is simply inadvertent data leakage. Here's an example from the Google doc we were talking about earlier. I shared my Google doc with someone and then asked them to share it with someone else. In spite of the fact that I was the owner and they were just added as someone who could change the document, they were able to share my document with someone else who could then make changes. I wasn't asked whether I approved of that sharing or not. This is a big risk when it comes to network connections. Once information has been passed

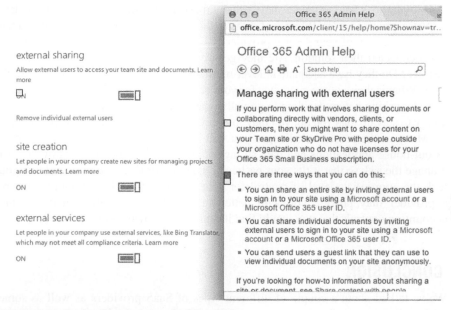

FIGURE 3.15 Setting Permissions with Office 365

Used with permission from Microsoft.

along out of your hands, it's next to impossible to protect it. We'll talk about this in greater detail when we talk about social networking since the same holds true to an even greater degree there.

How do you control your data? You have a similar concern when it's in-house, of course, but once you have put it in the hands of an Internet-accessible provider, you run into a circumstance where someone may either accidentally or deliberately send data to someone outside of your organization that should remain internal only. Certainly this can be done through copy/paste or screen captures or other methods to collect data to send along to someone else but it's much easier if you can, as in the case above, simply give someone access to the information or the document. Typically, you'll have control over that, as in the case of Figure 3.15, where I can control whether people in my organization can share information outside of the organization inside of Office 365. This is targeted at the SkyDrive functionality, and documents created using Office Web Apps.

Another concern, particularly if you are an IT security manager, is that of groups within the company going off and enrolling in SaaS solutions without taking into consideration the risks to the business or fully vetting the security implications of allowing critical data outside of the organization. They may also not have regulatory or audit requirements in mind when they are selecting a vendor. The ease of enrolling and the difficulty in knowing when this sort of behavior is happening make this a significant concern for some businesses.

Moving to a SaaS provider may actually make your disaster recovery or incident response process easier. While any disaster that affects your business locations may miss the location of your service provider, it's worth digging into how your provider has architected their solution. Are they geo-diverse so they can withstand a regional disaster? Do they have adequate failover mechanisms? Are their services highly available? What is their uptime guarantee for your service? These are all questions you may consider asking before deciding to go with a particular provider. If they have no more ability to stay up than you do, you may lose more by going with them than you gain.

Many of the security challenges you will have arise with both in-house as well as out-house applications and data storage strategies. The challenge is how to best manage the risk so that it fits your particular appetite for risk. You may find that you lack the appropriate level of control for your data due to lack of resources where a provider may provide you with better authentication as well as auditing and accounting controls that you would find it difficult to provide on your own.

CONCLUSION

We've talked about a couple of different types of SaaS providers as well as some of the advantages and security concerns of moving to that model as a way of meeting your business requirements. Certainly, having services easily and readily available no matter where you are, where the access is to an external site, and not your internal network can have the potential to make your business more agile and responsive. You also need to be concerned, though, with disaster recovery/business continuity policies and strategies that your provider has to ensure that your business will remain open if they are impacted by a disaster.

There are a lot of other SaaS providers that we didn't discuss offering a wide variety of solutions from marketing to communications to financial services. These providers not only offer business services but also personal services as well. One that springs to mind is Mint.com, providing an in-the-cloud way to manage your personal finances just as you might using a traditional application like Quicken. You would access your financial records through a Web browser rather than being tied to your desktop. This gives you a lot of freedom and the ability to make use of a mobile interface rather than needing a desktop or laptop. While we haven't talked about mobile yet, many SaaS providers have the ability to offer a mobile application to interface with their Web-based services. This also has its advantages as well as its concerns.

There are a lot of issues to be concerned with as you are evaluating a move into the cloud for some of your business processes. There are no clean answers since every business has a different appetite for risk based on how their industry is regulated, how they view risk, and the resources within their company that they most want to protect. There are also managerial concerns to take into consideration since cloud-based services can provide greater flexibility for people to perform their duties somewhere other than their desk under the watchful eye of their manager. Your business may not be prepared to let go of that sort of control since it takes a very different style of managing people and work expectations.

CASE STUDY 3.3

Milo Binkley, Director of IT Security at BC Publishing, discovered a group inside the mid-sized publishing house had signed up with Jive Software for social business services. He realized that this was placing the company's information outside of the traditional control of IT and in the hands of an external provider. He also realized that he had no policies in place to better guide this behavior or ensure that groups came to an advisory group or other controlling body to ensure the provider chosen could adequately protect the company data. While the group who signed up was concerned about empowering their employees and the business with enhanced functionality and flexibility, they weren't as concerned with placing important business data with a service provider.

At the same time, though, he was evaluating a move into the cloud for other business functions like e-mail, calendaring, and other communications needs. Part of the reason for this was the requirement for remote workers needing access to internal systems in order to get e-mail and maintain their calendars. This access has been provided through a VPN with two-factor authentication but that infrastructure has been costly to maintain, both in terms of technology costs and human resource costs. Additionally, controlling the company's e-mail meant needing security gateways for things like virus checking and spam filtering. Moving these services into the cloud would provide better access with less need to support remote access services. The move would also help their disaster recovery and business continuity posture. The challenge was finding a provider that had the right mix of security features, functionality, and price.

Summary

Some things to consider from this chapter:

- What is your policy regarding storage of sensitive information outside of the control of your IT organization and how are you protecting your sensitive information from being stored with a cloud provider?
- What is the policy of users and passwords for the cloud service provider? Can you use a single authentication database under your control to protect users and passwords?
- What are you paying in infrastructure costs between hardware, rack and floor space, HVAC, and power?
- What value would you gain from outsourcing some of your business functions like customer relationship management or human resources?
- Could you save money by outsourcing your e-mail services to an external provider?
- Do you have a lot of remote workers who would benefit from accessing business resources in the cloud rather than making use of a company-owned VPN?
- What would the cost be to migrate any services you currently offer to an external provider?

Storage in the Cloud

INFORMATION INCLUDED IN THIS CHAPTER

- Definition
- Data leak prevention
- Provider types
- Uses

INTRODUCTION

Maybe for many people "in the cloud" is defined as a place where their music or photos get stored because popular services like Apple's iTunes Match and PhotoStream or Samsung's Music Hub give people the ability to store their music or other media types on a set of servers somewhere out in the Internet. This lack of specific location is what gives "in the cloud" a very amorphous feeling because you have no idea where your stuff or what it looks like while it's sitting out there. iTunes itself has a bit of a cloud-like nature to it because they are happy to "store" your purchases for you so you can download them when it's convenient to you. This provides something like a backup for you, if all of your purchases are through Apple. Amazon also has a cloud service where you can access your purchases any time that is convenient for you, from whatever device you happen to be on at that moment.

Consumer services aren't the only places that cloud storage is being utilized. There are several business reasons for using cloud storage and some can improve productivity. However, all are not entirely happy in the land of business cloud storage since there are a number of concerns including privacy, accountability, access control, and data loss. Where businesses have traditionally been able to control who has access to their information, once it has left the organization, even to a vendor site, there are issues around what happens to it and how it's protected. These are serious issues that businesses have to contend with.

Whether they realize it or not, this is something that businesses have to address in one way or another since it's easy to use these storage providers to store information or share it with other people or keep folders synchronized. People may well be using Dropbox, Google Drive, Microsoft's SkyDrive, or a number of other storage providers from inside the enterprise, whether the business leaders or IT is aware of it or not. This can be addressed by blocking all of these sites with proxies or fire-walls but instituting black lists like that can be a challenging task to keep up with. Having policies regulating the use, educating employees and then deploying data loss prevention (DLP) solutions can be more effective ways of dealing with the use of storage providers.

One story that comes up from time to time when you start talking about cloud access is where remote locations, whether those belonging to the company or those of an outsource, has an unstable or slow link back to the home location. Just in order to get things done, people may make use of a cloud storage provider to keep important business documents that they need access to on a regular basis. They would pull the documents from the corporate site and then push them up to the cloud provider, sharing them with associates as necessary. This raises a number of issues, of course, including documents being used for business purposes that may be out of date. It also brings up concerns about having no control over business documents after someone has left the employment of the company.

Uses of cloud storage

This may seem something of a no-brainer but let's walk through some scenarios where cloud storage can make some sense. Certainly from a personal standpoint, you have the situation where you are disposing of devices on a somewhat regular basis and having access to your media and other files from any device you happen to be on is convenient. From a business standpoint, however, many of the same scenarios still apply.

Collaboration

This is a theme we'll keep returning to over and over, it seems. One of the many things I do, in addition to writing, teaching and so forth, is consulting. When I go into a company on a consulting job, I'm walking in with my own equipment—laptop, phone, etc. Many companies have policies and rules around what your computer should look like in order to connect to their network and my system is much different, considering the nature of the work I do, than they would typically see with the systems they provided their employees. Additionally, from a protecting both of us perspective but mostly me, it's better if I don't have any access to their network. In case something happens, I don't want there to be any chance of the reason for the thing going wrong to be me or something I'd done.

However, in order to get the job done, there is a lot of data gathering and I'm not alone when I go on these jobs. If it were just me, I could carry around a large USB stick and keep passing it around from person to person, but there are a couple of us who may be working on any particular job and we all need access to the same data. Sure, we could do the copy from one stick to another, but there are problems with that approach, apart from the annoyance of having to copy files around to multiple USB sticks. For one, if one of the sticks is lost, there is likely critical or sensitive data on the stick. This could be mitigated through the use of encryption, but then you have the challenge of supporting the same encryption mechanisms on the systems you are copying from.

Rather than going into all of.the different problems and ways around it and the problems with that, the short answer is that we have a need to collect information in the form of documentation from the client. Additionally, we may want to share other documentation, notes, reports, and so on with the client and multiple people within the client. Sure, e-mail works but e-mail isn't very secure because most people don't use encryption and while I have certificates for my various e-mail accounts, they would need to have the root certificate authority certificate installed on their system to verify my certificate plus their mail client needs to be able to support Secure Multipurpose Internet Mail Extensions (S/MIME) and decryption and it's just not nearly as interoperable as using a file sharing service. I did mention that I wasn't on their network, right? This rules out file shares on their network and while we could certainly establish a file share at our location and provide access, it would be a hassle with Virtual Private Network (VPNs) required and credentials and everything. The easiest, quickest, most scalable, and most secure way to accomplish this is to just use a Web-based file storage service.

This style of collaboration and information sharing can be accomplished in other ways. As another example, I'm using cloud storage to transfer files back and forth with my technical reviewer. We could use e-mail but if there are other people we want to be able to see the documents, like my editor for example, having one place where they are is far more convenient than to deal with the version issues you get by e-mailing documents around. You either have to put the version into the file name or, hopefully, it can go into the document properties somewhere. Either way, e-mail can be challenging.

Large file transfer

E-mail isn't the most efficient way to transfer files. Many servers have a limit on the size of files that can be attached to messages so it's not even possible in some cases to send files above a certain size. You may want to share a very large file, like a video of your child's first steps, with someone like his or her grandparents. You probably don't want to do something like post it to YouTube where it may be viewable by a lot of people you don't want to see it. You could make it private but there is always the risk of it accidentally being made public. You could send it to Facebook but, similarly, you may lose control over who sees the video. Plus, maybe your parents want the video locally. Using a cloud storage provider and sharing a folder with them so you could upload photos and videos that may be easier dumped into a folder than sent via e-mail.

I have taught a forensics class online the last few years and each year I use a very damaged Windows XP image to allow students to do some practicing with a full system image and make use of the tools we learned about during the semester. The learning management system we use has a file size limit so I post it to a cloud storage site and then share the folder with them so they can download it at their convenience. This works pretty well and since the compressed image is something around 2 GB, it just wouldn't work through e-mail or the learning management system. It used to be that we would have file transfer sites where you could FTP into them and transfer files. Then in the late 1990s, certain people started to discover these FTP sites and how insecure they were and they began using them for storing pirated movies, music, and software, not to mention child pornography. On top of that, FTP has always been a cleartext protocol so usernames and passwords, when they were required, were transmitted in the clear. Add it all up and FTP has really fallen out of favor in a lot of circles. This is where cloud storage picks up where FTP leaves off because cloud storage typically uses encryption to transmit information, making sure your usernames and passwords are encrypted as well as the information you are sending to or retrieving from the server.

Backups

Cloud storage can be used for backups and while it's not perhaps as convenient as something like an external drive, it's always available no matter where you are as long as you have Internet access where using an external drive means you need to carry your drive around with you. Similarly, you may also use cloud storage to offload files you don't need locally but don't want to just archive completely. We used to call this near-line storage, as opposed to online storage (your local hard drive) or offline storage (tape drives, CDs, DVDs, or even external hard drives stored away in a desk drawer). Again, as long as you have access to the Internet, you have access to your backup. This can be very helpful if you travel a lot. It can also be helpful if you have unreliable hardware or make a lot of changes to your systems. There are a lot of providers getting into the backup space. While some of these providers do a lot of advertising to individuals, like Carbonite for example, others may be able to provide backup services to businesses.

While both businesses and individuals have backup needs and their requirements are similar, they are not identical, nor are the support costs to a provider for each client space. Businesses may generally have higher bandwidth needs simply because of the volume of users associated with each business. Additionally, while reliability and sensitivity are important to both classes of users, there is probably more liability on the part of the backup provider when they take on a business user. This has to do with the value of the information that is stored. Intellectual property has a lot of value and as much value as there may be to an individual for their pictures, videos, and other documents, it's much easier to place a specific number to business documents and intellectual property.

Synchronization

You may have several systems and there may be a set of files that you want to be the same across all of those systems. Maybe you want all of your music and photos on your home system to be copied over to your work system so you can have music at your desk and a slideshow of your spouse and kids for your screen saver. Every time you got more photos or music, you'd have to copy it to a drive and take it into work. Or, if you had a laptop, you may be able to copy it over the network. Much easier is simply using synchronizing your data into a cloud storage provider then syncing your work system with the same cloud folders. Having access across devices and platforms is very important. As an example, I use a laptop and a desktop as well as a tablet and a smartphone. While I don't store a lot in the cloud as a place of primary storage, there are some things I do place into the cloud simply for the reason that I can put it up there on one of my devices knowing that it will automatically show up on other devices. When you work with a number of computing devices, having an automatic process to get your data to all of those devices or at least the devices you choose to participate in that process is incredibly valuable.

Security

Let's pull all this together, now. We have a number of cases where using a cloud storage provider is very useful. It can be an aid to productivity and smoothing out some business processes. Not to harp on the word collaboration too much but providing ways to share data with colleagues and business partners can help speed work and decisions. Giving people ways that they can easily collaborate can not only make processes more efficient but you may even find new ways of accomplishing tasks. Once you've opened the doors, people can be creative in how they choose to work with one another and if people are comfortable with how they are working, they will be more productive. However, we don't want to open the doors all the way without taking a look at some issues that could stand to be examined. You want to know and understand the privacy policy for your provider, their data retention policy as well as their data destruction policy. Additionally, are there logs that are available of transactions to be able to trace information that has been accessed, moved, deleted, or shared with others. All worthwhile questions to contemplate.

Privacy concerns

The cloud storage providers all have terms of use or something like them and they will also have something that looks or smells like a privacy policy outlining how they are allowed to handle any data you store with them. This should be a big concern to any business looking to move to a cloud model or thinking about releasing the reins so that their internal users can make use of cloud storage for business purposes from inside the enterprise. A little of digging around can turn up these policies for review. Not everything is a concern that should have you jamming on the brakes in your plans to move processes and storage into the cloud. Some portions of these policies may just stand a little light scrutiny more so you are aware of them than to make you say "hold on, can't go any further."

We can start with the Dropbox service and then move on to others to talk about differences. You'll find that these policies are very similar across the providers. Dropbox has a privacy policy and since it can change based on alterations in their service, new laws and regulations, we'll be looking at the one dated April 2013. The first thing to note is that Dropbox is collecting information from you that they will store just in order to keep you registered. This includes a username and password. Usernames and passwords are a commonly sought-after objective for attackers since it can gain them access to information within that account but may also lead them to be able to compromise other systems. How well they can protect your username and password will be covered below under infrastructure.

Not surprisingly, they collect information, including personal information, for marketing purposes. Under Personal Information in the privacy policy, it states "(iii) to better understand your needs and interests, (iv) to personalize and improve your experience, and (v) to provide or offer software updates and product announcements." You can of course, opt out of such communications but that doesn't mean they are going to remove your personal data from their systems, in part because it helps them to identify you and even though they may not be e-mailing you any longer, they are still tracking what you do in order to make their products better.

On top of marketing information, they also collect data related to where you are. Currently, Dropbox doesn't use GPS information from the mobile platforms that it supports but it reserves the right to one day collect that information. It does, however, collect information now that can be used to locate you with some degree of accuracy. Of course, it does this just because it's a network-based service and in order to communicate with it, you are providing your IP address. There is nothing at all you can do about this if you expect to receive a response from the server you are communicating with. How accurate can your IP address be at locating you? Well, Figure 4.1 shows a map of what one geo-location service thinks my location is. It's not particularly accurate but in the grand scheme of how large the Internet is, it's really not all that far off either. Interestingly, other Web sites have different ideas as to my location and none of them are right either, but similarly close. The point here being that any Internet service will have your IP address. While in many cases this is largely irrelevant, any service that has you authenticate yourself can map you to a location. While this is nothing newsworthy, it is worth keeping in mind. This is not to say that Dropbox or any other storage provider is keeping a mapping of your logins correlated with your location but if it was desirable for marketing purposes, they could make use of it.

In addition to your IP address, providers also have access to a wealth of information collected in their logs. Again, this is simply a result of your interaction with them. Storage providers, just as any other Web service, can get access to what browser you are running and the operating system and version you are running it on. In fact, Dropbox has this to say in their Privacy Policy about the correlation of your personal information and your location: "We also collect some information (ourselves or using third-party services) using logging and cookies, such as IP

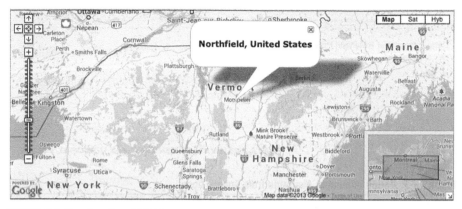

FIGURE 4.1 Geo-locating IP Address

Google and the Google logo are registered trademarks of Google Inc., used with permission.

address, which can sometimes be correlated with personal information. We use this information for the above purposes and to monitor and analyze use of the service, for the service's technical administration, to increase our service's functionality and user-friendliness, and to verify users have the authorization needed for the service to process their requests."

Your IP address isn't the only way to track you, particularly in light of social networking. Anything you post publicly may have information that you don't want to share. Many digital cameras, particularly those in smartphones, have the ability to place location information in your photos. When you share those photos, you are providing information regarding your whereabouts to people who may be interested in knowing when you are away from home. On top of that, let's say there was someone you didn't want to know the details about where you are. Stalker may be too easy a word since most people don't have stalkers but there may be a lot of people you'd rather not know specifics about where you are or where you've been. There are a lot of different ways to track you in a digital world if you are not careful.

What does all of this mean? Is your personal information at risk? Will it be shared with anyone? If the provider you choose is adhering to the Safe Harbor principles, the company is supposed to notify you that they are going to share your data with anyone. However, there may be exceptions to this. Box.com has this to say in their Privacy Policy, "We may disclose information to a third party to (a) comply with laws or respond to lawful requests and legal process, (b) to protect Box, agents, customers, and others including to enforce our agreements, policies and terms of use, or (c) in the good faith belief that disclosure is needed to respond to an emergency, or protect the personal safety of any person." The short version is that if law enforcement provides them with a warrant or subpoena, they will generally have to comply.

Safe Harbor

It's worth discussing Safe Harbor here, particularly in the context of privacy. Most of the providers you will run across will say they adhere to the Safe Harbor principles and since they do as a short-handed way of indicating some guidelines they operate under with respect to personal information that has been entrusted to them. Safe Harbor in a general sense is an example of actions that won't violate a particular rule. Specifically, in this case, Safe Harbor is a set of guidelines that, if followed, will not violate the European Union Directive 95/46/EC on data privacy, also called the Data Protection Directive. The Safe Harbor Privacy Principles were developed by the US Department of Commerce, as a way to allow US companies to certify that they adhere to the EU's standards so they can do business in Europe.

The EU requires that companies certify they adhere to these principles and then recertify each year. The principles that companies must adhere to are as follows:

- **Notice**: If data is collected from users by a company, the users have to be informed what data is being collected and the manner in which it is being collected.
- **Choice**: Users have to be given the ability to opt out of having their information provided to third-party businesses.
- **Onward transfer**: Any company that wants to send user data to a third party has to be sure that the third party also uses adequate data protection principles.
- **Security**: A company has to make reasonable efforts to protect the data that it has collected. This can be challenging since reasonable efforts can change over time, based on technology advances and changes in security best practice.
- **Data integrity**: Data that is collected should be for a specific purpose and be applicable as well as reliable to that purpose.
- **Access**: Users have to be provided access to the information stored about them and make any changes necessary to correct or delete if it is inaccurate.
- **Enforcement**: There has to be a way of enforcing these principles.

The Safe Harbor Privacy Principles aren't the first notable Safe Harbor provisions in the data space. When the Digital Millennium Copyright Act (DMCA) came out, there were Safe Harbor provisions in it to protect service providers against legal action in cases where the providers' users were violating the act.

Data retention

The only law currently in existence in the United States requiring the retention of data is Sarbanes–Oxley (SOX) that requires any data that has been used to create financial reports be retained for 7 years. This impacts public companies in order to provide transparency to the shareholders. This could include evidence of usage that was used for billing purposes. Beyond that, though, there are no requirements for data retention on the part of cloud storage providers, though they will generally have their own requirements around storage and retention of information with respect to log files and other usage artifacts resulting from the service.

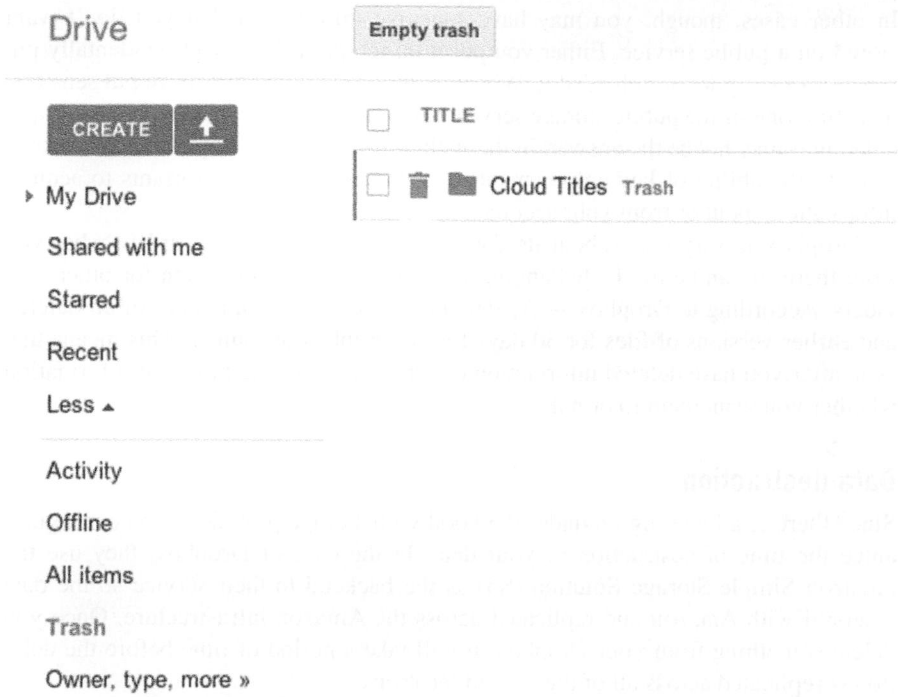

Drive   Empty trash

CREATE   ↑

▶ My Drive

Shared with me

Starred

Recent

Less ▲

Activity

Offline

All items

Trash

Owner, type, more »

☐   TITLE

☐   🗑   📁   Cloud Titles Trash

FIGURE 4.4 Google Drive Trash

Google and the Google logo are registered trademarks of Google Inc., used with permission.

While knowing how long they will have information about when and where you have used the service is interesting, what's more relevant is how long they are keeping your data around. Like any good business based in a digital space, most of these hosting providers perform backups. They may also use replication to store your data in multiple locations for online or near-line access at any point. When you delete information from your storage folder at a cloud storage provider, is it really deleted? Google has instituted functionality in their Drive service that is similar to what you are likely used to from using a graphical desktop environment. They have a Trash folder. You can see in Figure 4.4 both the link in the left-hand navigation bar as well as the one document that I have in my trash folder in my Google Drive. The thing about the Trash link, though, is that it's hidden under More so if you don't know it's there and don't have a need to recover any data, you may not recognize that Google is still storing information you thought you had deleted. Box.com, SkyDrive and others use similar functionality to allow the restoration of deleted files, just as you have on your desktop.

While in some cases, that's a good thing, since people accidentally delete files all the time and having the ability to restore can be a lifesaver when it's needed.

In other cases, though, you may have sensitive information that you don't want stored on a public service. Either you put it up temporarily or you accidentally put it into a sync folder or uploaded it. Whatever the reason, you may have put sensitive data onto one of the public storage services and want to make sure it's gone. Simply deleting it may not be the answer. In these circumstances, you may also want to keep in mind the ability of law enforcement to issue subpoenas and warrants to acquire information about or from your account.

Dropbox is very clear about its data retention policy with regard to what you store there. It can be more challenging to locate similar information for other providers. According to Dropbox—"By default, Dropbox saves a history of all deleted and earlier versions of files for 30 days for all Dropbox accounts." This means that even after you have deleted information on Dropbox, it is retaining that information whether you want them to or not.

Data destruction

Since there is a lot going on under the hood with storage providers, you can't guarantee the time of destruction of your data. In the case of Dropbox, they use the Amazon Simple Storage Solution (S3) as the backend to their service so the data is stored with Amazon and replicated across the Amazon infrastructure. Once you delete something from your Dropbox, it will take a period of time before the deletion is replicated across all of the cached locations.

Infrastructure

This is the cloud after all and the foundation of any cloud function is the collection of technologies that are commonly based around the World Wide Web. HTML, JavaScript, XML, AJAX, PHP, and so on are commonly the backbone for providing these types of services. Additionally, there is probably a database hanging around somewhere even if it's only tracking user information and associated login information. How is all of this protected against attack? The common attack types on Web technologies are injection attacks and issues with authentication and session management. Additionally, there are some attack types related to poor input validation like Cross Site Scripting (XSS). The question is, what is your cloud storage provider doing to make sure they are protected against attack, which could compromise your data?

Protecting yourself

According to Google's investor information, they made $43 billion in advertising revenue in 2012. Make no mistake, they make a large amount of money knowing as much as they can about you and while they may not share the contents of your documents with other people and they also can't use the contents of your documents as though the documents belonged to them, they do use the contents of your documents to learn more about the sorts of things that are of interest to you so that they can target advertising at you.

Revenues	Full Year		2013 (Unaudited)	
	2011	2012	Q1	Q2
Google Web sites	$26,145	$31,221	$8640	$8868
Y/Y growth rate (%)	34	19	18	18
Q/Q growth rate (%)	NA	NA	0	3
Google network members' Web sites	$10,386	$12,465	$3262	$3193
Y/Y growth rate (%)	18	20	12	7
Q/Q growth rate (%)	NA	NA	−5	−2
Total advertising revenues	$36,531	$43,686	$11,902	$12,061

In millions, except share amounts which are reflected in thousands and per share amounts.

While most of the cloud storage providers encrypt your data to protect it while it's sitting on their drives, that doesn't protect your data from them since they typically have the keys for the encryption. This isn't always the case, though. Some providers, like Tresorit, have encryption that takes place on the client side so the encryption keys are with the client. While there have been very few publicly reported breaches of online storage providers, there is always the possibility of it happening. If you are concerned about the sensitivity of your data that you are pushing up to a cloud storage vendor, you can encrypt it beforehand using any of a number of utilities that are available. Windows, for example, provides the ability within the operating system to encrypt files and folders. When you select the Properties on either a file or a folder, you can click on Advanced and get a dialog box that will allow you to check Encrypt contents to secure data. You can see the check box in Figure 4.5. There are a number of third-party utilities, as well, that will allow you to encrypt data. Once you have encrypted it, you can upload it and as long as you don't upload the keys as well to be stored with it, you can leave it there without concern about it being opened and compromised. This is a process, though, and something you may want to consider for only your most sensitive information. If I were to store, for example, my Christmas card list, I may not want to bother encrypting it unless it had addresses associated with names. If it did, I may be concerned about the leakage of that information, especially since it's not mine. Files can be encrypted on a case-by-case basis, of course, based on their sensitivity.

The storage providers we have been primarily talking about so far all have two-factor authentication, which ensures that you are using something you know and something you have to protect yourself from your account being compromised. Multifactor authentication is the idea that there are three primary authentication factors that can be used to identify someone—something you know like a password, something you have like a smartcard or cell phone, and something you are. Something you are is where biometrics comes in and you would use a fingerprint or

FIGURE 4.5 Encrypting Files on Windows

Used with permission from Microsoft.

an iris scan to identify yourself since those features are unique to every person or at least not something that can be easily proven to be not unique.

Given how ubiquitous cell phones are and their ability to receive messages no matter where you are, the cell phone has become a good second factor on top of the password. The provider would send a message or code to your phone either through a text message or a call and you would use that code as a second authentication factor. If an attacker were to get both your password and your cell phone in order to compromise your account, you are likely in more trouble than just having your account compromised. In Figure 4.6, you can see how Microsoft uses a second factor authentication. While the selection for sending a message to my phone (and you'll notice my entire number isn't shown in case someone has gotten to this point with a stolen password), I also have the option to receive a phone call or to get an e-mail. Once I have the code, I can enter it and prove that I am who I say I am.

Encryption

Employees at the storage provider may have access to data that is stored with them even though there are policies and procedures at each company designed to protect

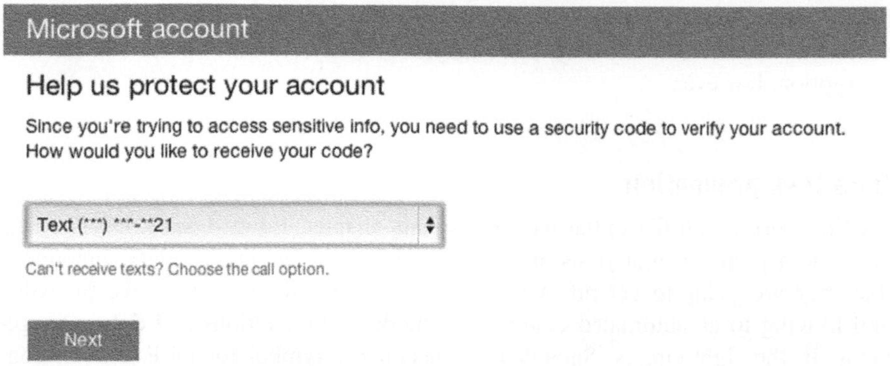

Microsoft account

Help us protect your account

Since you're trying to access sensitive info, you need to use a security code to verify your account.
How would you like to receive your code?

Text (***) ***-**21   ⇕

Can't receive texts? Choose the call option.

Next

FIGURE 4.6 Multi-Factor Authentication with Microsoft

Used with permission from Microsoft.

your information and more importantly, the provider from any legal entanglements resulting from your information being stolen or removed. However, the provider isn't the only one to take into consideration when you are deciding to place your data with a storage provider and deciding how to accomplish that. While it's certainly not news to people in the business, the intelligence agencies of the United States have long been in the business of gathering digital intelligence within the United States. In the late 1990s, it was rumored that the Federal Bureau of Investigation (FBI) had a piece of software called Carnivore that was capable of devouring large amounts of data and analyzing it. At the time, I was working at GTE Internetworking and we didn't believe that even if it did exist, Carnivore was capable of consuming the nearly 10 gigabits per second worth of data our OC192 links were capable of generating given the hardware of the time.

However, now, computing power has increased, our data access has increased due to a wider bus in the common Intel processors we are using today and it may be possible for a few systems to consume a large amount of traffic and keep up with it in real time. The NSA has been accused of not only spying on phone calls around the world but also of infiltrating the networks of service providers, meaning they are capable of capturing traffic between data centers as well as potentially traffic coming in from subscribers. Theoretically, if you are simply using one of these service providers being monitored just for business the NSA won't have much interest in you but the fact that it's being monitored may be cause for concern.

The best way to protect yourself from any level of monitoring is to make use of encryption to protect your data, not only in transit from your network to that of your service provider but also at rest. When your data is sitting on a drive at your storage provider, it is potentially at risk from a breach or a rogue administrator. While the data may be encrypted by your provider, the keys used to encrypt it are owned by your provider. If that's the case, a breach may be able to make use of stored keys and an administrator may also be able to get to the data from the inside. You can protect yourself against that sort of attack by encrypting the data yourself before transmission into the cloud. If what you are storing with a cloud provider isn't sensitive in any way, there may not be any reason to go to the effort of encryption, however.

Data loss prevention

As I'm working on the initial writing for this chapter, Edward Snowden is in the news on a pretty regular basis and, in fact, the NSA has just recently announced that they are going to get rid of 90% of the system administrators like Snowden and moving to an automated cloud-based model for operations and data management. In the right circles, Snowden has become a symbol for DLP, though consumer media has been more focused on the international drama around his leaving the country and the US government trying to get him back and facing off against other governments.

Why is Snowden the symbol for DLP? Because at the center of everything, what he really did was walk out of the NSA offices with a lot of documents on a USB stick, which he shouldn't have been able to do. Not only was what he did a policy violation but there should have been technical controls that prevented him from using the USB stick to begin with. What does copying data onto a USB stick have to do cloud-based storage? In the end, both have the potential to remove critical or sensitive data from an organization and once the data is gone, it can put the organization at risk either by giving a competitor an advantage or by providing information for further infiltration. Perhaps even risks in other areas but no matter what the risk may be, having sensitive or critical data leave the control of the organization is not a good thing.

In order to protect a company from this sort of thing, we use DLP. DLP has become big business and it comes in a number of forms since there are a number of ways you can have data leave your facility. This was highlighted in late 2012 and early 2013 with the report from Mandiant regarding Advanced Persistent Threat 1 (APT1) indicating that this group that had been identified was infiltrating desktop systems through malware and other social engineering techniques and once they had a foothold on the desktop, they were using the access to shared storage on the network to grab as much data as they could and send it out to storage facilities under their control. The amount of data that has been stolen from companies around the world using these techniques is simply impossible to count. But the strategy documented highlights the challenge of detecting and stopping data loss.

Let's start out by identifying some of the ways that data can be extracted from a company and moved into the hands of either a hostile entity or a competitor.

- Copied to a USB drive
- Carried out of the building in hard copy form
- Copied to shared cloud storage
- Copied to storage controlled by the hostile or competitive entity
- Extracted through Bluetooth from a rogue device in the area

- Extracted from sniffed network connections
- Posting to social media
- E-mail

These ways of getting data out of a system could be used either with the knowledge of the user, whether maliciously or otherwise, or without their knowledge as a result of a system compromise. What you need is a way to detect when sensitive data is going somewhere it doesn't belong. There are a lot of ways for data to leave a system, as outlined above, but when you think about it, you could catch them with either a network DLP solution or an endpoint DLP solution. Those two types would catch the different ways sensitive data would leave the organization.

A network DLP solution would be set up on the perimeter of the network and it would have to scan all network traffic looking for evidence of sensitive data as it passes through the DLP system, whether it's a device or software running on a system. If it detects communication that may include sensitive information, it can trigger an alert. The difficulty is that if the communication is encrypted, as in visiting a Web site over Secure Sockets Layer/Transport Layer Security (SSL/TLS), a network DLP will not be able to determine whether there is sensitive information being transmitted. This would be the case for any of the cloud storage providers that all use SSL/TLS to protect information in transit.

You can also get endpoint DLP that has an advantage over network DLP because it has the ability to see data before it gets encrypted. It also may have the ability to block transmissions of e-mail, instant message, or uploads through Web sites. Preventing sensitive information from being sent in e-mail at the endpoint can keep the data from being stored on a server, even if that server is corporate controlled. Endpoint DLP can also prevent data from being copied via Bluetooth or over to your mobile device (smartphone, tablet, etc.).

CONCLUSION

Cloud-based storage solutions can be incredible ways of bringing efficiency and collaboration to a work environment. One of the biggest considerations you have to make while looking to transit to cloud storage, though, is how to protect your most sensitive information and also gain control over how it's stored. This is also the case even if you are not trying to transition to cloud storage as a strategy since people in your organization may well have found ways to implement cloud storage themselves for either their needs or for the needs of their individual groups. As a result, getting ahead of it with policies, education, and technical answers to protect your sensitive information, like DLP solutions, can go a long way to protect your business.

When you start developing your policies, you need to be aware of the different information that these providers collect, especially in the case where the industry you are in is regulated. Health care particularly has regulations about how you can handle the data you have and what you can do with it. To a lesser degree, any business that handles credit card data has some rules they are expected to comply with. These aren't regulations but instead are guidelines you would be expected to follow in order to protect the information entrusted to you by your customers. You should want to protect it in order to keep those customers and their business.

The world we are in is growing much smaller, much like a very small community where everyone knows everything about everyone. The reason for this is the move to digital technology for more aspects of our life. There are advantages to this, of course, where we can easily keep in touch with friends and relatives but there are disadvantages too where it's a lot harder to maintain your privacy and moving your personal or professional information into the cloud can do more than simply fray at the edges of your privacy. It can take enormous chunks out of information you may have otherwise considered to be private.

Summary

Some points to consider from this chapter:

- Without policies and technical support like firewalls and proxies, employees may already be using cloud storage.
- Do you have a strategy in place for DLP to ensure sensitive information isn't leaving your organization?
- Encryption will help protect any information you may be storing in the cloud. What are the encryption in transit and at rest policies for your provider?
- What is the data destruction policy for your cloud provider and does it match requirements you may be bound by?
- What is the retention policy for backups at your cloud provider? Do those retention policies match with any legal or regulatory requirements you have?
- What would you be using cloud storage for? Convenience? Easy access from external sources? Cost savings?

CASE STUDY

Small businesses can gain enormous benefit from implementing cloud storage solutions because it allows even the smallest of businesses to immediately have information technology infrastructure without having to expend a lot of money in hardware, software, engineering, and maintenance. Additionally, if you are a business that is more decentralized, making use of the cloud can enable sharing and storage of information among people who are employed by your organization without needing to find ways to give those people, who may be all over, access to your network. IP Architects is a security consulting organization that has run into some of these scenarios and has solved them by moving some of its operations into the cloud. John Pironti of IP Architects says he decided to use a cloud storage solution for his business because of the availability of information from anywhere, both for him when he's on the road and for the consultants he employs who are geographically diverse.

Additionally, cloud storage gives IP Architects disaster recovery capabilities because his data isn't stored at the business and is protected redundancy and backups that would be challenging for them to implement themselves due primarily to cost considerations. Using cloud storage, IP Architects gets long-term archive capabilities at a reasonable price and rather than having the backup on tape or some other offline storage medium, the archives are online or near-line and far more readily available.

When it came to deciding what vendor to use, Pironti took into consideration the cost as well as the availability metrics and how well the solution would integrate with his current applications. Additionally, since he provides security consulting, the provider had to have encryption capabilities, including the ability to manage and escrow keys used for the encryption. Finally, he had to ensure that the provider had strong authentication, including multifactor, as well as logging capabilities and an audit trail over how and when data was uploaded. In the end, Pironti selected Box.com as his cloud storage vendor after using a matrix comparing his requirements to the capabilities of the different storage vendors. Pironti says they were the best fit for his company given his current needs as well as what he expected to need in the future.

Further reading

Why Stalkers Love Your Geotags, 2013. About.com Internet/Network Security. Retrieved December 3, 2013, from <http://netsecurity.about.com/od/securityadvisorie1/a/Why-Stalkers-Love-Your-Geotags.htm>.

Mohamed, F., 2013. NSA Revelations Threaten Cloud Companies. The Huffington Post. Retrieved December 4, 2013, from <http://www.huffingtonpost.com/2013/11/06/nsa-revelations-cloud_n_4226695.html>.

Virtual Servers and Platform as a Service

INFORMATION INCLUDED IN THIS CHAPTER

- What is virtualization?
- Benefits to virtualization
- Virtualization in the cloud
- Delivery speed

INTRODUCTION

Virtualization offers a lot of benefits to businesses, as well as users. On the computer I'm writing this on, I have Parallels installed and I run an instance of Windows 8 and another instance of Kali Linux. I regularly run virtual machines because I have applications I either want to have access to or need to have access to and they run on different operating systems. It's far more convenient to have multiple operating systems running on a single machine than it is to have multiple machines. I have one laptop to carry around and I can bring up other operating systems as necessary, based on where I am and what I'm doing. This is much easier on my back, needing only one laptop rather than several, but it's also a lot easier on my wallet because I don't have to buy a new system or laptop just to be able to install a new operating system. I do, though, need to buy the license if I'm running an operating system like Windows. I can't get around that legally.

While you could multiboot operating systems as well, using virtual machines is far more convenient. If you multiboot, you'll consume a fixed amount of disk space to accommodate a separate partition for the additional operating system. In a virtual machine, you can set up a dynamic disk that only takes up the amount of space used rather than the entire amount of space allocated to the partition. You also need a way to sync up bookmarks from your Web browser and also have a way to get to e-mail and perform other, similar business-related tasks in the second partition. While it's not entirely onerous to maintain two separate sets of application to handle business communications, it can cost time to do that, which could be better used actually performing work. This doesn't even consider the time it takes to shut down one operating system and boot up another.

The same advantages that apply to me, apply to bigger businesses and on a bigger scale. Where I don't have to wear by back out lugging around a bunch of laptops or desktop systems, a business can save on rack and floor space by consolidating their all of their operating systems onto a smaller number of physical systems. Once you have a smaller number of physical systems, you save on power, as well as HVAC. Businesses will also save a lot of money when they consolidate systems because where I may save a few hundred by not having to purchase another system to host another operating system, server-class hardware with redundant power supplies, lights-out management and all of the other exciting features that come with server-class hardware costs multiple thousands of dollars.

We've been having this lovely, meandering discussion about cloud-based technologies so you may be wondering what the deal is with the sudden veer into the oncoming traffic lane of virtualization. Many cloud computing services rely on virtualization in order to work. This is especially true when it comes to platform as a service (PaaS). PaaS can be used to very quickly spin up a Web service or application. Some of the services we have discussed up to this point actually use the PaaS services of other providers in order to deploy their own services. One of the great attributes of cloud computing is building upon the backs of others. While this has long been common in business, being able to take advantage of someone else's expenditure in creating a large data center with network performance and reliability is an enormous benefit. Take advantage of the work and expenditure these companies have put into making all of this work.

History of virtualization

It may be surprising that the idea of virtualization goes back to the 1950s. In fact, while the PC world that you may be most familiar with is now really jumping on the virtualization bandwagon, larger systems have been virtualized very successfully for more than 40 years. First things first, though. While virtualization was introduced as a concept in the late 1950s, it wasn't until the next decade that a virtual machine was actually implemented. IBM was behind the first push into virtualization in the early 1960s. While they were working on their Control Program/Cambridge Monitor System (CP/CMS) operating system, they began developing prototypes and test systems to support the development of an operating system that was capable of supporting timesharing and virtual operating systems.

One of the biggest challenges was memory, especially considering the limited amount of memory even the largest of systems of that era had. Without adequate memory, it was difficult to support a number of programs running at the same time, much less having multiple operating systems, each with multiple programs running inside it. The solution to the problem was virtual memory. Virtual memory involves moving data out of physical memory to another location temporarily in order to swap in other data. On a system where there is one user, as in a personal computer running DOS in the early 1980s, this may be accomplished with the use of memory overlays.

With only one program running, the user has full control of the system, and can swap memory out any time they want. When you have multiple users on a single system, you need the operating system to make decisions about what information can be swapped out of memory and stored elsewhere.

There are a few challenges with respect to virtual memory. One of the first is deciding how to decide what information to move out of physical memory. There are a number of ways this can be handled including first in, first out; last in, last out; first fit; and best fit or worst fit. There are a lot of algorithms that can be used to move information out of memory so the next decision is where to store it. Physical memory is considered primary storage because it's fast, or at least the fastest way to access large amounts of information on a computer. The next best scenario is to use your permanent storage in a temporary way. The hard drives we use today are far removed from the storage options available in the 1960s, though IBM did have a platter-based hard disk in the early 1960s when they were developing the first virtual machine. However, the systems were at least as likely to be using magnetic cores for long-term storage. These magnetic core storage devices were neither fast, nor large.

While there were hard drives, they were neither fast nor large. However, they were the best option for moving information out of primary storage in a way the information could later be retrieved and put back where it came from. This brings up another problem. The programs and their associated data are all different sizes, so are we going to just pull entire programs out of memory in order to make room for other programs? It's an option, though maybe it makes more sense to chunk the programs up into a collection of bits that's larger than a byte or a word but smaller than the full size of the program. In fact, virtual memory is typically implemented in pages. The size of a page is not universally defined, but instead is up to the specific implementation of the operating system and its virtual memory. The advantage to using pages, though, rather than swapping out entire programs, is that the remainder of the program may be able to continue to execute if the pages in memory have the operations next in line for execution on them.

Now we have pages, a place to store them and a way to decide which pages we are going to pull out of physical memory. What we are missing is a way of determining what page is missing and where on the disk that page happens to be so it can be retrieved. As it turns out, the best way to handle this is a specialized piece of hardware and the early implementations of virtual machines didn't have this piece of hardware. The first virtual machines available commercially, though they lacked the hardware necessary to make virtual memory efficient, were the IBM System/360s, available in 1965. The System/370, announced in 1970, would include the hardware necessary to fully implement virtual memory.

In the 1980s, UNIX workstations were becoming popular among technical users like engineers but business software like spreadsheets was commonly written for Microsoft's Disk Operating System (DOS). The company Insignia Solutions created an emulator that could run DOS programs inside a UNIX workstation. While it is considered an emulator because of the translation required between instruction

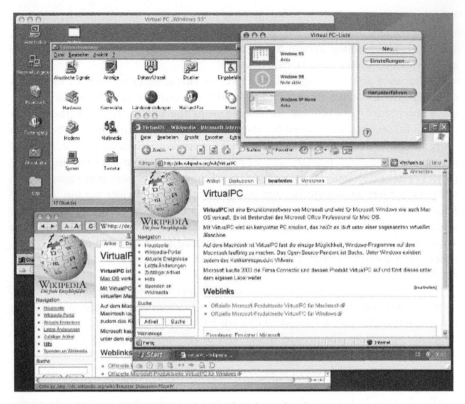

FIGURE 5.1 Microsoft Virtual PC Running Multiple Operating Systems

Used with permission from Microsoft.

sets due to the different processors in use with PCs and UNIX workstations, it offered a virtual machine running inside of whatever Unix-like operating system the user had. Later, it gave the ability for Macintosh users to be able to get access to DOS and later Windows applications without having to have a second system.

In the mid-1990s, Virtual PC was released by Connectix as another emulator program, allowing Macintosh users to run Windows programs. Figure 5.1 shows multiple instances of Windows running inside an Apple Macintosh. Remember that in the mid-1990s, Apple wasn't yet using the same Intel processors that Windows ran on so running those programs required an emulator capable of doing the translation between the Motorola and PowerPC processors and the Intel instruction set. Connectix followed with a release of Virtual PC to run inside of Windows but this came after VMWare entered the space in 1999 with the release of their Workstation that allowed you to run a virtual system inside of a host operating system.

Over time, virtualization became more mainstream. Microsoft bought Connectix to acquire the Virtual PC technology to offer their own virtualization solution.

Different emulation and virtualization software was developed for Linux, including Xen and KVM, which was a set of kernel extensions allowing virtualization to be handled within the kernel. Sun Microsystems also developed a virtualization technology that was included in Solaris. Sun also owned the processors in their systems so they were able to add processor support for their virtualization technology. Meanwhile, back at IBM where it all began, their mainframes now have logical partitions (LPARs) that partition a system into multiple LPARs with each partition running a separate operating system.

How virtualization works

Virtualization requires software that is capable of providing the look of a hardware platform to a guest operating system. This requires that it respond to all interactions with the system Basic Input/Output System (BIOS) in a way that's consistent with how hardware would respond. This requires that it is able to see those interactions, including input/output attempts, interrupts, and memory accesses. The operating system, and the subsequent users of that operating system, sees an abstract device with a set of hardware that has nothing at all to do with the underlying hardware of the host system. A virtual machine can present multiple hard drives and multiple network interfaces where there may not be multiples in the host system. You may offer up an Small Computer Systems Interface (SCSI) to the hard drives on your guest operating systems where you have only Parallel AT Attachment (PATA) drives on your physical system. Figure 5.2 shows the configuration screen from a Parallels virtual machine showing not only the devices that are configured for that machine but also a set of devices that could be added.

In 1974, Gerald Popek and Robert Goldberg defined a set of requirements of systems that were going to implement virtualization, including an analysis of instruction sets for processors and what needs to be in place for the instruction sets to allow for virtualization. According to Popek and Goldberg, instructions fall into three categories. The first category is privileged instructions. These are instructions that would get trapped if the software using the instruction is running in user mode but not if the software was running in supervisor mode, like the kernel would be. The second type of instruction is control sensitive instructions that attempt to alter the configuration of the system in some way. Finally, we have behavior-sensitive instructions that rely on the system to be configured in a certain way like having a register set or the processor's mode.

The problem is that processors may implement a series of privilege levels to protect the most important instructions and access. When an operating system is up and running, only the host operating system has the access to execute privileged instructions. Applications would run in the least privileged mode. Any access to the privileged instructions, such as an instruction that does interrupt handling or performs input or output, has to be run through the kernel. A virtual machine monitor (VMM), also called a hypervisor, may not run in supervisor mode because it

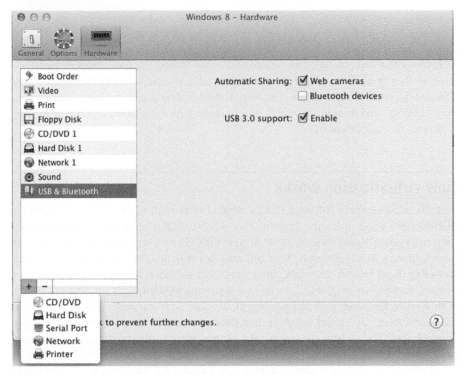

FIGURE 5.2 Hardware Configuration with Parallels Virtual Machine

isn't the operating system. As a result, it may trap and emulate in order to provide the same sort of functionality that the host operating system has with regards to the underlying hardware. The guest operating system calls a privileged instruction and the hypervisor traps that instruction and handles it through hardware emulation rather than allowing it to pass through the underlying hardware.

In order to better support virtualization, the Intel processors commonly found in personal computers needed a set of extensions added to them. Both Intel and AMD, who has a line of processors whose instruction sets are compatible with the × 86 processor from Intel, have implemented a set of processor extensions to support hardware virtualization. Intel released a line of processors in 2006 that hard virtualization extensions and AMD released their virtualization compatible processors in 2006. One feature that these processors have is the ability to support extended page tables to allow for page table virtualization within the memory management unit.

Hypervisors

The hypervisor, or VMM, is the software layer that sits underneath the guest operating system allowing it to believe there is really hardware in place. There are a

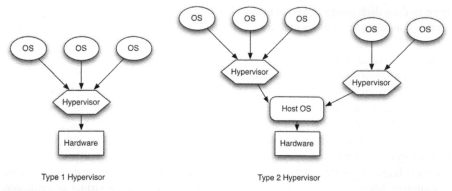

FIGURE 5.3 Two Types of Virtual Machines

number of hypervisors available commercially today from VMware, Oracle, Microsoft, and Parallels, as well as those available for Linux like KVM and Xen. There are two types of hypervisors. The first type is capable of running on the bare metal without an underlying operating system of its own. The second type would run on top of a host operating system. As an example, I am running Mac OS X on a MacBook Air while I am writing this. I have Parallels installed as a hypervisor. Since it runs on top of Mac OS X, it is a type 2 hypervisor. VMWare ESXi Server or Microsoft Hyper-V Server are type 1 hypervisors that run on top of the bare metal and don't require a host operating system.

Either type of hypervisor is capable of running multiple guest operating systems but with a type 2 hypervisor, you may run multiple type 2 hypervisors on top of your host operating system and each of those hypervisors may have multiple operating systems. As an example, I have had both Parallels and VMWare Fusion installed on a Macintosh in the past and I could run both of them at the same time with guest operating systems running on top of the individual hypervisors. Figure 5.3 is a graphical representation of the two types of hypervisors. With type 1, you can see it sits right on top of the hardware while with type 2, you can see a more traditional, host operating system sits on top of the hardware while the hypervisor is on top of the host operating system.

Snapshots

Remember the old days where you wanted to have a number of systems that looked identical and you ended up using something like Ghost to take an image of your hard disk and you could then use that image to copy onto other hard disks, maybe one at a time or possibly streaming over the local network until you had your image copied to the other systems and you could then boot them up. Perhaps you have something like a Kickstart or Satellite server for Linux systems to copy your images from. Then, if you had a case where you wanted to capture a particular configuration of a system with a set of applications on them or number of settings, you may have to do a disk image again and store that image. There are a number of use cases where you want to grab an image of a system at a particular point in time. With a virtualized system, you can not only easily create a system image that can be moved from one system to another as a baseline, you can also quickly and easily take a snapshot of your system configuration and settings at a particular point in time.

The one scenario that always comes to mind for me when we talk about snapshots is quality assurance and testing. When you are testing, you want to get your system into a stable configuration with all the right tools and applications in place and then you want to run a test. If you are running a destructive test or one that makes changes to your system or application, you probably have to do a lot of work in order to get yourself back to a state where you can start the next test since the tests may not be cumulative where one builds on the results from another. With a virtual system, you can take a snapshot when you have your system set up the way you want it, run your test and then reset back to the snapshot that is serving as your steady-state baseline.

Platform as a service

You may be wondering by this point where all of this talk of virtualization is going. Sure, virtualization is cool but you bought into a book about cloud computing and other technologies allowing you to extend your reach and allow faster, more efficient business processes. What's all of this virtualization stuff all about? Well, virtualization is what makes the next technology possible. Without virtualization, we wouldn't have the idea of PaaS. In fact, previously, technology was such that you could offload some of your hosting requirements to a provider. This might be for the purpose of getting risky systems out of your own data center or it may be because the provider had better bandwidth. There are a number of reasons you may have offloaded system hosting. However, in a hosting model like that, you may likely have paid big money because you were buying the use of real, physical hardware and you may have required several systems to provide you with a traditional Web layer, an application layer and a database layer. On top of that, you may have wanted multiple systems at each layer for load balancing or redundancy. That's a lot of systems and the hardware required for all of that was costly both to acquire as well as to keep operating.

With PaaS, you get all of the features of the more traditional hosting model with a lower price and far more flexibility and speed. The reason for the flexibility and speed is because of the use of virtual machines. Using a virtual machine with a base image, you can very quickly and easily get a system up and running and PaaS providers make use of virtual machines. This makes provisioning a lot easier because there is no more hardware involved. Provisioning a PaaS solution can be completely automated and in fact most providers have automated it. As an example, you can see in Figure 5.4 the screen that allows you to select a system image for an Amazon EC2 instance.

Using Amazon to create a server instance, it's literally just a handful of minutes to get a system up and running to a point where you can get into it and start

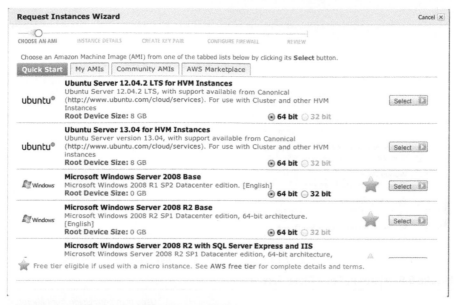

FIGURE 5.4 Creating an Amazon Virtual Machine

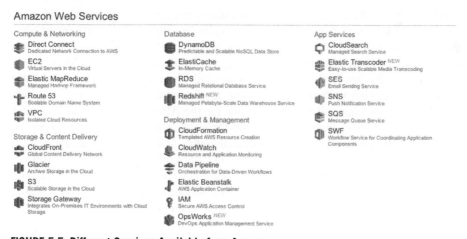

FIGURE 5.5 Different Services Available from Amazon

adding your content for whatever you want to use the system for. Amazon also provides a lot of common applications that you can quickly and easily get up and running. You can see the list in Figure 5.5, including a Domain Name System (DNS) server, a database server, a search service, and a number of other applications where Amazon has done the work of building and configuring the system for you and all you need to do is add the specific functionality or data that you want the system or

FIGURE 5.6 Microsoft Azure Cloud Services

Used with permission from Microsoft.

service to have. We are using a lot of modular concepts where we can reuse work that has already been done rather than everyone having to essentially remake the wheel before they start adding their own specific baseball cards and streamers to it.

Amazon isn't the only provider offering these services, of course. Microsoft is another provider involved in the PaaS space and Microsoft is well known for not only their operating systems but also their development tools. After all, Microsoft got their start writing a BASIC interpreter for the Altair 8800 personal computer in the 1970s. Without that interpreter and the success it offered, there may not be Windows, Office or any other Microsoft application. Microsoft offers an application development platform with their PaaS offering, currently called Azure. Microsoft's development environment is called Visual Studio and with Visual Studio 2012, you can develop directly for Azure, creating Web services. Figure 5.6 shows a dialog box from Visual Studio, creating a new application for Azure.

Advantages of PaaS

We've already gone over some of the advantages of using a PaaS provider. It is much quicker to get systems up and running to a point where you are doing the real work for your specific application or content. You don't want to spend all of your time or money on infrastructure. Speed is a big factor because you can spin up a new server very quickly and get yourself up and running in a matter of minutes, ready to start pushing content or applications. Another aspect of speed is being able to quickly respond to demand. Depending on your architecture, of course, you can start up new server instances and add them to your application in order to respond to the demand you may be seeing.

There are also advantages to using someone else's infrastructure, particularly in the case of smaller businesses. If you are a small business, you need to hire someone to be a system administrator. This may not be the only job this person has and so they will need to juggle between doing system administrative tasks and other jobs. Or maybe you have a full-time system administrator. You may have a jack-of-all-trades who is good at a lot of things, as many system administrators are but hasn't been able to focus on one specific area to get really good. You may also not be able to pay for a really top rate system administrator. When you are using a service provider, you are taking advantage of a much larger talent pool and people who are focused specifically on their jobs. You can do a hire-by-proxy of the best talent by outsourcing to one of the large service providers who are well stocked with highly skilled and knowledgeable people. You benefit from these people managing these services 24 hours a day and knowing them inside out.

It's also cheaper to outsource to a platform provider in some cases. In addition to the savings we have talked about before where you save on buying systems plus electricity, rack and floor space and cooling costs, you also only pay for what you use, generally at reasonable rates because the cost of the whole service and the utility cost is spread out over a large number of customers. The smaller customers get the benefit of being on the same platform with larger customers because the costs of all the infrastructure used to support the operation get spread out over all of the customers. When it comes to costs, the pay what you eat model can save you a lot of money up front, when you are trying to get a service off the ground, particularly if you are basing your business around the service you are offering. When you aren't getting a lot of traction or traffic early on, you aren't paying a lot. In fact, with the larger providers like Amazon and Google, you can get started on a free service until you begin to actually start getting a lot of usage.

Just as a pricing example, Google charges $0.08/h for on-demand frontend instances and $0.05/h on reserved frontend instances. This is after the 28 free hours for frontend instances. You will also pay for network bandwidth and disk usage. You will pay $0.12/GB for your outgoing bandwidth with Google, at the time of this writing. Incoming bandwidth is free. Data storage is $0.18/GB. You will also pay for using application programming interfaces (APIs) like per operation for the datastore API. There is also a blobstore API, an e-mail API, a channel API, and others. Using any of these will cost per usage.

Amazon also uses a pay as you go model and also uses on-demand and reserved instances. The difference is that with on-demand instances, there is no long-term commitment. You use what you need and you pay for it as you use it. When it comes to reserved instances, you pay an upfront cost while reducing the hourly cost for your usage. Amazon also has tiers for different instance sizes. The different sizes give you more speed, more capacity, more storage space, depending on whether you choose small, medium, large, or extra large. This is another advantage, of course. You can see the different size selections in Figure 5.7. Migrating from one size to another can be much easier than trying to upgrade a physical system.

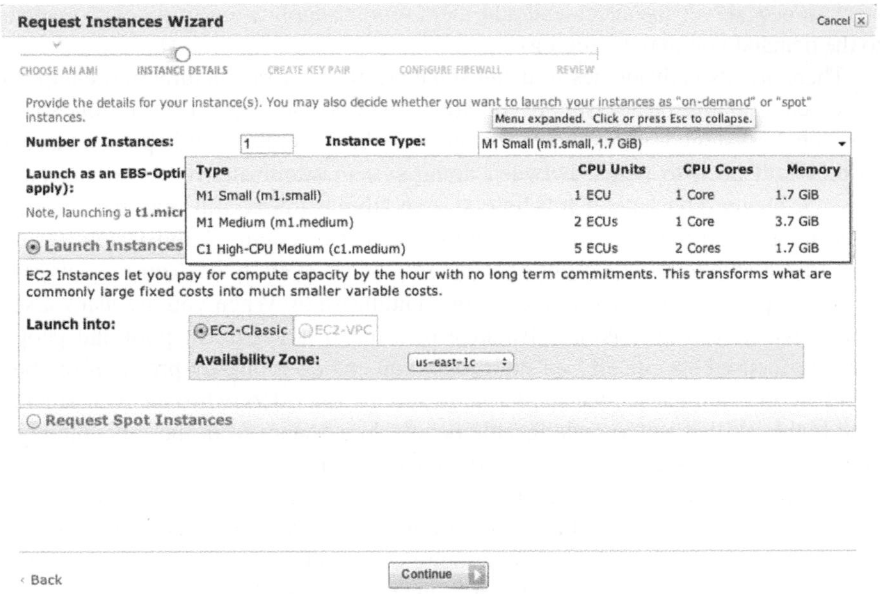

Request Instances Wizard   Cancel ⓧ

CHOOSE AN AMI   INSTANCE DETAILS   CREATE KEY PAIR   CONFIGURE FIREWALL   REVIEW

Provide the details for your instance(s). You may also decide whether you want to launch your instances as "on-demand" or "spot" instances.

Number of Instances:	1	**Instance Type:**	M1 Small (m1.small, 1.7 GiB)			▾

Menu expanded. Click or press Esc to collapse.

Launch as an EBS-Opti...
apply):

Note, launching a **t1.micr...**

Type	CPU Units	CPU Cores	Memory
M1 Small (m1.small)	1 ECU	1 Core	1.7 GiB
M1 Medium (m1.medium)	2 ECUs	1 Core	3.7 GiB
C1 High-CPU Medium (c1.medium)	5 ECUs	2 Cores	1.7 GiB

⦿ **Launch Instances**

EC2 Instances let you pay for compute capacity by the hour with no long term commitments. This transforms what are commonly large fixed costs into much smaller variable costs.

Launch into: ⦿ EC2-Classic   ◯ EC2-VPC

Availability Zone: us-east-1c ▾

◯ **Request Spot Instances**

‹ Back   Continue ▷

FIGURE 5.7 Instance Sizes from Amazon

PaaS also gets you scalability that I've hinted at a bit so far. Upgrading from a smaller instance to a larger instance under the Amazon Elastic Compute Cloud is quick and easy, giving you more performance. You can also get the ability to place your instance into multiple regions. This could give you the ability to be more resilient and scalable. You can have load balancing across multiple systems as well as multiple regions. Using multiple systems will allow you to handle traffic peaks.

Building a business

This easy-to-use infrastructure has allowed a number of companies to bring up services quickly and allow them to scale, just as we discussed above. One business that has made use of those services is Instructure who develop a learning management system (LMS) called Canvas. Canvas allows learning institutions like colleges, universities, and even high schools or middle schools to place learning content like quizzes, lessons, reading assignments, links to outside sources, or other content online. It gives you a gradebook and a place to store all assignments digitally so there are no more lost papers resulting from transporting them around from classroom to office to home to be graded. An LMS can provide a well-structured environment for students to find their way through everything related to a class. It is also a way to have all of the information about their classes in one place.

Instructure makes use of Amazon as its service provider. Canvas itself is open source and it's an application you can easily install inside an Amazon instance.

Canvas - Learning Management System powered by TurnKey Linux

FIGURE 5.8 Building a Canvas Instance with Amazon

Amazon offers a marketplace where you can purchase Amazon Machine Instances (AMIs), sometimes with specific applications already installed. Turnkey Linux offers a Canvas instance that you can very quickly set up. Figure 5.8 shows the page in the marketplace where you set up a Canvas instance. I was able to get to this page with a simple search and then another click indicating I wanted to get a Canvas instance. With just one more click, I can have Canvas up and running.

Not all businesses are based on open source models. Another business using Amazon infrastructure is Flipboard. Flipboard is a personalized magazine, filled with content from providers you have chosen yourself. Flipboard not only uses Amazon server instances to operate its business, but also uses service instances for content distribution to user devices. Another business built around a mobile application that uses Amazon is Urbanspoon. Urbanspoon is an application used to search for restaurants through the use of categories, locations, and prices. They make use of Amazon to store content that is used in user profiles as well as restaurant reviews.

In addition to small or new technology business, a large number of established and big businesses are using PaaS providers to power their operations including Autodesk, Ericcson, The Guardian, Lionsgate, and Netflix on Amazon as well as BMW, Toyota, Harris International, Herbalife and Wellmark Blue Cross and Blue Shield using Azure. Not surprisingly, a large number of businesses are also using the Google Cloud platform including Ubisoft, Rovio, Best Buy, and Khan Academy.

Security considerations

One of the biggest challenges with PaaS and security has more to do with user behavior than it has to do with how well secured the services themselves are. Certainly you've come away with the impression that PaaS services are very easy to use as well as inexpensive to get off the ground. The fact that some of the providers have free, get started offerings doesn't hurt. Because of that simplicity, you may have organizations who think they have a need for a Web service who don't really understand the complications involved with spinning up a Web service and ensuring that it is protected from attack, including and especially the data that may be stored there.

Small businesses can easily and quickly get Web services up and running but groups within large organizations may also get Web services up and running quickly and neither case may consider the possibility of data loss or leakage or the damage to the company. Even if there is no sensitive data, a poorly administered Web service may cause reputational damage to a company. If the service is put up in the name of the company, even if it doesn't have the blessing of management, the company is going to take the hit from any problems that may result from the use of that service, including a poorly designed or written application. While this may not be a huge risk, it is something to consider. With the ease of use and installation of services, it's easy to start to lose control over your information and your reputation. This is where a little education and awareness training goes a long way and where offering partnerships with IT and management can ensure that those are the first places groups go when they have a need to offer up a Web service.

One advantage of using the larger providers is that they have often taken security into consideration and they are using encryption in all the right places to make sure your information, including your authentication credentials, is protected. Amazon, for example, generates encryption keys when you create an instance. Those keys are used, in part, to authenticate you as well as being used to encrypt sessions when you are logged onto the system. You may also have the ability to use two-factor authentication to better protect your interactions with your service provider. This can help to protect against unauthorized users, especially in the case where login information gets breached.

There is a risk from PaaS providers that is very nonspecific because it doesn't really affect companies or individuals who use the service. Free and inexpensive computing power can draw people who may have malicious intents. Cloud computing has been used in the past to break passwords using a distributed computing model to apply a lot of computing power. There are a number of utilities available that can do password cracking using the cloud computing resources, including the graphics processing units (GPU) of an Amazon EC2 instance. In 2010, a German used Amazon servers to launch password cracking attacks. He says setting up 100 nodes to crack passwords took just a few clicks and didn't cost a lot of money. Having access to cheap computing power could potentially open the door to large-scale attacks, though the providers are regularly on the lookout for such things.

CONCLUSION

PaaS offerings provide a lot of enticing options for getting servers out of your data center, getting yourself out from under the burden of maintenance, updates, and security. At the same time, you free yourself from those obligations, you open the door to fast access, speed of deployment, resilience and potentially fault tolerance and redundancy. An advantage to PaaS is the ability to quickly do a proof of concept without taking a lot of time or resources to get the infrastructure in place to support it. With the free tier of these services, you may be able to do the trial without investing any money and then easily migrate it to a reserved instance when you have completed the trial and are ready to go production with it.

Making use of a provider will give you the benefits of using shared resources including lower costs for infrastructure as well as highly skilled and capable administrators that may be difficult for your business to find and hire if you are small or remote. When your infrastructure is in the cloud, you may have more options when it comes to locating your business as well as where your employees can be located. If your infrastructure is scattered around using cloud-based services, including the infrastructure you use to interact with customers and partners, you aren't constrained by needing to be inside a traditional firewall to get access to business-related services. Shared services like those from a PaaS provider can also give you a more reliable and secure infrastructure because the provider may be implementing firewalls, intrusion detection, and other security technology that you may not have the resources to implement yourself. The provider will do this because they need to protect themselves as well as their customers. If they can't protect their customers, they may not have as many customers.

Underneath all of this, of course, are a large number of virtual machines. Amazon, for example, is known to use the Xen hypervisor on Linux systems. Virtualization has offered a lot of benefits itself, including cost savings from lower hardware costs, less electric usage, less floor space, and less cooling required. Virtualization also offers a lot of flexibility and quicker system build times. Certainly you can deploy virtual machines yourself and save a lot of money that way but one advantage to using a provider is the number of possibilities for getting different operating systems deployed. Between your provider and a marketplace, you can get instances of a variety of operating systems and applications that can get you up to speed quickly.

Summary

Some points to consider from this chapter:

- PaaS may offer you flexibility and speed of delivery.
- Virtualization has a lot of benefits, particularly for testing purposes or if you have a need for the support of multiple operating systems.
- PaaS providers may provide tools for rapid application development, like Microsoft's Azure.
- Server virtualization can provide a lot of cost savings when you calculate Heating, Ventilation and Air Conditioning (HVAC), power, rack, and floor space.
- Cloud computing may provide a way to get high-speed computing for short-duration tasks without having to purchase systems yourself.

Social Media

INFORMATION INCLUDED IN THIS CHAPTER

- Social networking
- Engagement
- Gamification
- Security concerns

INTRODUCTION

Coincidentally, the news this morning had a story about Facebook privacy concerns. While these concerns have been floating around for years with one version of "Facebook owns my life" stories or another, there are real issues to consider. The first issue is what you may be doing without realizing it because you don't understand the settings on your Facebook account or on what you post. Perhaps there are some defaults that you haven't bothered to change. This can expose you to having your postings become public, sometimes embarrassingly so. Even beyond embarrassment are the personal ramifications. Looking at Figure 6.1 you can see some Facebook postings that were completely public and were retrieved on the Web site www.weknowwhatyouredoing.com using the Facebook Graph API. The site collects public posts from Facebook under the categories "Who wants to get fired?", "Who's hungover?", "Who's taking drugs?", and "Who's got a new phone number?" These are examples of postings that the poster probably didn't mean to be public, though there are likely a large number of other posts that are public that don't fall into any of these categories.

The reality is that social networking has become an integral part of our lives. It has allowed people who haven't seen one another in years or even decades to get back in touch. It provides news and information to those who may not normally consume news from traditional sources. It's not only a news source, it's a way of entertaining people and also misinforming them by allowing the nonsense that used to be chain letters to spread much farther, much faster. The sheer volume of false messages due to the networked nature of social media gives them a lot of weight and standing. Here's an example. I was checking through my Facebook news feed this morning and ran across a message referring to male versus female peppers and how peppers with three

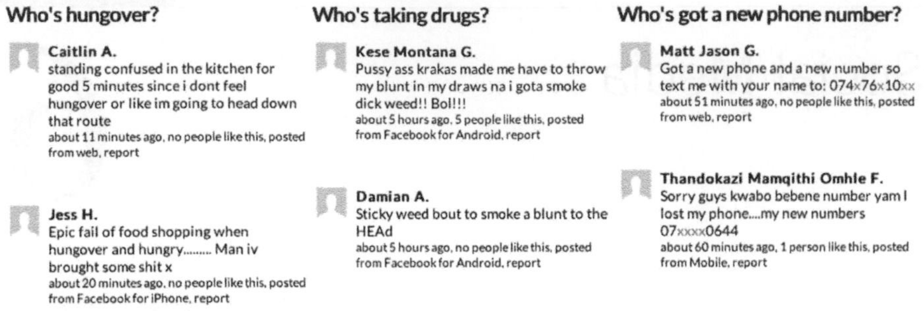

Who's hungover?

Caitlin A.
standing confused in the kitchen for good 5 minutes since i dont feel hungover or like im going to head down that route
about 11 minutes ago, no people like this, posted from web, report

Jess H.
Epic fail of food shopping when hungover and hungry......... Man iv brought some shit x
about 20 minutes ago, no people like this, posted from Facebook for iPhone, report

Who's taking drugs?

Kese Montana G.
Pussy ass krakas made me have to throw my blunt in my draws na i gota smoke dick weed!! Bol!!!
about 5 hours ago, 5 people like this, posted from Facebook for Android, report

Damian A.
Sticky weed bout to smoke a blunt to the HEAd
about 5 hours ago, no people like this, posted from Facebook for Android, report

Who's got a new phone number?

Matt Jason G.
Got a new phone and a new number so text me with your name to: 074x76x10xx
about 51 minutes ago, no people like this, posted from web, report

Thandokazi Mamqithi Omhle F.
Sorry guys kwabo bebene number yam I lost my phone....my new numbers 07xxxx0644
about 60 minutes ago, 1 person like this, posted from Mobile, report

FIGURE 6.1 Potentially Embarrassing Facebook Status Posts

bumps or lobes on the bottom are male and those with four are female. Of course, this isn't true but a friend of mine shared it from someone else and very quickly, people start to believe this thing that just isn't true and not only that, but continue to spread it from one person to another.

Social networking provides a way to interact with customers in ways that were much harder and much more expensive previously. It provides an intimacy and a connection that is difficult to match. Using social media can provide better customer service, better marketing, and a far better handle on what your customers really think of you. Some believe it's the next step in engaging customers and building loyalty, as we'll see later on in the case study as well as through a discussion of gamification.

History and impact of social networking

The various networks we have created for computers have always been social in nature. One of the concepts of the ARPANET was easier collaboration of scientists around the country. That and, of course, cost savings to keep from having to buy a dedicated and very expensive computer every time a new project got funded by ARPA. If you think about it, social networking is really just another way of communicating and collaborating on a much grander scale than was possible in the early days of the ARPANET, but the goal of communication of collaboration continues, well past the days when research was the primary aim of connecting computers together. I remember one of the fascinations for me when I first sat down on an IBM mainframe attached to the BITNET was being able to send messages to people across the world.

In the late 1970s, USENET was created and provided a way for people to join groups of people they have something in common with to engage in discussion and, quite often, arguments that degenerated into what were called flame wars. This was particularly true anytime the discussion turned to a topic where the two (or more) sides were fueled by deeply held beliefs. I recall emacs versus vi being particularly heated. UNIX versus VMS was also a source of debate that I recall. Certainly there were many others, and I haven't even touched on religious or political debates from the real world. There must have been endless discussions and debates on those topics

```
>>Well, you could write a lisp function to do it...
>
>You gotta be kidding!
>
>Go into recursive hades for eternity just to do yank'n'stuff?
>
>Emacs is losing its edge...
```

Come, come. Look at the following function to do exactly what is needed.
And, it even prompts for the parameters (unlike VI). It isn't that hard.
Plus, before using Emacs, it had been 3 years since I used lisp. I'm
rusty, but it's easy writing useful code. Which just goes to show
you that in Emacs, if you don't have the function, you can write one. Can
you read News inside of Emacs? [I could go on forever...]. Anyway,
this function doesn't use recursion...

```
;; Function to yank to a regular expression.
(defun yank-to-re (reg re)
  "Yank into REG from the point until the point where RE is found."
  (interactive "cYank into register :\nsRegular expression :")
  (let ((ppoint (point)))
    (if (re-search-forward re)
        (set-register reg (buffer-substring (point) ppoint)))))
```

FIGURE 6.2 USENET Posting on Emacs vs. Vi

on USENET, just as there were in real life. Fortunately for us, Google has an archive of discussions from USENET, and you can see a sample in Figure 6.2 of a thread called vi versus emacs.

In the 1980s, there was also software that allowed multiple users to communicate with one another all at the same time. Again, I'm familiar with some of this software from my BITNET days. I remember Chat, Forum, and Relay. The whole thing was really brilliant. On BITNET, we had the ability to send short messages to other people on the system we were on as well as other systems, if those systems were attached to our network. This was very much like text messaging for computers and the messages were short—documentation I can find today to bolster my memory indicates that the messages were probably under 132 characters. Using that messaging system, we were able to join public chat forums where messages were relayed to everyone who was participating in the forum. Figure 6.3 shows a list of commands that were common across the various chat forum services.

The University of Maine, the source of a lot of activity on the BITNET, had CSNEWS/UMNEWS, which was a newsletter, mailing list, forum, and messaging system all wrapped up in one. Figure 6.4 shows the banner from the very first newsletter. Andy Robinson, one of the creators of CSNEWS/UMNEWS, reminds me that they had check-ins and check-outs, allowing you to advertise whether you are online and available or not. Robinson says this was the first social networking site because it included many of the basics of Facebook. Of course, Facebook has a lot of additional functionality that would have been very difficult if not impossible with the technology that was available at the time.

```
*************** Relay Commands ***************
/Bye . . . . . . . . . . . . Signoff from Relay
/Channel <num> . . . . .Change to channel <num>
/Contact <host-nick> . .Show Relay contact info
/Getop . . . . . Try to summon a Relay operator
/Help. . . . . . . . . . . . Prints this list
/Info. . . . . . . . . . . Send RELAY INFO file
/Invite <nick> . . .Invite user to your channel
/Links . . . . . . . . . . .Shows active relays
/List. . . . . . . . . . . List active channels
/Msg <nick> <text> . . . .Sends private message
/Nick <newnick>. . . . . . Change your nickname
/Names <channel> . . . . .Show users with names
/Rates . . . . . . . . .Display message rates
/Servers <node>. . . . Show relays serving node
/Signon <nick> <channel> . . . .Signon to Relay
/Signon <nick>,SHIFT . . Forces uppercase shift
/Signon <nick>,UNSHIFT . Forces lowercase shift
/Signoff . . . . . . . . . . Signoff from Relay
/Signup <full name>. Signup or change full name
/Stats . . . . . . . . Display Relay statistics
/Summon <userid>@<node>. . Invite user to Relay
/Topic <subject> . . . . Topic for your channel
/Who <channel> . . . . Show users and nicknames
/WhoIs <nick>. . . . . . .Identify a nickname
```

FIGURE 6.3 Commands on Relay Chat System

```
##    ## ### ###      ### ###### ###### ### ###
##    ## ## ### ##    ##  ##  ## ## ## ### ##
##  ## ## ## # ##    ##     ##    ##  ## ## # ##
## ## ## ## ##    ##     ## ## ## ## ## ##
##   ##   ## ###    ###### ###### ## ##
                CAPS User's NewsLetter
                  Volume 01 Number 01
                      04/05/84
              Editor: Andy  Robinson (ANDY@MAINE)

     Staff:
Andrew T. Robinson (ANDY@MAINE):          editor;
Michael Johnson    (CSNM059@MAINE):       editor;
Barry Gates        (CS23124@MAINE):       editor;
Richard Fortin     (CS23011@MAINE):       editor;
Sean Colbath       (GROUP604@MAINE):      staff writer;
Tim Willsey        (CS23003@MAINE):       staff writer;
Prof. G. Markowsky (MARKOV@MAINE):        faculty advisor;
         NewsLetter Contribution Sink Machine: CSNEWS
      Contributions from readers welcomed and encouraged!
```

FIGURE 6.4 VM/COM Newsletter

With permission from Andrew Robinson.

This was in the early 1980s. By the late1980s and early 1990s, AOL, CompuServ, and other online service companies were providing ways for people who had computers with modems to connect. Initially some of these ventures were created around gaming and games but eventually they became multipurpose, including the very same chatting capability we had on the mainframes. The thing about personal computers is that they were designed to be single use so there weren't communications capabilities built in as there were with multiuser systems that needed those capabilities for coordination and control among other things.

Along with multiuser forums, services like AOL provided e-mail as well as the ability to send messages directly to other users, much like the Short Message (SMSG) utility mentioned earlier on the IBM mainframes. This instant messaging required that the other user be online in order to send them an instant message. The name gives it away, of course. If you were to send it and the user were to get it later, that wouldn't be very instant and the store and forward nature of that would be closer to e-mail than a message sent and received instantly.

Eventually, once all of the smaller networks got hooked up to the NSFNet to create what we now call the Internet, there was still a desire to have this capability to have real-time communication rather than the store and forward nature of e-mail, which may still be slow depending on how regularly the mail server and the user were online since not every site was full time. The Relay program was inspired by several programs that were forerunners and it, in turn, inspired a Transmission Control Protocol/Internet Protocol (TCP/IP)-based version called Internet Relay Chat (IRC). Prior to Relay, there were a number of chat hosts spread across the BITNET, and Relay provided a way to consolidate those systems into a unified network. The same was true with IRC. A number of systems were bound together into a network so when you connected to one host, you could gain access to others who were connected to the same network.

Social networking sites

It's now the turn of another century and the Internet is purring along nicely. Businesses have been figuring out what it is and getting up to speed on how to make money using it. We have e-mail, instant messaging, and still chat rooms in the form of IRC for communication, and marketing folks are trying to figure out how to make the best use of a Web site. What's missing? One thing that's missing is an asynchronous form of communication that is less formal than e-mail, providing speed of communication like instant messaging without requiring the recipient to be online in order to receive the message. Having that middle ground helps offer a better and more engaged form of communication.

What we end up with to accomplish that task is social networking. Messages on a social networking site are stored so they can be viewed whenever the user wants and can be viewed over and over, just like e-mail. It also has something closer to the immediacy of instant messaging but with the advantage of being public, just like IRC and similar real-time public discussion forums. Social networking allows people to meet and collaborate just as with public discussion forums but with a more connection-oriented approach, like an e-mail system with contact lists. You can store the people you know and keep track of what they are doing.

As I write this, NBC's Today Show is unveiling their new studio and they have included a space called the Orange Room where they will be watching social media and reporting it as news. This includes trending topics, which can indicate something that is happening that should be reported. They will also be reporting on the response to news stories. This morning, for example, there was a story about a rising tide against the continued use of the name Redskins for the Washington football team, since some feel it's offensive. They were able to break down the response by geographic region and tie that to locations where there are large populations of Native Americans. Adding in the aspect of where this story is important throws in an interesting twist that could be much harder to obtain without the Internet technologies that are being used.

There are a number of different ways to implement social networking or social media, and it all depends on the purpose or goal of the site. Some sites have specific reasons to pull people together and others are more generic in nature. One of the early implementations of a Web-based social networking site is Classmates, targeted at allowing high school classmates to connect and organize reunions and get-togethers. One of the problems with Classmates was there were tiers of membership on Classmates, and in order to truly interact with your classmates that you found there, you had to be a paid member. To me, this really limited its usefulness. Other sites are business oriented, like LinkedIn, allowing people to extend their professional network in order to get sales leads or job opportunities or just solve problems in their professional world. Many are just general purpose but a service like Twitter is less connection oriented than a service like Facebook so the audience you reach or the group you pay attention to in both of those sites can be completely different between them.

There are and have been a large number of social networking sites around the world, with some being niche sites for specific purposes and others being more general purpose but more geared toward specific geographic regions. As a way of discussing some of the foundations and purposes, I want to present a small number of commonly known sites. Some of this is for historical perspective, but there are also some significant differences between the different social networking sites, particularly when it comes to business involvement in these sites.

Friendster

Friendster was a very early social networking site, developed in 2002 by a Canadian programmer. The name came from putting the word friend together with Napster, which was a peer-to-peer file-sharing network popular at the time. Friendster was a way of developing online circles of friends, providing a way for people to connect with one another and also extending the circle of people they know. In the first few months, Friendster had several million users, proving once again the interest people have in reaching out and connecting to one another, even through technology. Friendster's popularity inspired the launch of Dogster, which was a similar idea for dogs to have circles of their own friends.

MySpace

MySpace was a response to Friendster by the marketing company eUniverse. Because it was created by a marketing company, it had a leg up in the quest to acquire subscribers. eUniverse had a large mailing list for their clients, and it used this mailing list to get subscribers to MySpace. Very quickly, MySpace took over from Friendster in the volume of subscribers. MySpace became more than just a place for friends to connect; it became more of a platform. It was a place for musicians to give access to their music to other MySpace members. They could populate a playlist on their page so that anyone who visited could listen to a number of songs they had. This would give more exposure to these artists and hopefully gain new fans. On top of music, MySpace was the first social networking site to offer a place for game developers to provide Web-based games. MySpace was the leading social networking site for several years and had several offers to buy them. Given its popularity, it became a target for the spread of malware. Between the application development platform on MySpace and the links that users may share with one another, it wasn't that difficult to infect systems with malware.

One advantage MySpace had in the race to develop a solid platform and lure users in was well-understood technology. MySpace was initially developed in ColdFusion, which had been around for the better part of a decade at the time MySpace was developed and there were development tools available for rapid application development ColdFusion. Friendster, on the other hand, was written in Java Server Pages, which had only been released a couple of years before by Sun Microsystems. Java Server Pages are a very feature-rich platform but in the early 2000s, they were not nearly as mature as they are today.

MySpace has experienced a decline in the last several years, though they relaunched the Web site in 2012 with a completely new design. This was after MySpace was sold to Specific Media Group and Justin Timberlake the year before. Timberlake announced the redesign of the site on Twitter, and the redesign now supports logging in through Facebook.

Facebook

When you have books and movies that center on the creation of a particular product or brand, it's probably safe to say it's a well-known story but let's go through the highlights quickly. In 2004, Facebook was launched by Mark Zuckerberg with the help of friends Eduardo Saverin, Andrew McCollum, Dustin Moskowitz, and Chris Hughes. Zuckerberg, rightly or wrongly, became the focus and public face of Facebook and remains so to this day. He is chairman and CEO and became the second youngest self-made billionaire in history in 2012. None of this is apropos of much of anything other than to suggest that at a very young age, Zuckerberg was instrumental in creating a Web service that has become something more than simply a social networking site.

Facebook allows users to add Friends to a contact list. The reason I refer to them as Friends and not as friends is because a Friend is little more than a contact in a list because they may not even be people you know well who you add as a Friend.

Facebook has a news feed that you would typically go to when you log into Facebook. The news feed has status updates and posts from people on your Friends list. As a result, there is a lot of advantage to have people in your Friends list who you may not know well because they may have interests that align with yours or maybe you just want to pay attention to what they are doing because it's interesting. Just as an example, I have several celebrities on my friends list because either I wasn't sure if they'd accept the request or because I thought it would be interesting to see what they say or just to express support. As an example, I am friends with Julie Brown who is an actress, comedienne, and singer because she's very funny and I've been a fan for over 25 years. She recently posted Figure 6.5 and it made me chuckle. Facebook and the little jokes and quips and memes that we spread through it can lighten a day sometimes.

Facebook started as a college thing, beginning only at Harvard and then slowly extending beyond until anyone could join. Now, businesses can have pages on Facebook. Where businesses used to need Web sites in order to advertise their services and provide a way for customers to get in touch with them and learn more about them, now Facebook has become the place where businesses live. Many smaller businesses only have Facebook pages and no Web site. In addition to having a place where customers can get access to information, Facebook also provides a more direct place where customers can easily interact with the business because there is almost always a place to comment on Facebook, either generally or on against a specific post. As an example, I was poking around Facebook looking for examples and I came across one

FIGURE 6.5 Facebook Posting

from the Ford Motor Company where they have made an announcement about a product and people who follow the page are able to comment on it. When they comment, they may get responses from the company, as happened in this particular case.

This level of conversation and dialog can be very important to a business, and it helps create engagement and loyalty in customers, in part because they feel as though their ideas and grievances are heard. Using Facebook and other forms of social media, you can get nearly unrivaled and direct access to your customers. This is really a double-edged sword, considering that it exposes you and your business to accountability from your customers, whether warranted or unwarranted. Your customers have the unprecedented ability to praise you or say very bad things about you in front of a very large audience of people. The Ford Motor Company page I mentioned earlier has nearly 2 million likes and over 20,000 people talking about it. This doesn't include people casually driving by the page, so to speak, to see what Ford may have to say. If someone were to post something bad about Ford, there is a chance of tens of thousands of people or more reading about it.

Like MySpace, Facebook also offers a platform for developing applications including games. Facebook offers several application programming interfaces (APIs), including the primary API that gives programmers the ability to post anything on behalf of a user as well as retrieving information. The Graph API is HTTP based and gives access to a wide range of data. You can test queries and build requests using the Graph API Explorer, which you can see in Figure 6.6. The Graph API Explorer can provide support while you work on building your application. The Graph API is also the entranceway into Facebook that the Web site referenced earlier, www.weknowwhatyouredoing.com, uses to gather public information looking

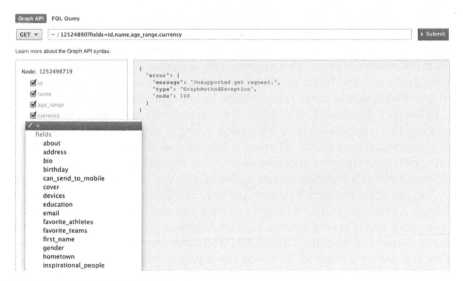

FIGURE 6.6 Using the Graph API Explorer

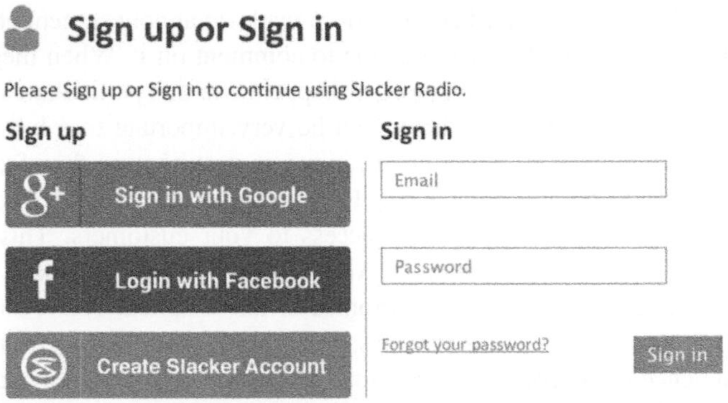

Sign up or Sign in

Please Sign up or Sign in to continue using Slacker Radio.

Sign up

8+   Sign in with Google

f   Login with Facebook

Ⓢ   Create Slacker Account

Sign in

Email

Password

Forgot your password?

Sign in

FIGURE 6.7 Signing Up with Slacker Radio

for potentially embarrassing status updates. In addition to the HTTP-based Graph API, there is also a JavaScript API.

Like MySpace, Facebook has been a target for malware. Considering its popularity and the fact that there is a programmatic interface into Facebook, it's not surprising that malware authors would try to make use of the platform to acquire targets. The Koobface malware is one that attacked both Facebook and MySpace users. Among other things, it attempted to gather login information to Facebook, Skype, other social media sites as well as FTP servers. Technically speaking, Koobface (an anagram of Facebook, by the way) is a worm since it was capable of spreading without user involvement by making use of user contact lists.

Facebook provides a lot of services, not the least of which is making use of their APIs to provide login services. You may have noticed the number of locations now that are allowing you to skip creating a special login account if only you'll use Facebook to authenticate yourself. You can see an example in Figure 6.7, where you can create an account for Slacker Radio or you can simply use existing Facebook or Google credentials to authenticate yourself. This can save a lot of businesses the need to create and secure their own login functions, including storing usernames and passwords, not to mention dealing with forgotten passwords and backup authentication.

Facebook's Graph API provides a way of gathering interesting information, including the information we've mentioned a couple of times previously. We've talked about gathering public information but you can also use the Graph API to gather private information and visualize it in a way that can be very revealing. Wolfram Alpha is a Web site created by Wolfram Research, and it's based on what has been Wolfram Research's primary product for the last 25 years, Mathematica. Wolfram Alpha can generate a lot of fascinating statistics about your Facebook life, if you give it access to your account. Figure 6.8 shows a graph of all of my Facebook friends clustered by how they are related. While each of them are just dots, if you swing your cursor over any of them, you can pop up a little box indicating who they are. You can see the box for my old friend from my BITNET days, Jennifer Murphy (nee Wyman). Wolfram Alpha calls all of this personal analytics, and Jennifer is a

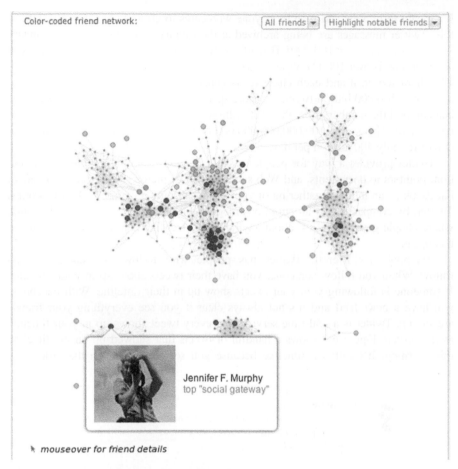

FIGURE 6.8 Graph of Facebook Friends from Wolfram Alpha

With permission from Jennifer Murphy.

social gateway meaning that she has a lot of friends who are not in friends network. As a result, she is a gateway for me to even more people. Using personal analytics, you can get a number of views on the people who are Facebook friends, where they are, who else they know, and how they are all clustered (or not) together.

Twitter

Twitter is another social networking phenomenon, though in an entirely different way than Facebook is. Where Facebook has privacy concerns because many Facebook users expect what they say to be private and don't always realize that there are a lot of controls over how your information is shared, Twitter is almost entirely public. When I send a message out on Twitter, called a tweet, it is public. It's designed to be public.

It's meant to be seen and read by anyone who cares to go looking for it. Because of this, Twitter messages are being archived at the Library of Congress. As of January 2013, there were over 100,000 GB worth of tweets being stored, which, in case you are counting, is over 100 TB. When you consider that each tweet has something under 140 characters in it and each character is generally one byte, we are talking about more than 100,000 billion tweets or, more specifically, as long as you can wrap your head around the number, more than 100 trillion tweets. Let me put this into a different perspective. That's over 100,000,000,000,000 tweets. And counting, by the way, at a clip of roughly 400 million per day.

Twitter provides a way for people to share thoughts, comments, ideas, information, pointers to documents, and Web sites, as well as pictures. You may think about Facebook as an intimate gathering of your friends around a campfire sharing stories. Twitter, by comparison, is an enormous megaphone on top of a very large building, where people go to shout just about anything they feel like and anyone who cares to listen, can.

Facebook has friends. Twitter has people who follow you and who you follow. When you follow someone, you have their tweets show up in your timeline. If someone is following you, your tweets show up in their timeline. With Facebook, you have a news feed and it's not always clear if you see everything your friends are saying. Twitter is a real-time service, and every tweet shows up in your timeline as it's posted. Figure 6.9 shows a handful of tweets that showed up on my timeline this morning. It's called a timeline because you see the tweets in the order they

FIGURE 6.9 Tweets on Twitter

were received in and just to make sure you recognize that, you see how long ago they were posted. The figure in the upper right of each tweet is the number of minutes ago each tweet was posted.

The difference between Facebook friends and Twitter followers is that becoming a Facebook friend requires the approval of the person you are requesting the connection with. Twitter, on the other hand, is a very open social network where all you have to do is follow someone and you get to see everything they have to say. This does bring up the issue of being careful what you say on Twitter because if you say it, people will see it. The same is true of all other social media, of course, since it's easy enough to reshare something someone has posted, but with Twitter it's not even about resharing, called retweeting, it's simply the fact that everything you say is public and can be seen by someone interested enough to go searching for it.

Twitter makes use of hashtags to highlight particular topics. This makes it easier to search for topics that may be of interest to you. It also helps to keep an eye on the pulse of what people are talking about in the Twitterverse. The trending list is the topics that people are most talked about, and Figure 6.10 is the trending list from the morning I'm writing this. Often, you can see something jumping out indicating some big piece of news that is either ongoing or that has just happened. Looking over this particular list, nothing jumps out at me aside from iOS 7 since today is the first day it's available. This is, though, a good way of keeping track of news events that may be worth following up on. It's also a good way of businesses knowing whether their customers are saying things about them. Considering that today is the first official day that iOS 7 is available, it's a good bet that people will be posting a lot of comments up to Twitter and Facebook and any other place they can about their troubles and woes with the new operating system as they spend time getting used to how it's different from the old version. Apple is probably spending time reading through Twitter to see what people are saying in order to get feedback on what people would like and what they don't like.

Twitter is a direct pipeline to a number of companies. Tweeting a negative comment about a company and including a hashtag or even a reference to the

FIGURE 6.10 Trending Topics on Twitter

FIGURE 6.11 Interactions with a Company over Twitter

company's Twitter account can get a direct response from someone in the company, providing a customer a way to air grievances and potentially get them resolved, turning an upset customer into a satisfied one. I've been known to use Twitter to try to get easy, direct access to someone at a company, as you can see in Figure 6.11, where I contacted a company about something I had ordered from Amazon but was being fulfilled by the company I contacted. I got a response and ended up getting what I needed. This was an example of good customer service, and Twitter helped it happen.

Not many years ago, blogging was a popular activity, and the best way to keep up with a lot of blogs was to use Really Simple Syndication (RSS), which was a way of being notified when a new page or blog post got put up. You would get a sample of it through RSS and then you could go to the blog site and read the full page. The world seems like it continues to be more fast paced and sometimes, 140 characters is enough to express a sentiment that could be drawn out to several pages. So, we get microblogging with Twitter where people can express opinions just as they can on a blogging site. We also have a place that acts like an RSS reader. This is one of the things I use Twitter for, actually. It gives me a quick heads-up about things that I may want to look into in more detail.

Twitter can also be used for audience interaction. As I was digging through Twitter and old tweets, I ran across one that was simply the hashtag #dunkgirl. In Times Square, about a year ago, there was a large video screen that had an audience interaction component to it. The screen showed video of people in Times Square standing in front of and underneath it. Superimposed on that was a graphical component, including a large ball that would bounce around based on interaction with the audience. If you saw the ball approaching you on the screen, you could strike out at it in some way and it would bounce off in another direction. In addition to that, there was a short segment where a man and a woman appeared on screen and you were requested to vote on which one you would like to see in a dunk tank. In order to do that, you sent out a tweet with the appropriate hashtag. This is one example of an audience interaction component with Twitter. There are a number of them, including on news shows where tweets may be put onto a scroll or they may use a particular tweet to indicate a preference for one thing or another, much like a vote. This audience interaction increases engagement, and Twitter has become a great way of engaging with customers and audience members.

The engagement level is so high, actually, that people often simply post without thinking and this can be a significant challenge. You may recall Anthony Weiner and all the furor over various things he posted to Twitter. When it comes to Twitter, no matter whether you believe it's private or not, messages can be permanent. Including the consequences for the posts. Companies may look into your social networking activity before hiring you. And, as in the case with Weiner, you may lose out on something really big if you aren't careful about what you do.

Google+

It's hard to have a discussion about social networking and not include Google since they have been trying so hard to get into the game for years. Google tried Wave and Buzz as ways to get into the social networking space and eventually, in some cases fairly quickly, they dropped out. Buzz was gone in less than 2 years. Wave was effectively done less than 6 months after its public release. Currently, Google's social media offering is Google+, though they have also added on something called Google+ Hangouts. Hangouts adds video and text messaging to Google+ and takes over for what used to be Google Talk. Google+ is almost a hybrid of Twitter and Facebook since it includes some capabilities of each of those services. The one thing it offers that the other two don't is a way of segregating the people you know into clusters, which you probably already do in real-life anyway. You may have a group of people who are work colleagues, another group who are work friends, another group who are high school friends, college friends, business associates, and so on. If you have something to say to one group that isn't strictly relevant to another group, you may limit the conversation to just the people it's relevant to. They call this feature Circles.

The features list for Google+ is long and, as mentioned earlier, includes features that may resemble those of Twitter's and Facebook's. In place of a news feed or a timeline, Google has a Stream where you can post comments. Google+ also has Hangouts where you can chat with friends or have video conversations. Where Facebook users have the ability to "Like" something, Google+ users get a + 1 feature, indicating that it's something they are interested in. Google+ also has the ability to track what's happening and trendy with "What's Hot." There are also games available, though they don't get a lot of visibility and there aren't many of them. While the hashtag to indicate a primary word or topic within a post originated with Twitter, Facebook has since picked it up, as has Google+.

Crowdsourcing

It's hard to argue against having people do your work for you. Crowdsourcing is another aspect of making use of the social and collaborative aspects of the Internet. In 1997, before we were using Web sites to communicate socially, there were mailing lists, and one of the mailing lists I was on at the time was for fans of the band Marillion, who have long been one of my favorite bands. They hadn't been able to tour in North America for a few years at that point and with a new album on the horizon, those of us in North America were anxious to see them in concert. The economics of visas and getting equipment and everything else involved meant that they may not be able to afford to come over for the new album. As a result, one of the North American fans, Jeff Pelletier, proposed that we help fund the upfront costs of the tour. Initially, the band balked at the idea since they didn't want to feel like they were taking advantage of the fans. In the end, the fans put up $60,000 to help defray touring costs and we got a North American tour. We also got a special CD recorded at one of the tour dates that was only for those fans who had put up money. Some of us who jumped in early got signed copies of the album.

Since that time, Marillion has used a similar concept to get fans to prepay for albums so they could fund recording. The fans that put up money generally get their name in a book that goes with a special release of the CD. This is done as a thank you for the trust and generosity shown by the fans. When the album is ready, the fans who prepaid get the special edition of the album and everyone else is free to buy the normally priced retail version. There are a number of other examples of crowdfunding with the Web site kickstarter.com used to fund creative projects like art, books, and movies, including the Veronica Mars movie that is supposed to finally see the light of day as a result of funding generated on Kickstarter. If a project has enough people willing to help fund it, it can get done and avoid the commercial requirements that are typical of businesses who like to see a return on their investment. When it comes to a crowdfunding model, people are putting up money for something they are interested in and the only result they want to see is the end result. They are not looking for monetary gains. The Pebble watch is another example of a crowd-funded project where those who helped fund the development got an early release of the watch.

Funding isn't the only function that can be handled by the crowd. Crowdsourcing can also be a way for small businesses to get work done that may otherwise cost them a lot of money or time. While there are a lot of crowdsourcing models, what it ultimately provides is a way for an organization or a person to propose a task or project that needs to be accomplished, and either a group or an individual will volunteer to undertake the task or project.

In some cases, the person or group who takes the task will be paid for it, but there may also be cases where someone volunteers to take on a task simply for the experience or because it gains them the prestige of having accomplished the task. Your business may need a logo done, a Web site created, or maybe there is a large amount of data that needs to be processed in some way. In most cases, these are one-off tasks that you wouldn't necessarily need a full-time person for. You'd normally contract it out in some way. This is an easy way to throw out your project to a very large group of people where you can then make a decision about who you want to take the project on for you. You may even be able to get people to try out for the task in some way before handing it over.

This can be done through a number of Web sites dedicated to crowdsourcing or it may be as simple as tossing an idea out to one of a number of social networking Web sites like Facebook, LinkedIn, or Twitter. Each of these will have a different audience, though any of them provide the ability for your request to be seen very quickly by millions of people. Making use of our social networks and the basic interconnectedness of people can be very beneficial. It doesn't also have business benefit, of course. The X Prize is a crowd-sourced model that involves a competition for the best solution to a big problem facing society at large, intended to inspire innovation and creative solutions to complex problems. While there is certainly a monetary advantage to the winning team, there is also a competitive aspect to these prizes where the winners can say they competed against some very strong teams and came away being the best.

Gamification

Yes, if you aren't familiar with this term, it is exactly what it suggests. The idea of gamification is to introduce gaming elements to a variety of interactions in order to increase interaction. This can include engagement with customers over social media. One socially oriented application that springs to mind when I consider gamification is Waze, which is a GPS navigation app that introduces elements of gaming like collecting candy that has points as you drive as well as being awarded points for reporting traffic slowdowns, police on the road, and other impediments to getting where you want to go in a timely fashion. Waze uses all of the cloud-sourced information collected from all of the users of the application to generate a real-time picture of what the state of a navigation pathway is. This adds weighting to different routes based on whether there are significant slowdowns or construction or other potential problems that a driver may encounter. Based on all of that information, Waze may reroute you to a faster, less busy road to get to your destination. This works because people are incented to use the app and feed it information. Without that incentive there may be far fewer people adding data, which would make the app far less useful. The game-like features drive use, making it more useful for people who may not be drawn by the gaming aspect.

Plenty of other sites include gaming elements. Foursquare, for example, is a social networking site that allows you to check-in at locations. You get points and badges, rewarding your use of Foursquare. It also encourages you to continue to visit locations. If you have the most check-ins in a 60-day period, you become mayor of the place. The advantage to this particular service is you get to see other people who are at a particular venue or location, which may give you the opportunity to meet up with those people. Using this, you can more easily connect with friends who may also be at the same venue.

One company driving the use of gamification and social media is Rockit Media, Inc. Rockit has developed a platform that can help companies better engage with their customers. One way they do this is by allowing customers to receive alerts from the company about events, savings, and other relevant information in a way that the customer chooses. This might be a text message, an e-mail, or an alert on an app. Rockit also can provide games to engage the customers and give them a sense of accomplishment. Once customers start getting a sense of accomplishment, they may well like to share their accomplishments with their friends. This may well be done over social media where a large number of other people will see it. I'm always reminded of the old Breck commercials at this point that did a great job of explaining exponential progressions with the line, and accompanying visual, "she tells two friends, and they tell two friends and so on and so on." This is just as true of social networking as it is about word of mouth networking except that social networking spreads the word so much further and so much faster.

Earlier we were talking about engaging with audiences and customers in a way that seemed fun and interesting where a particular outcome could be influenced by those customers and audience members. This is another example of gamification. If you are watching a TV show and it asks you to tweet with a particular hashtag in order to vote, you are going to continue to watch that TV show and perhaps continue to tweet to see if your vote was on the winning side or not. You are engaged in an activity that ties you to the television show, and you aren't going to tune away which means they get to keep showing commercials to you. They increase the number of eyes they have for sustained periods of time, increasing the rate they can charge for ads. You are engaged in not only watching the show but also interacting with it.

Human resources

Social media can be very useful when it comes to your human resources department. This can go a couple of ways, actually. Where a site like LinkedIn can be used to look for likely candidates for jobs, other social networking sites could be used to look for candidates as well. In addition to looking for candidates, some companies are doing research about their prospective employees on social networking. When you are applying for the perfect job that's exactly what you've always hoped to do at a great company, you don't want that photo of you mooning out your college window to hold you back. After all, your actions can reflect on the company you work for and some companies take that very seriously.

Some companies have been known to require their social networking passwords. This can be a potential source of liability for the company, and case law regarding its legality hasn't been settled yet. At some point there may be laws against it. When you are using social networking sites to investigate your employees in order to make hiring decisions, you run the risk also have being held negligible for a bad hire if there was anything questionable that was turned up. Obviously, this is something each company must consider carefully and make their own decision as to whether to use this strategy when it comes to hiring decisions. It's definitely worth keeping an ear on case law and any new legislation in this arena since it's still a moving target at this point.

Security considerations

There are a number of considerations when it comes to social networking and security. Some of these are personal in nature, while others are considerations that are more relevant to individuals, but the fact is that if you are using social media for your business, you are having individuals perform that interaction. Rather than continuing to talk in the abstract, let me give you an example. You employ someone to monitor social media and interact with your clients or customers in some way. In the process of performing their duties, they click on a link that takes them to a Web site and their system becomes infected with a virus. This is something that individuals have to be concerned with but it can also have an impact to a business. As a result, if you have a business that makes use of social media in some way, educating your employees on appropriate interactions with the Internet will be beneficial in not only keeping them protected but also protecting your business. Social networking has become a popular way to infect users with malware. Again, this isn't surprising since it's such a large target. Millions of people use social networking on a regular, if not daily basis, and that many people is difficult to ignore if you are looking for usernames, passwords, or other sensitive information.

One of the big areas that is of concern from a security perspective is the use of passwords, or more accurately, the reuse of passwords. It's common for people to reuse the same password or variations on the same password across multiple services. This is widely known so compromising a password on one service may offer at least an indication of what a user's password may be on another service. Fortunately, some of the social networking sites are offering protection against account compromise by implementing multifactor authentication. Google uses your cell phone to provide additional protection to your Google accounts. When you use a new system with a Google service, you can get a text message sent to your phone with a code that authenticates that you are really the one logging in. This assumes that someone hasn't stolen your phone in addition to your account information.

Facebook also implements multifactor authentication with what they call login approvals. This works in the same way that Google's multifactor authentication works, by sending a text message to your phone. Making use of this service requires that you share your cell phone number with these companies and trusting them to not use that number in a way that could put your privacy further at risk. Twitter also uses phone numbers and e-mail addresses to ensure that you are really the one trying to login. Cell phones, with their ubiquitous nature, are a pretty good secondary verification that doesn't require the deployment of a large number of tokens or smartcards to millions of users.

As noted previously, you may make use of Google or Facebook to provide authentication services for you. These are certainly not the only companies that are capable of providing authentication services but they are some of the predominant ones. If you wanted to offer a service that required user authentication, you could make use of an open authentication implementation, relying on a third party to verify that someone is who he or she claims to be. This does mean that you have to trust the third party to verify the identity at least to the extent you find necessary.

Social networking sites can pose a lot of challenges to a business, not the least of which is policy decisions around how best to make use of social networking and how much to allow employees access. Some people feel that if there is a potential to waste time, businesses are obligated to prevent that behavior to maintain productivity. If you do allow employees to access social networking sites for business purposes, you will want to ensure that you have adequate antivirus and intrusion detection in place to protect your systems.

You may also consider your company's reputation when it comes to social media. Without further dragging company names into the mud, some companies have had their social networking strategies hijacked. The moment you establish a social networking account like a Facebook page, you open the door for users to interact with you. This can often be a good thing. With Facebook, though, anyone can get onto your page and write anything they want. If you can get it removed, you can't get people who have seen it to unsee it and the comments may damage your reputation. Where it gets tricky is in the case of Twitter with hashtags. When you start using a hashtag like #ricwritesgoodbooks or something based on your company, anyone can then make use of that hashtag and pollute the search results. Anyone looking for those hashtags will get all of the results, including the negative comments.

CONCLUSION

It didn't take long after computers were built on a more regular basis than one-offs before people began discussing the possibility of connecting them together. Once they were connected together, it was almost as much about allowing people to communicate with one another as it was about anything else. Humans are social creatures and they find new and different ways to communicate at every stage of technological development. Over the course of 40 years, we have refined and further refined our ability to communicate with one another. At this point in time, we have not only the ability to communicate with one another but the ability to quickly and easily communicate with large numbers of people all at once and have them be able to communicate back with you. Where previous types of media have been more one way or limited two way, like books, magazines, and newspapers, social media is multiway. I post something, a friend of mine comments on it and then shares it to an entirely different group of friends. And so on and so on.

Business can take advantage of this phenomenon to better engage their customers. The challenge there is that businesses should expect to get responses from their customers. Social networking has also been a target of malware authors, so businesses need to be aware of that if they jump into the social networking space and engage directly rather than just using social networking sites as additional advertising space.

Summary

Here are some ideas to consider from this chapter:

- The Internet has a long history of services being geared toward social services.
- Social networking sites like Facebook, Twitter, and Google+ have a lot of potential for engaging with customers.
- Some elements of social networking may be more public than you realize.
- Social networking could be used for human resources—either finding hires or checking on them.
- You could use social networking for background checks.
- Your company's reputation might be impacted by interactions with social media since you can provide a platform for people to say negative things about you.

Further reading

Library of Congress Is Archiving All of America's Tweets. *Business Insider*. January 22, 2013. Web, September 18, 2013.

Bhasin, K. 13 Epic Twitter Fails by Big Brands. *Business Insider*. N.p., February 6, 2012. Web, January 22, 2014. <http://www.businessinsider.com/13-epic-twitter-fails-by-big-brands-2012-2?op=1>.

Mobile Computing

INFORMATION INCLUDED IN THIS CHAPTER

- Remote e-mail
- Smartphones
- Apps
- Bring your own device (BYOD)

INTRODUCTION

As I'm writing this, I can't help but wonder where you are reading it. Is it a hard copy? Do you have an actual book in front of you with paper pages and a spine? Perhaps more likely, you are reading this on an electronic device like an e-reader or a tablet or maybe even your phone. Why would I wonder where you are reading it? According to the Pew Research Center, use of e-readers is increasing and in some demographics, there is a significant increase year over year in the last couple of years. While the ability has been around for years, an increase in capability, speed, and storage coupled with sharp decreases in prices has put the ability to read books, magazines, and newspapers electronically in the hands of a lot of people.

My first experience with a tablet was a few years ago after the first iPad came out. I was heading to a job where there was a major virus outbreak, and I was looking for an entertainment device. I picked up an iPad for portable entertainment like movies. I quickly discovered Angry Birds but while I was on-site, I found the most important feature of the iPad as far as I was concerned. I was able to acquire reference books and keep them on my iPad where I could look up information at any time, whether I was online or not. I was able to have a portable reference library with me wherever I went. At that point, I was sold. It was, prior to that experience, that I would never read books on an electronic device. I liked paper. I liked holding the book. I quickly discovered that reading on a tablet is very comfortable and has a number of other benefits, like being able to have multiple bookmarks and perform quick searches for a particular word or phrase.

Of course, I have found a large number of other uses since that time for not only the iPad but also Android tablets. Since this chapter isn't about reading on electronic devices, we'll spend some time talking about the variety of other capabilities that mobile devices bring. We've been spending a lot of time talking about cloud services and mobile devices and cloud services go hand in hand. It's hard to imagine one without the other, frankly. It's almost like one made the other possible, or maybe it's just a coincidence that both happened at roughly the same time and they are completely unrelated. Mobile devices and cloud computing and storage give us the ability to do anything from anywhere, and there are definite advantages and disadvantages to this freedom and flexibility.

Smartphones

While Blackberry had been doing the smartphone thing for years, it's hard not to give credit to Apple for helping with the smartphone explosion. I had a Blackberry for a while and the Blackberry Messenger has a great feature where you could send what was in essence a text message and you'd get a notification when it was delivered and read. Apple has since implemented this same feature in their iMessage application. You could also send text messages from the Blackberry but when I had that phone, it was extra money to send text messages, and the Blackberry gave you the ability to send those messages to another user without paying text-messaging fees since it was tied up with the data you were already paying for. It does require that the other person have a Blackberry himself or herself and you had to have their Blackberry PIN. Otherwise, you can certainly send text messages to someone but you miss out on the delivery verification. Blackberry messages are also bounced through a server, which may expose them to viewing by someone other than the sender and the recipient in spite of the fact that it looks like a direct, person-to-person message. It's tough to take my security hat off, and Blackberrys were marketed very strongly to executives and management who may be transmitting sensitive information back and forth.

Before we get too far ahead, we should talk about what a smartphone actually is. A smartphone is a cellular or mobile telephone that's built on an operating system providing advanced features that aren't typical to basic phone functions like making and receiving calls. In the 1990s, the personal digital assistant (PDA) was a popular business accessory. Whether it was the Palm or a Pocket PC, having calendaring, e-mail, fully functioning contact lists with more detail than just names and phone numbers or notes, the PDA was critical. A smartphone initially was just a phone with PDA functions. The Blackberry also had and still has the capability of running applications that you install onto the phone. While several applications came pre-installed, like e-mail and messaging, people have been able to develop third-party applications to increase the functionality of the Blackberry since 2000. It wasn't too long after Blackberry started getting big that the leader in the PDA space introduced a device that was PDA and phone in one. Palm introduced the Treo 600 in 2003, and it had the functionality of the Palm Pilot merged with a phone.

About the same time, in 2003, Android, Inc. was formed with an intention to develop smarter mobile devices. Two years later, the company was acquired by

Google in an attempt to get into the mobile market. Two years after that, Apple released the iPhone, and Google helped found the Open Handset alliance that resulted in the release of the HTC Dream a year later running the Android operating system. While there are other operating systems in use on mobile devices, the two predominant platforms are Apple's iOS and Google's Android. Currently, the Android has a larger share of the market, partly due to the generally lower cost of Android phones and partly due to the fact that it simply runs on a wider range of phones with different sizes and form factors. This is because far more manufacturers make Android phones than iOS-based phones.

At the time of this writing, the total number of smartphones in the world is something close to 1.4 billion, according to ABI Research. That's 1.4 billion out of roughly 5 billion mobile phones in the world and numbers are increasing. This is a longer, but data-backed, way of saying that the trend of smartphone use is increasing and smartphone adoption will continue. When you put a smartphone, capable of accessing e-mail and other information at any moment from any location, you have a tool people are going to be using more and more for business purposes.

My first smartphone was a Blackberry and I got it because I was looking for a way to have access to e-mail from anywhere I was and I was also looking for a device that would merge the PDA functionality I had with a Handspring with the phone I was also carrying around. At the time, the calendaring feature on the Handspring, which ran the Palm OS just like the Palm Pilot, required that it be synced to your computer in order to get your calendar updated. If you forgot to sync your PDA, you didn't have the latest meetings in your calendar so you might actually miss one if you were running from one place to another.

My first iPhone came because I had changed jobs and the job I was at didn't use the Blackberry. My choices were a Windows phone or an iPhone, and the iPhone seemed like a much more interesting platform at that time. As a starting point, it didn't rely on extra technology to get the messages to the phone. Additionally, the number and type of apps that were available even then on the iPhone convinced me that it might be helpful to have when traveling. One of the useful features is the ability to refer to a map that would place you on the map somewhere reasonably close to where you were in actuality. If you travel a lot to places you have never been to before, this is a very helpful feature. You might think of it like your own personal concierge and tour guide in addition to your assistant.

One of the challenges with early smartphones was the difficulty in getting applications for them. There wasn't one place to go to get apps for your PDA and smartphone. Apple resolved this issue by creating the App Store and giving users a single place to come and get apps. Having the single place made apps easier to find and when they are easier to find, users can quickly buy apps and add functionality to their phone. Apple didn't do this strictly out of the goodness of their heart, of course. They get 30% of the sale of each app for providing the infrastructure and oversight over the App Store. Figure 7.1 shows the Apple App Store, including a list of apps that Apple recommends. Of course, Apple also has exclusive say over what apps you can have on your phone based on what they allow into the App

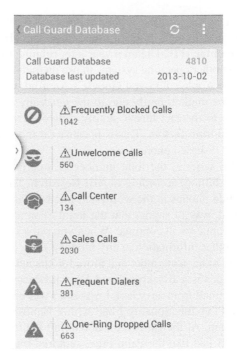

FIGURE 7.1 Using Call Blocking on Android Phone

Store. Apple has a set of policies that prohibit certain types of applications and while this may help protect users, it does leave developers of an application that's been rejected with no option for distribution.

Eventually, I switched over to an Android and specifically, the Galaxy series from Samsung. One of the primary reasons, initially, was a desire for a larger screen. I had also grown tired of the problems with keeping information on the phone under my terms and being able to easily store and retrieve pictures, music, and other files. I was also finding with the setup I had that I couldn't make changes to contacts on the phone and my laptop and not have one side written over and the changes lost. In the end, I found that Android gave me a more useful and productive phone. Widgets provide the ability to have live, active content on the phone without actually launching an app. I can quickly check the weather, for example, by just looking at my phone and not needing to find the app and launch it. More importantly, though, I gained caller ID and, even better, the ability to block calls from numbers I never want to see again. Not only will the call blocker app block calls I don't want to see but it makes use of a database of known problem phone numbers so I can benefit from the experience of others. You can see the categories and how many numbers listed in each category in Figure 7.2.

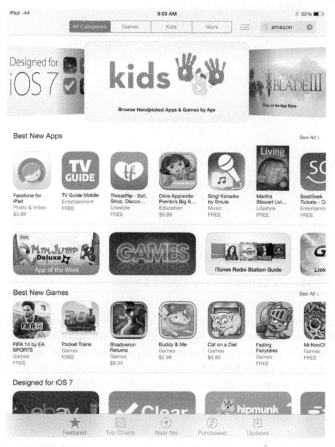

FIGURE 7.2 Apple's App Store

Apps

Android has its own app store, too. In spite of that, there are significant differences between the Android app store and the Apple app store. One of the first and largest differences is the gatekeeper for entry into the app store. Apple requires that you pay money to be an Apple developer. They charge an annual fee for developers to get access to create and sell their apps. Once you submit your app, Apple has to approve it before it shows up in the App Store. They have their own set of criteria for denying access, and they have created some controversy in the past by denying apps from competitors. Perhaps the largest controversy came in 2009 when Apple rejected the Google Voice app. There were concerns about preventing users from making use of Voice over IP services on their iPhones, raised by federal regulators. Another similar concern with the app store is the lack of transparency in the process.

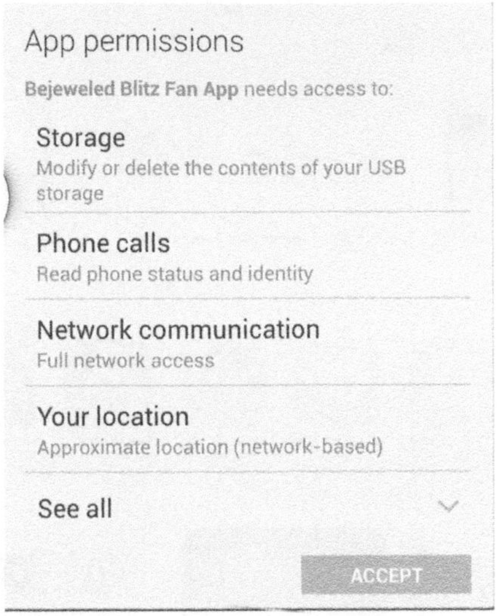

App permissions

Bejeweled Blitz Fan App needs access to:

Storage
Modify or delete the contents of your USB storage

Phone calls
Read phone status and identity

Network communication
Full network access

Your location
Approximate location (network-based)

See all

ACCEPT

FIGURE 7.3 Permissions Requested by App Under Android

Google, on the other hand, has its own app marketplace called the Play Store. This is not the only place where you can get apps for the Android devices but it is the predominant one. Google requires a registration fee to place apps into the Play Store. This is a much lower bar than the one from Apple to get into the App Store, but it is still a bar. Google does not have guidelines for what apps are allowed and what apps are not allowed, which can leave the Play Store exposed to serving up malicious apps to its users. However, unlike Apple devices, Android apps are required to request specific permissions and you, as a user, will be presented with the permissions requested by the app when you install it. Figure 7.3 shows the permissions that have been requested by some random application I selected while writing this. Google has implemented features to protect users from malicious apps, and hardware vendors like Samsung have implemented other features to better protect users.

When you install the application, you don't get the option of turning off any of these permissions or restricting the application in any way. What you get is the information needed to make a decision about whether you trust the app maker and the app to do the right things with those permissions. Unlike Apple, Google does not do any vetting of the applications that are put on the Play Store so it's entirely possible that malicious apps may find there way onto your phone before they are recognized as malicious apps. According to Symantec, a company known for its antivirus offerings, and Google Play store took on 1000 malicious apps in August, 2013. This is not a total of 1000 malicious apps as of that month. This is 1000 malicious apps added in that month alone. There may be a tendency on the part of unsophisticated users to assume that if an app is available through the app store, it must be trustworthy. This may be even truer if the app has a high rating. The problem is that ratings can be inflated much like stuffing a ballot box. If you have a malicious app and you want a lot of people to install it, you might create a lot of false reviews and ratings to make it look like it's a great app.

The Google Play Store isn't even the only marketplace for apps for the Android. Where you would have to jailbreak an iPhone to install an application that hasn't been sanctioned by Apple, you can easily use an alternative to the Google Play store to download and install apps to your mobile device. There is a trade-off here between an expanded app universe and the safety of your device. Apps that are only available through an alternate app market may very well be malicious. Again, it's important to be aware of the risks of installing apps on your Android device, no matter where you are getting them. One alternative, however, is the Amazon app store, and Amazon doesn't add just any app to their store. If you are on an Amazon Android device like the Kindle Fire then you get all of your apps from and Amazon app store, which means you get a limited selection of apps to choose from.

Beyond the potentially malicious nature of the apps themselves is the potential for serious vulnerabilities in the operating system software itself. Where Apple restricts the use of iOS to just Apple devices, Android is open to a wide variety of hardware manufacturers. This means that there is a wider range of hardware that has to be supported that increases the complexity of the operating system. Anytime you add functionality and certainly when you increase complexity, you run a much higher risk of vulnerabilities. On top of that, each hardware manufacturer may create a custom version of Android layering additional features and applications on top of the core Android OS. Once you buy a phone from HTC or Samsung, you are locked into getting updates from that vendor or through the phone carrier you use once the vendor has released the new version. This means a lot of companies are now responsible for generating different versions of the operating system with fixes for security vulnerabilities. Suddenly you have a big challenge when it comes to keeping up with versions because there are simply too many versions out there.

On top of all of that, with so much hardware, vendors are more likely to orphan a piece of hardware and not release updates for it. As an example, I had the original version of the Motorola Xoom for a while. I already had an iPad but I wanted to be able to compare them side by side so I could offer advice on the pros and cons of each if I was asked by a business I was doing consulting work for. At some point, the Xoom became orphaned on Honeycomb. While Motorola may have stopped issuing fixes for the Xoom 1, anyone investigating vulnerabilities and creating exploits certainly wasn't stopping looking for those. They have time on their side since there would be no fixes forthcoming and anyone who had bought the Xoom and found it a perfectly reasonable tablet might still be using it for a long time and be vulnerable to exploitation. With so much hardware and the software fragmentation that comes along with it, there are a large number of devices in the wild running very old software that could have critical vulnerabilities in them that aren't likely to be fixed.

The same may also be true of apps that are available on mobile devices. Some developers have a strong commitment to improving their software and issuing bug fixes on a regular basis. You can see this with the number of apps that seem to be constantly updating or expecting to be updated. On the iOS platform, you have to specifically go in and force apps to update. This can mean that there may be significant vulnerabilities in an app on a large number of devices because people may not pay attention to keeping their apps up to date. On the Android side, you can set apps to update automatically. This has pros and cons, of course. It's nice to get the updates without having to do anything to get them, but it's also possible that you may get an update that causes your app to stop working. Especially in the case of Android with so much different hardware and also different size screens, you may well run into situations where apps stop working the way you expect or simply stop working altogether. The one case where you would have to update an Android app manually if you had automatic updates on is where the permissions for the app have changed in some way. Once there are permission changes, you have to approve the permission changes. In some cases, though, whether it's on the Apple or Android platform, there is software that is simply orphaned by the developer. It will never get updates and may be an exposure to the user.

We've been talking a lot about Android and Apple as though they are the only two device types on the market. This is certainly not true, but they are good examples for other platforms that will have the same issues. Microsoft has recently updated their Surface tablet and they are continuing to try to get traction in the phone space with their hardware partners. They also have an app store for their operating system and it will have the very same potential for problems that we've been talking about on the other platforms. Like Apple, Microsoft has an approval process, and they also have a certification process that you have to follow to get your app certified to be able to run on one of their devices. Once you submit an app to Microsoft, it will get checked out, just as with Apple, and Microsoft will either approve or reject your app. Again, while there are certainly downsides to this process and I certainly wouldn't expect Apple or Microsoft to find all potential security vulnerabilities in an app, the fact that someone is taking even a cursory look will weed out some of the risk posed by apps on your mobile devices.

Jailbreaking

Another way of extending capabilities of a mobile device is jailbreaking it. This involves exploiting a vulnerability in order to introduce unauthorized applications onto the device. This is how iPhone users get more applications and gain more direct access to both the operating system as well as the file system. In addition to the lack of control, there are a couple of legitimate concerns around jailbreaking. The first one is the possibility of introducing malware onto the phone since there isn't the strict control over apps that get added after the jailbreak. Jailbreaking doesn't prevent you from adding apps through the App Store, it just adds an additional means of obtaining apps. Once you have performed a jailbreak on your phone, you not only get access to an additional set of apps, you also get the ability to replace the default apps that Apple provides.

The network providers are concerned about the impact of jailbreaking on their network and that is a mixture of issues. The first is that jailbreaking may open the door to malicious software, and malicious software may generate a lot of network traffic. If a large number of iPhones were suddenly involved in a botnet and that botnet were called into service to create a distributed denial of service attack, it would be a critical issue for the network provider. There are a number of applications that are available through Cydia, the jailbreak equivalent of an app store, that may create more network traffic through the provider's network.

They are also concerned, apparently, about the possibility of malicious software on the mobile devices attacking the network from the inside. They may be concerned that a mobile device running an OS that has been jailbroken could start sending malformed protocol requests to the network and that could have a negative impact, including the possibility of knocking cells offline, causing an outage. Any phone that has jailbroken software on it could potentially have more direct access to the cellular radio and that could be of some concern to the network providers. Apple also has concerns with devices that have been jailbroken, but that's mostly a concern about the user experience. If the user jailbreaks their phone, they won't be getting the experience Apple wants them to have, and they have legitimate concerns about an increase in support requests to repair phones that have been altered in this way.

Android is an open-source operating system and, as a result, there have been a lot of groups who have created distributions to run on mobile devices designed for Android. All of these distributions are based around a particular version of the operating system, but they may have added additional features or created a different look to the phone that may be more appealing to users. These custom ROMs, as they are called, are easily available, though it may take some effort to install one of them on your device. This is because there is a boot loader involved. The boot loader is the component of the operating system that locates and boots the actual operating system kernel. The phone manufacturers generally protect the boot loader in order to keep from having the custom ROMs installed on the phones, protecting the integrity of the device, its functionality, and the user experience they expect you to have.

Android is a very developer-friendly operating system. You can see this just by looking through the settings menus where you will find a Developer Options menu, as shown in Figure 7.4. Anyone can download the Android Developer Kit (ADK) and turn their phone or tablet into a development system, including using the ADK tools to directly interface with the phone as long as the phone is plugged into the computer where the ADK tools are located. This is part of why you can see the USB debugging switch. If you enable USB debugging, you can send commands directly to the phone over the USB cable to perform actions like rebooting the phone or installing software to it.

The difference between custom ROMs and a jailbroken iOS is that custom ROMs don't unlock any new, otherwise unsupported apps. In order to get additional access on your phone or tablet, you need to get root access on your phone. It's called root access because it's named after the superuser account under UNIX/Linux systems. iOS and Android are both UNIX-based operating systems. Android

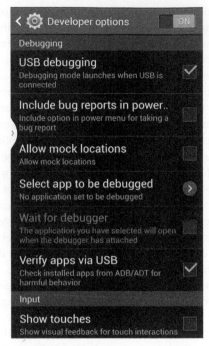

FIGURE 7.4 Developer Options on Android Phone

is based on Linux while iOS is a custom version of Mac OS X, which is based on BSD UNIX. Normally, you would have the access of a regular user but after getting root access, you have complete control over the device to make any changes you want to make. This is, of course, a potentially dangerous proposition, depending on how skilled you are with these types of operating systems. In reality, the difference between a custom ROM on an Android device and getting an iPhone or iPad that has been jailbroken is fairly large. In the case of the iOS device, you can get direct access to the file system where you otherwise can't. This can include making changes to operating system files. In the case of Android, you can get to the file system at any point if you want to install a file manager. In the case of my Galaxy S4, it came with a file manager already installed when I took it out of the box. This provided me the ability to move data easily between the internal storage and the SD card I installed to get some additional storage space.

Providing mobile access

The easiest way to provide mobile access is to simply open up ports through your firewall and allow your mobile devices to connect directly to your mail servers to pull mail. POP3 and IMAP access don't really solve the problem of calendaring unless you want to rely on all of your devices getting an invitation and updating their own local calendar. That's not really the promise of mobile devices, however. You need to have a way to at least get your mobile devices access to their mail and calendar. If there are other features like notes or reminders, it's helpful to have access to those as well.

In order to get more entrenched in the enterprise space, Blackberry offered a server for free that could get e-mail out to Blackberry users. One of the challenges with mobile access is how to allow the mobile devices to get access to information that's typically inside the corporate perimeter, like e-mail. In the case of Blackberry, you registered your device on the Blackberry Enterprise Server (BES) and if you received an e-mail, the BES would be notified and it would push the e-mail out to you over the air. This was a way round having to allow external connections into sensitive internal infrastructure. You could allow the outbound connection through the firewall and not have to allow inbound connections from anywhere in the world. It was a pretty good solution to a sticky problem.

Microsoft has had software capable of synchronizing mail, calendar, etc. to a mobile device since 1996. Early on, it was ActiveSync and targeted at the PDAs. By 2002, they had moved the functionality into the Exchange Server and it was called Exchange ActiveSync (EAS). EAS provides a number of ways to provide functional interactions with the Exchange Server, including calendar interactions like accepting or declining calendar requests as well as enforcing password policies and setting security features. EAS also provides the ability to look up addresses from the global address list, which can be critical functionality in sending messages to people who aren't on your personal contact list.

Microsoft also uses push technology, just as Blackberry does with their BES. EAS will push out e-mail as well as contacts that are stored on the server and the calendar. This allows you to be constantly updated with changes that are made from any device you access the Exchange Server from. If you make changes to your contacts from your desktop, your mobile device will automatically pick it up because ActiveSync will send out all the changes to the mobile device. Figure 7.5 shows some of the other settings available with EAS.

In addition to the sample shown in Figure 7.5, EAS has other capabilities that provide fairly extensive control over mobile devices that fall under EAS. You may disable removable storage like a micro SD card, and you may also disable any camera that is built into the mobile device. EAS also allows control over what apps may be installed and also what apps may be blocked. Attempting to control the apps that get installed onto a mobile device can be a daunting task but in some cases, you may want to protect your network and your sensitive data by restricting the apps that can be used to a small number that are relevant to business needs.

Physical security

Mobile devices have generally been getting smaller, particularly when you compare them with the bricks that used to be required to house the transmitter and an

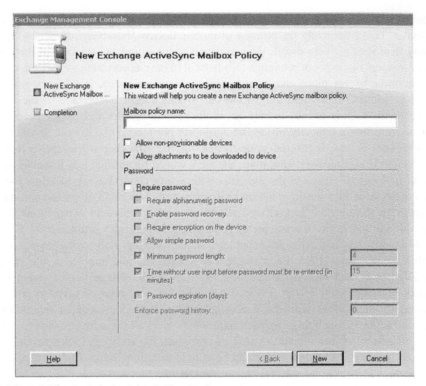

FIGURE 7.5 Microsoft ActiveSync Policy Settings

enormous battery. In spite of Samsung's introduction of devices now called phablets like the Galaxy S4 and the Galaxy Note, which are quite a bit larger than other mobile devices. Even saying that, the mobile devices are generally small enough to easily get lost. Losing the device is one of the largest considerations for mobile device security. This is another place where something like the EAS server can be helpful. EAS has the ability to require that devices use passwords, and if someone gets the password wrong some previously specified number of times, EAS can require the mobile device wipe all of its data. This protects any sensitive information from being removed from someone who may have stolen the phone.

This is not to say that you need EAS to perform a device wipe after a number of failed passwords. This is a common preference setting on smartphones, though with EAS, you can require that it be set. You can also perform a remote wipe at any point you believe the device has been lost or stolen. This is also becoming possible with manufacturer functionality like the Find My iPhone feature that's available with Apple's iCloud. Samsung, similarly, has a location function for their devices that also includes the ability to remotely lock or remotely wipe a device.

In order to fully protect mobile devices, there are a number of best practices that should be utilized.

1. **Locking**—Mobile devices should have a screen lock to prevent unauthorized users from gaining access. In most cases, this will also prevent any programmatic access from a computer like using iTunes or the Android File Transfer app. You can't get access to any of the information on the device without unlocking it first. This is how it should be, of course. If all you have to do in order to gain access to the information on the mobile device is plug it into a computer, there isn't much point in locking it to begin with.

2. **Use strong authentication**—Locking phones is a pretty common strategy but often the authentication used is a simple four-digit number. With four-digit numbers, there are only 10,000 possible combinations. Screens on smartphones, where the digits are generally shown since smartphones no longer have physical keyboards any longer, tend to show fingerprints. While there may be technology used to resist fingerprints, over time a lot of presses in the same places will leave fingerprints. That makes it a lot easier to guess the four-digit PIN. Better than using a four-digit PIN is using a passphrase, which most smartphones tend to support. This makes it more complex and, hopefully, harder to guess. Android phones also use patterns to unlock the phone. This can also leave a trace on the surface of the screen, making it easier to guess how to unlock it, but without the trace, a random pattern can be even harder to guess.

3. **Biometrics**—Android phones have had the ability to perform facial recognition natively for a while now. The iPhone has apps that you can buy to add facial recognition to the phone. While this isn't perfect, it can provide some ability to ensure that the person holding the phone is the owner. Android offers backup authentication mechanisms in case facial recognition fails. The newest version of iOS, version 7, also offers biometric capabilities by allowing users to unlock their phone with a fingerprint. Since it took the Chaos Computer Club just a matter of days to break the fingerprint authentication, this is also not perfect. Over time, it will improve, and you can use biometrics to better secure your phone.

4. **Antivirus**—It's rapidly getting to the point where there is enough malicious software out there that antivirus is not a bad idea to consider on mobile devices to protect your data as well as the functionality of the device.

5. **Find your phone**—As noted previously, you can enable a phone locator. This is important for a number of reasons. The first is just simply to recover a lost phone to minimize the costs associated with having to replace that phone. On top of that, if a phone has been stolen, you want to recover it as quickly as possible. While you can include a strong password and encrypt the device, if the password is obtained either by guessing or through another means, the data on the phone has been compromised. Additionally, while you may be able to remote wipe the phone, that requires the phone be talking to the cellular network and have data access. Someone who was deliberately trying to obtain a

FIGURE 7.6 Security Configuration Settings on Android Phone

phone because of the information that's on it may put the phone into a Faraday bag or Faraday cage in order to protect the phone from getting those remote wipe commands. A Faraday cage is designed to keep electromagnetic signals from getting to the phone as well as preventing those same signals from getting out to the network from the phone.

6. **Know your apps**—Always be careful about the apps that you are installing. Malicious apps get into even the Apple App Store from time to time, so you want to make sure you know what you are installing.

7. **Encryption**—The iPhone has been encrypting data on the phone by default since the 3.x line of iOS. Android also has the ability to encrypt storage, though it's not commonly turned on by default. Android phones also allow for extensible storage through micro SD cards. The phone will also encrypt the external storage device. Encrypting your data is critical to preventing someone who has your phone from getting access to your data. The only way they could get to the data would be to guess your passcode, which should provide decrypted access to all of the data on your device since it's part of what is protecting your data. The current encryption standard is the Advanced Encryption Standard (AES), and the major mobile operating system vendors support AES to encrypt data on your device. Figure 7.6 shows the settings on an Android device to encrypt the primary storage as well as the secondary storage

(SD card). Encryption is particularly important on the SD card because while the phone itself may require unlocking before yielding information, it's trivial to remove the SD card and access any data that may be stored there.

While these are all protection strategies you should be implementing on your phones, you shouldn't expect they will provide unbeatable protection on your phone. Some of it still comes down to appropriate handling by the users. If the users are careless with their phones and with the data they keep on the device, your organization will take on the risk of your users. Where possible, not only should you have the paper policies in place but also the appropriate EAS policy. Google also has several options for configuring security policies for mobile devices. If you get Google Apps for Business, you get access to completely configure a policy for any smartphone that uses your company's Google Apps account.

Bring your own device

The price of smartphones has come down, and the functionality has improved to the point where a good-sized segment of the population has their own smartphone. Where it used to be that you relied on your job to provide you a cell phone or a pager, we're well past the economic threshold where people find it useful to get their own devices and it's affordable to do so. When people get their own smartphones, they get interested in being able to check work e-mail and generally be connected to what's going on with their work lives. Some of the softswitch and private branch exchange vendors even provide apps on smartphones to get access to their work phone.

Allowing users to make use of their own devices to gain access to corporate resources is typically called Bring your own device (BYOD), and it brings up a number of issues when it comes to the security of your network. Where it often starts is someone in executive management getting a shiny new toy like a Blackberry or an iPhone or an iPad and wanting to be able check their mail and maybe have their phone calls rerouted to their new smartphone when they are away from their desks. As soon as an executive gets access to critical corporate infrastructure from outside the infrastructure, it's not hard to make the leap to letting everyone have it. This is mostly because you need to make the infrastructure changes allowing it, no matter how many people end up having access.

This is not to say that there aren't scalability issues to take into consideration but that's generally a different discussion than how to grant access to e-mail and other network infrastructure. This may include getting wireless network access, since mobile devices have 802.11 interfaces for network communication. Many businesses separate their wireless access from the rest of the network, requiring that users who get wireless access use a virtual private network (VPN) connection to gain access to internal, corporate resources. One reason for this because wireless communication can be intercepted by anyone close enough to get the signal. In the case of wired communication, you have to have physical access to the network,

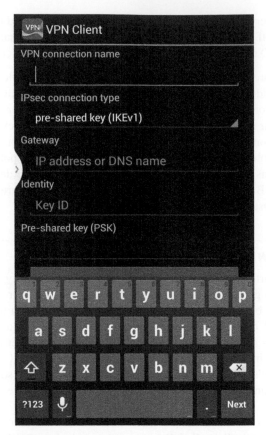

FIGURE 7.7 Configuring Virtual Private Network (VPN) Client on Android Phone

meaning you have to be inside the building. With wireless, I can often pick up the signal in the parking lot outside of the building and even if the wireless network makes use of Wired Equivalent Privacy or WiFi Protected Access, there is a risk of those messages being decrypted because they may be vulnerable to attack.

Employing an IPSec VPN over the top of a wireless network adds privacy by encrypting the messages as well as authentication because IPSec often employs better authentication than the wireless protocols do. This also ensures that you limit the entry points to your network by making everyone go through a VPN instead of exposing your whole internal network to the wireless network that anyone may be able to get access to with enough time and effort. Fortunately, mobile devices based on iOS and Android have the capability of initiating VPNs built into the operating system. When you connect to a wireless network, you can also connect to the corporate VPN, allowing you access to your e-mail and other enterprise resources from your mobile device. You can see the configuration settings for creating an IPSec VPN connection from an Android phone (Figure 7.7).

Boundaries

Depending on who you are, you may read this differently. From a corporate or an enterprise perspective, you are extending the perimeter of your network out to the end user device that could be anywhere in the world. From an end user perspective, the unacknowledged boundary is allowing work life to intrude into private life. You get used to having your phone with you and checking it just to kill time, whether it's e-mail, Facebook, Twitter, or just a game of Candy Crush or Angry Birds. At some point, you get your corporate e-mail on your phone and you're checking e-mail at all hours of the day and night just because you have access to it. This is a boundary that used to be clear but has been slowly eroding, as mobile devices get cheaper and more accessible, whether it's a laptop or a mobile phone or a tablet.

When you connect your personal device to your network, any EAS policy in place will be pushed down to the device. As discussed previously, EAS has the capability to have extensive control over the device including disabling a lot of functionality that would be desirable for personal use even if it may not be desirable for business use. The question is how much control would you as an owner of a personal device would allow the business to have over your smartphone. The business needs to protect its interests but where those interests and your own personal interests diverge, the business interests will win in the case of an ActiveSync server because the policy gets pushed to the phone regardless of whether it's a personal phone or not.

This is a decision that each user has to make. Whether to allow the business to have control over their device, including the ability to wipe it, just in order to have some access to business information like e-mail. Keep in mind that in cases where an employee leaves the company, the company may wipe the device in order to ensure that all company data that is stored on the device is removed. A remote wipe may remove business-specific information or it may remove all information on the phone, including personal pictures and contacts. It may also simply remove everything from the phone, leaving it totally unfunctional. The degree to which the remote wipe operates depends on the service ordering the remote wipe and the operating system on the mobile device being wiped.

We've covered one aspect of boundaries by talking about protecting your corporate network from direct access from a mobile device. This is primarily because of the potential risks of using wireless networks. Wireless networks, because you have little to no control over where the signal goes to, provide a certain amount of risk. As an example, Figure 7.8 shows a list of all of the networks that are available from where I sit, without any additional effort on my part. Using a VPN gateway as a boundary between the network where your mobile devices, including laptops, connect and the inside of your network is a good idea. While you may consider this to be a complication, it's likely that you have a VPN gateway in your network already so this is just another use of it. The VPN could also provide a way for your mobile devices to gain access from outside of your network as well if the gateway is already in place. Your VPN gateway then becomes the boundary between your internal network and all mobile devices, regardless of type and location.

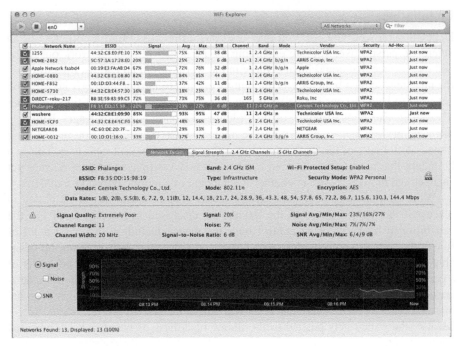

FIGURE 7.8 Using WiFi Explorer

CONCLUSION

Mobile devices have provided a lot of capability for users to be productive no matter where they are. There are a number of challenges by enabling mobile devices for business use, including the risk associated with extending the edge of the enterprise network. This is what invariably happens when you allow access to corporate information like e-mail from mobile devices. Wherever that mobile device is becomes the edge of your network, whether the access is from a WiFi hotspot in a coffee shop or whether it's being accessed over the cellular data network of your cell provider. While this was previously true by opening up a VPN gateway to allow remote access from your remote workers, especially if you allowed split tunneling, it's even more true with mobile devices because of the potential for greater volumes. Using a push technology rather than pull will help alleviate this risk.

We are coming to a point where antivirus or some other malware protection software will become commonplace on mobile devices. One of the reasons for this is because they present an enormous foothold for those who have malicious intent, particularly when it comes to stealing information. Where there is an opportunity, there will be people lined up to take advantage of the opportunity, and right now one of the biggest opportunities is mobile devices. There is already malware in the wild affecting Android, iOS, and Blackberry. You can expect more malware instances on all the platforms as mobile usage continues to rise.

There is no stopping adoption of mobile technology at this point nor should there be any attempt to stop it. Mobile technology may be blurring the lines between work and home life, but in the end, if used wisely, it has the potential to improve the work-life balance because you don't have to be chained to your desk any longer to be productive. You can be at your kids' soccer game and still be available for business calls, just as though you were at your desk, and you can still answer important e-mail messages from anywhere you are. It's worth being vigilant, however, that just because you can be productive from anywhere you are that you don't allow your business life to take over your family life, just because you have that ability.

Summary

Some ideas to take away from this chapter:

- Smartphones have been around for well over a decade, and you could also consider them just an extension of the PDA.
- The Blackberry introduced the push to phone concept with a server at every business who wanted to implement the Blackberry for their users.
- The iPhone and the Android OS have dramatically increased the desire for smartphones.
- Getting remote access to e-mail can be a security challenge, particularly if the e-mail is stored within the corporate network.
- Cloud-based e-mail services like Google Apps for Business and Microsoft Office 365 help with the security challenge associated with mobile devices trying to pull e-mail remotely from a corporate network.
- Cloud services can push security policies to a mobile phone to better protect the business.
- BYOD raises some challenges with corporate networks but security policies can help mitigate them.

Further reading

Rainie, L., Kickuhr, K., Purcell, K., Madden, M., Brenner, J. The Rise of E-reading. Pew Internet Libraries RSS. Pew Research Center, April 4, 2012. Web, September 23, 2013.

Unified Communications

8

- Voice over IP
- Presence
- Instant messaging
- Video over IP

INTRODUCTION

While it's common knowledge that Alexander Graham Bell invented the telephone, the complete story is far more complex. Bell was working on a patent for an acoustic telegraph. Up to that point, the fastest way to communicate over long distances was the telegraph, which was capable of transmitting simple signals. Because of the way patent law was written in Britain, a patent had to be filed there before any other country or the patent wouldn't be awarded so Bell made arrangements to file his patent overseas and wait for acknowledgment of its acceptance before moving forward with a patent in the United States. Bell wasn't the only one working on a patent for a means of transmitting sound over distances. Elisha Gray was also working on a similar patent. When Bell got around to putting his patent together, by coincidence Gray filed papers with the patent office at the same time.

There is some debate over who actually filed first, but Bell was the one who was awarded the patent. This may not be particularly meaningful except that Bell had men he was in business with and the intent of the patent was to make money with it. One of the ways he did that was to open the Bell Telephone Company to hold the patents that were critical to creating telephony service. Bell's father-in-law encouraged the creation of the New England Telephone and Telegraph Company, which merged with the Bell Telephone Company within a couple of years of the creation of both. Gray, on the other hand, was a part owner in a company that supplied Western Union with telegraph equipment. Gray's company was eventually purchased by Western Union and it became Western Electric.

Somewhere in the middle of all of this, Thomas Edison was also working on a patent that was critical to the success of the telephone. When the telephone was

FIGURE 8.1 Telephone Operators

Seattle Municipal Archives, Seattle, WA.

created by Bell, the receiver portion used a piece of parchment paper to sense the vibrations from the sound waves. This led to a very weak signal. Edison, completely separately from both Gray and Bell, developed a carbon microphone. The carbon particles are placed between a diaphragm and an electrode and the sound waves pressing against the carbon particles makes changes to the electrical resistance. The carbon particles created a much stronger signal and the Edison carbon microphone continued to be used in telephones from the late 1800s up into the 1980s.

Early on, there were a large number of telephone companies, and each telephone company had their own lines. In some cases, there were multiple phone companies in the same geographic area, and each company strung its own lines with a single line running from the central office (CO) to the subscriber. This might lead to a large number of lines strung through a city on a number of different poles. Early on, there was a need for a way to pass phone calls from one provider to another and even later, there had to be a way to get phone calls from one geographic location to another geographic location. Think state-to-state or even country-to-country. Early on, this was done through the use of telephone operators. One CO with a telephone operator would connect up a call using a plug board to another CO where there was another telephone operator. You can see a number of telephone switchboard operators in Figure 8.1 along with the cables with their ¼″ TRS plugs. A TRS plug or connector has a tip, ring, and sleeve providing three connection points. These connectors continue to be used today, though they were invented for use in the phone network.

When we transmit data through the Internet, as we have been discussing in previous chapters, we are doing packet switching. This is because the communication stream between two ends is broken up into individual packets of varying size, and each packet finds its own way through the network that is determined as the packet is traversing the network. At each stop along the way, the waypoint, called a router, makes a determination about where to send the packet next. Packets may arrive in a different order than they were sent. The system on the other end is responsible for putting the packets back in the correct order. When it comes to a voice network, there is nothing on the receiving end that would put pieces of the communication back into a correct order. As a result, the communication from one end to the other needs to be nailed up from beginning to end. You can think of this as the line that runs from your house to the CO, if you still have a traditional phone line in our house. Anytime you pick up the phone, you get a dial tone because there is a dedicated circuit from you to the CO.

While it took several years to work out the kinks of multiple phone companies and how to connect them all together in a way so Joe in southern California could call Albert in eastern Maine. The switchboard operators performed the same role that routers do in a packet-switched network, except that they did it once when the call is placed and left it up until the call was completed. A phone network doesn't use packet switching because there aren't packets. When your stereo receiver creates sound to send out your speakers, and yes, I realize that in a wireless world this is also old tech but bear with me here, it doesn't chunk the sound signal into small packets. It's an endlessly modulating signal that looks like a wave. You can see a series of sound waves of different frequencies in Figure 8.2. In order to carry information that never really stops but continues flowing, you need an end-to-end circuit to carry the signal over.

Signaling

While the switchboard operators originally managed this circuit-switched network, it wasn't very sustainable, as the phone network got larger. More lines and more need for speed as people placed calls required the creation of a mechanical circuit switch. Early telephones didn't have a way to dial a number. They relied on an operator. You picked up your phone and it sent a signal to the operator who answered and placed the call for you. Eventually, phones got the ability to dial numbers with a rotary dial. These types of phones were sending pulses into the network that indicated the numbers that were being dialed. The pulses provided information to the early switches to indicate the number the caller wanted to place a call to.

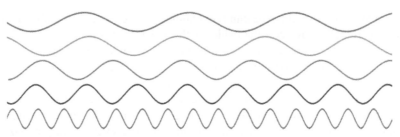

FIGURE 8.2 Different Frequencies of Audio Waves

This was the first round of in-band signaling where all of the information about the call was done through the same line that the call itself was on.

Decades later, the pulse tones gave way to dual-tone multifrequency. This was typically called Touch-Tone and instead of a rotary dial, it used square buttons on the phone which, when pressed, would emit a dual-tone sound that would be sent to the CO that the phone was connected to. These tones would then trigger behavior at the switch at the CO by initiating a call. Even later, additional functionality using the * or # keys was possible including redialing the last number that tried calling or blocking your own number from showing up with caller ID on the other end.

All of these capabilities relied on the ability of the phone company to signal between the CO and the phone as well as between COs, regardless of how they were connected to one another. In order to set up a call, messages need to be sent from the phone to the CO indicating a desire to place a call and then the CO needs to allocate space in the network for the call to take place, whether it's a local call through the same switch or whether it's connecting to a user on a remote switch. The circuit the call will take place over needs to be nailed up so a lot of components along the way need to know what's happening. This was previously done with a chain of telephone operators relaying information to one another through the different exchanges or phone company offices. As the phone network became more automated, it was apparent that there needed to be an automatic way of performing signaling across the network that was efficient as well as capable of handling all of the features of the phone network as it was, plus being able to support additional features.

Initially, the signaling, as noted above, was done in-band. This means that the tones that were being used to send messages between parts of the phone network were being sent down the same lines that would also carry the voice once the call was connected. The reliance on the lines used to carry the voice or bearer signal meant that signaling was limited to audio, which was an analog waveform. Eventually, the in-band signaling was replaced with out-of-band signaling, meaning that all of the overhead of setting up calls through the network, including transmitting billing information, was done using a different channel from the one being used to carry the voice or audio. Using a different channel meant that digital information, or packet-based communications, could be used, which opened the door to a lot of different types of information being sent through the network, far more efficiently.

In 1980, the International Telecommunications Union (ITU), a special agency of the United Nations, defined Signaling System No. 7 (SS7) to succeed Signaling System No. 6. Signaling System 5 and those before it were all in-band signaling protocols while SS7 used out-of-band signaling. SS7 has two different modes it can operate in. The first is associated mode where the signaling traverses the network in the same way the call does, leading the call through from switch to switch. Quasi-associated mode is where the signaling traverses an entirely separate network designed for SS7 traffic. The call continues to traverse the public switched telephone network (PSTN), separating the signaling entirely from the media. The SS7 goes through a series of signal transfer points through the SS7 network. North American phone networks generally use quasi-associated mode where associated mode is more common in smaller phone networks.

Digital lines like those in the T-carrier family (T-1, T-3, and so on) as well as those from the Integrated Services Digital Network (ISDN) use separate signaling from the bearer channels, though they are all generally bound together. In the case of ISDN, for example, you get two bearer channels, called B channels, and one data channel, called a D channel, in the basic rate interface (BRI) implementation. You may also get a primary rate interface that uses 23 bearer channels and an associated data channel for all the signaling associated with the line. This is carried over a T1 in North America, though it's carried over other types of lines in other parts of the world.

H.323

And this is where we get off the traditional telephony train and join up with the world of Voice over IP (VoIP). The reason for spending so much time getting to the point of where signaling has separated from the audio stream of a call is because when we talk about VoIP, we talk about several different protocols that encompass both signaling and media. The first standardized VoIP was H.323, released by the ITU in 1996, which is really a set of standards providing the ability to transmit both voice and video across a packet-switched (data) network. When you look at a packet capture of an H.323 call, you won't ever see any H.323 messages because H.323 actually specifies a process and a set of standards that would be used to set up a call. The various protocols associated with H.323 are binary protocols, meaning that you wouldn't be able to easily read them visually. In the case of Figure 8.3, I've used Wireshark to analyze the packet because it pulls it apart for me and has all the components of the message broken out, making it much easier to see what's going on.

H.323 not only specifies what messages and protocols should be used during call control, but it also specifies a network architecture, including the various components that would be involved in a call. The following are the various elements defined for an H.323 installation. Not all of these elements are required.

```
▽ H.225.0 CS
  ▽ H323-UserInformation
    ▽ h323-uu-pdu
      ▽ h323-message-body: setup (0)
        ▽ setup
            protocolIdentifier: 0.0.8.2250.0.4 (Version 4)
          ▷ sourceAddress: 1 item
          ▽ sourceInfo
            ▽ vendor
              ▷ vendor
                H.221 Manufacturer: Equivalence (OpenH323) (0x0900003d)
                productId: Callgen323 pogacsam
                versionId: 0.9alpha4
                terminal
                ..0. .... mc: False
                ...0 .... undefinedNode: False
          ▷ destCallSignalAddress: ipAddress (0)
            0... .... activeMC: False
            conferenceID: f8fdf93e-cd9e-d611-9ab2-000476222017
          ▷ conferenceGoal: create (0)
0070  00 3d 14 43 61 6c 6c 67  85 6e 33 32 33 20 70 61   .=.Callg en323 pa
0080  67 61 63 73 61 6d 00 00  0a 30 2e 39 61 6c 70 68   gacsam.. .0.9alph
0090  61 34 00 00 00 0a 01 06  12 06 b8 00 f8 fd f9 3e   a4...... .......>
00a0  cd 9e d6 11 9a b2 00 04  76 22 20 17 00 5d 0d 80   ........ v" ..]..
00b0  07 00 0a 01 03 8f 80 23  11 00 c0 fe f9 3e cd 9e   .......# .....>..
00c0  d6 11 9a b2 00 04 76 22  20 17 01 00 01 00 01 00   ......v" .......
00d0  01 00 02 80 01 00                                  ......
● 🔲 OCTET_STRING_SIZE_1_256 (... | Packets: 499 · Displayed: 499 (100.0%) · Load time: 0:00.... | Profile: Default
```

FIGURE 8.3 Packet Capture of an H.323 Message

- **Terminal**—A terminal is an endpoint. This would be any device that would initiate or terminate a call. This might be a soft client or it could be an IP phone. It may also be a video-conferencing system. The terminal implements the protocol stack required to handle call control as well as media handling.
- **Multipoint control units**—A multipoint control unit is responsible for handling multiway sessions. This might be a conference call, for example.
- **Gateways**—A gateway provides a bridge from one H.323 VoIP network to another network. This would enable a VoIP network to connect to the PSTN, for example. If you wanted to place a call to someone not on your own network, you would need a gateway to get that call off the network, whether it's to another VoIP network or to the PSTN.
- **Gatekeeper**—A gatekeeper can provide a number of services to an H.323 network. While it's nice to believe that you can trust everyone who jacks into your network, it's not realistic. As a result, you need a device to handle registrations on the network, including authentication and access control. On top of that, when a call comes your way, it's helpful for the network to know how to get in touch with you.

Figure 8.4 shows a very simple network with the important components in it. Depending on the vendor you are using and the size of your installation, you may have many more components in your installation. In general, though, you would have a terminal, represented in the figure by a phone that connects to a gatekeeper. The gatekeeper would take care of getting the phone registered with either an extension or a username. Once the phone is registered, the gatekeeper knows how

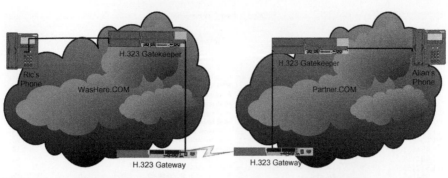

FIGURE 8.4 H.323 Network Diagram

to get in touch with the phone. When a call comes into the network, whether it's from inside or outside the enterprise, the phone infrastructure needs to know how to get to the user. The gatekeeper would keep track of that information.

On top of that, the gatekeeper would be in place to do what it could to protect the network. In performing admission control, the gatekeeper ensures that calls attempts come from legitimate users and registration attempts also come from legitimate users. Depending on the size of the network, the gatekeeper may only be able to protect the terminals from attack or traffic flood. Typically, the terminals would be the most sensitive point within the infrastructure as the least resilient. IP phones or terminal adapters generally have slower processors and maybe even lower speed network interfaces. As a result, they may end up failing if there is too much traffic or even malformed traffic. The gatekeepers themselves may still be susceptible to attack, while they protect the endpoints.

Any time a call has to pass out of the realm of the local network, it would need to pass through a gateway. This may be a way to get a call out to the PSTN, in which case the IP call would need to be converted to an analog call. If you have multiple networks connected to one another, the gateways would be responsible for getting a call from one network realm into another network realm.

As you'd expect, all of these different components communicate with one another using one of the different protocols specified by the H.323 standard. There are a number of different protocols that are used in order to set up a call. Different types of calls can create a different set of messages so we're going to focus on a very simple call flow using the network diagram in Figure 8.4. Ric is going to place a call to Allan. Again, we're going to use Wireshark to help us out here. Using the packet capture from Figure 8.3, I have used Wireshark to generate a ladder diagram, which is used to diagram a call flow showing the messages that are sent from one system to another. If there are multiple systems in the path, a ladder diagram can show the messages going from one system to another, indicating all the stops that messages make along the way. Figure 8.5 is the ladder diagram that Wireshark generated, and we'll refer to that as we follow a call through the network. Since the

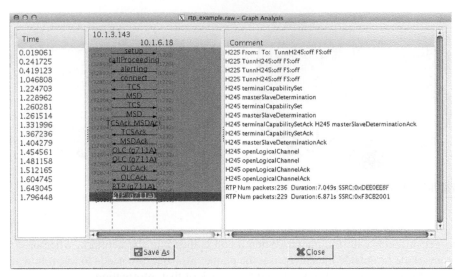

FIGURE 8.5 Ladder Diagram of H.323 Call

diagram only shows a portion of the network, I will supplement with additional detail that is missing from this particular ladder diagram to indicate where additional messages may be sent.

The first set of messages used to get the call up is part of the H.225.0 protocol that is responsible for call signaling and admission control. Before an endpoint places the call, it would send an admission request message to the gatekeeper, requesting the address of the destination endpoint. The gatekeeper will respond with an admission confirm message. These messages don't show up in the ladder diagram and aren't always required. Similarly, there may be gatekeeper requests that are sent from an endpoint trying to locate a gatekeeper to communicate with. Again, these messages aren't required, and they don't show up in this particular call flow. Once the endpoint knows who they are calling and where the callee is located, it can place the call.

In order to place the call, the endpoint would send a SETUP message to the gatekeeper that would send it along to the gateway on its own network. That gateway, in the case of our example network, would send the SETUP message on to the gateway on the partner network. The SETUP message would be passed on to the gatekeeper where Allan was registered and the gatekeeper would send it along to Allan's endpoint. Once Allan receives the SETUP message, he sends back two status messages. The first is a callProceeding message. The second is an alerting message. These messages indicate to the caller that the callee has received the SETUP message and the signaling portion of the call has been established.

Let's say that my good friend Allan has the phone number 212-459-7890. When I dial that number, my terminal adapter initiates all of the messages indicated above.

His terminal adapter sends back the responses as indicated but more importantly, the terminal adapter initiates the phone ringing. The status messages also trigger the ringback on the callee end. Without that ringback to indicate that the called phone is actually ringing, you get silence and confusion about whether the call is actually in progress. In the process of troubleshooting some issues on a VoIP network once, we were having problems getting the ringback to work. It's strange to listen to silence and then suddenly hear a voice on the other end. Without that feedback to indicate the call is in process and the phone on the other end is actually ringing, we have no way of knowing the call setup has succeeded and the phone on the other end is actually trying to get the attention of the person we are trying to call.

When Allan picks up the phone, the terminal or terminal adapter sends a CONNECT message back to my terminal adapter. This is an indication to my terminal adapter to initiate a negotiation around how we are going to exchange the voice portion of the call. We switch to a different protocol, H.245, at this point. You can see in the figure that we first negotiate capabilities between the two sets. During this process, there are a few things that need to take place. The first is determining an IP address and a port where media should be sent to. By media, of course, I mean the audio of the call. This may also include video, so you will often see the content of the call referred to as media since it can refer to either audio or video. In addition to IP address and port information on both ends, there is also a negotiation of the content of the call. As I said, we could potentially send audio or video so we need to decide which one we're going to do. On top of that, we have to decide the type of audio or video.

You're probably familiar with MP3 or AAC files on portable music devices. You're also probably familiar with WAV files, which are uncompressed audio. When it comes to audio and video, there are a number of ways to present the same information. Some of this has to do with the way it's put together but there is also compression to take into account. A traditional phone circuit has about 3000 Herz (Hz) of bandwidth used for voice. Any frequency below 400 Hz or above 3400 Hz just gets dropped. Think about this in the context of buying headphones where they often say they are good for a frequency range of 20–20,000 Hz. Typically, humans can't hear that whole range of frequencies but if you capture it, in order to transmit it, you need to have that bandwidth available to send that amount of data.

Because of the variability involved in capturing and transmitting audio, in part because of the different ways of capturing and storing it, the two ends of the call have to negotiate the codec that is being used present the video and/or audio. Codec is a shortened way of saying compressor/decompressor and different codecs describe how the media is going to be encoded, the sample sizes, the bandwidth being captured as well as whether the information is being compressed. What is really being negotiated is what codec is going to be sent via the Real-Time Protocol (RTP), which is used to transmit real-time media like audio or video. RTP encapsulates the individual chunks of audio inside of a set of headers that provides a timestamp and sequence number, among other pieces of data, allowing the recipient to put it all together into the right order.

Speaking of order, it's worth noting that in the case of a real-time stream where the playback is happening live, just as the source is being captured and transmitted live, the recipient won't be waiting for a message that may be missing. If packet 15 and then 17 arrive, the recipient won't wait to play 17 until 16 comes in. It will simply play 17 and if 16 then comes in, 16 will just get dropped. The reason, in case it's not obvious, is that if you wait to play media back, you get pauses. I don't want there to be gaps in the playback because then it sounds choppy and if the wait is too long, it can be difficult for the ear/brain to decipher what is actually meant. Keep in mind that these individual chunks of media are, perhaps, 20 ms of audio. If I wait a second or more for the next 20 ms chunk, it may be difficult to really understand what's being said. Similarly, we don't want to just insert the missing chunk when it comes in because then the conversation starts sounding garbled. It's better to just drop the occasional fragment of audio because our brains are really good at filling in missing chunks of information. Your brain takes in discrete chunks of information and makes them appear to be a fluid thing.

Session initiation protocol

In addition to H.323, the session initiation protocol (SIP) is a common VoIP. SIP was originally designed to provide a way for any session to be established between two parties. It didn't matter what type of session was being established because the protocol was entirely media agnostic. SIP could be used to establish an instant messaging session or a game session. It could also be used for audio and video, which is where it really took off. In fact, the original SIP specification was spelled out in Request for Comments (RFC) 2543 but that was later superseded in RFC3261 in order to update it with enhancements. On top of that, there have been a large number of additions to the 3261 standard providing enhancements and extensions. The reason for that is because SIP has been adopted for so many applications.

SIP has many similar applications to H.323, but one of the primary differences between them is that SIP was designed around the HTTP model. The messages look similar and the request/response model is the same as HTTP. This also means that where H.323 is a binary protocol encoded using ASN.1, SIP is a text-based protocol. This makes SIP considerably easier to implement and use because if you capture the messages, they can be easily read and understood since they are primarily in English and can be parsed visually rather than requiring a utility to pull the message apart to make it readable by average humans. Below you can see a standard SIP message, typically the first message in a simple call setup, taken from RFC 3665 that details basic SIP call flow examples. You can see that it's all in readable text and while some of it may look complicated, once you understand what the different components are, it's clear what's going on.

```
INVITE sip:bob@biloxi.example.com SIP/2.0
  Via: SIP/2.0/TCP
client.atlanta.example.com:5060; branch = z9hG4bK74b43
```

```
  Max-Forwards: 70
  Route: <sip:ss1.atlanta.example.com;lr>
  From: Alice <sip:alice@atlanta.example.com> ;tag=9fxced76sl
  To: Bob <sip:bob@biloxi.example.com>
  Call-ID: 3848276298220188511@atlanta.example.com
CSeq: 1 INVITE
  Contact: <sip:alice@client.atlanta.example.com;transport=tcp>
  Content-Type: application/sdp
  Content-Length: 151

  v=0
o=alice 2890844526 2890844526 IN IP4 client.atlanta.example.com
  s=-
  c=IN IP4 192.0.2.101
  t=0 0
  m=audio 49172 RTP/AVP 0
a=rtpmap:0 PCMU/8000
```

The INVITE message shown above is, as I mentioned, the first message in a call setup. This is analogous to the SETUP message in H.323. Each transaction is identified by a few of the elements in the SIP message. The first of which is the Call-ID. The Call-ID is meant to be unique across space and time meaning that there should never be another call with the same Call-ID, ever. This is done to protect against confusion if the call ever moves out of the network infrastructure where the call originates. This is why it needs to be unique across space because two separate call infrastructures should never be able to create the same Call-ID in case the call passes from one infrastructure into another.

Each call can be very complicated with a number of transactions occurring during the life of the call, including changing media streams or maybe adding in additional parties. Because of that, another identifier for the call is the CSeq or call sequence number. In the call above, you can see the CSeq is 1. Not only is the number important but the method that goes along with it because of the number of transactions that may take place during the life of the call. Some calls can be very simple, however. Again using a ladder diagram, you can see a very simple call setup using SIP in Figure 8.6. The INVITE is sent from the caller to the callee. The callee will send a provisional message, and you can see where the HTTP influence comes in, like 180 Ringing. This number code is very much like HTTP that uses numeric codes to indicate a particular response to a request. Where SIP has an INVITE request, HTTP has a GET request. The callee may also send back a 183 Session Progress just to indicate that the INVITE message has been received and is being processed. When the phone is answered, the callee sends a 200 OK, just like a successful HTTP request. Once the call is picked up, the media session negotiation is completed and the call can progress. Once the call is over, one of the parties hangs up and sends a BYE.

As indicated, this is a very simple call, and it also only indicates a peer-to-peer relationship between the parties. There is no intermediary to help determine the location of the callee in order to get the messages to the right location. While

```
         Alice                          Bob
           |                             |
           |          INVITE F1          |
           |---------------------------->|
           |        180 Ringing F2       |
           |<----------------------------|
           |                             |
           |          200 OK F3          |
           |<----------------------------|
           |            ACK F4           |
           |---------------------------->|
           |       Both Way RTP Media    |
           |<===========================>|
           |                             |
           |            BYE F5           |
           |<----------------------------|
           |          200 OK F6          |
           |---------------------------->|
           |                             |
```

FIGURE 8.6 Ladder Diagram of a Classic SIP Call

H.323 has gatekeepers and gateways to get messages around between devices and networks, SIP uses a proxy. The proxy model provides a number of benefits. You may recognize the proxy model, again from the Web space. Most people who interact with a proxy do so at their work where the business has implemented a Web proxy. The Web proxy takes requests from users and then forwards the requests on as though the request is actually coming from the proxy itself. The proxy ends up hiding the real requester from the recipient. This can also be true of an SIP proxy that could send the request on to the next hop as though it were from the proxy itself. Once you add proxies into the flow, though, the messages that get sent back and forth change a little. You can see a ladder diagram of a call with a pair of proxies in the middle in Figure 8.7. Each hop will send a provisional message like the 100 Trying or the 180 Ringing back to the hop before it. Those messages are not passed on but get consumed by the proxy or endpoint directly.

SIP also uses authentication to ensure that callers have permission to place calls through the network. The authentication may be requested as part of a call where the INVITE message would be challenged with an authentication request. SIP again takes from the HTTP model. SIP uses either basic or digest authentication for its users. With basic authentication, the username and password are easy to determine because they are passed in the message, albeit Base64 encoded. Base64 is not challenging to decode so simply capturing the message can yield the username and password. Digest authentication uses a hash of the username, password, and a nonce or random value provided by the server. This is also potentially breakable since you can capture the digest message as well as the nonce that was passed by the server and then generate your own digests with a list of passwords. Once you have the same digest value, you know what the password is.

```
      Alice           Proxy 1           Proxy 2           Bob
        |               |                 |               |
        |   INVITE F1   |                 |               |
        |-------------->|                 |               |
        |    407 F2     |                 |               |
        |<--------------|                 |               |
        |    ACK F3     |                 |               |
        |-------------->|                 |               |
        |   INVITE F4   |                 |               |
        |-------------->|   INVITE F5     |               |
        |    100  F6    |---------------->|   INVITE F7   |
        |<--------------|    100  F8      |-------------->|
        |               |<--------------- |               |
        |               |                 |    180 F9     |
        |               |    180 F10      |<------------- |
        |    180 F11    |<--------------- |               |
        |<--------------|                 |    200 F12    |
        |               |    200 F13      |<------------- |
        |    200 F14    |<--------------- |               |
        |<--------------|                 |               |
        |    ACK F15    |                 |               |
        |-------------->|    ACK F16      |               |
        |               |---------------->|    ACK F17    |
        |               |                 |-------------->|
        |            Both Way RTP Media                   |
        |<===============================================>|
        |               |                 |    BYE F18    |
        |               |    BYE F19      |<------------- |
        |    BYE F20    |<--------------- |               |
        |<--------------|                 |               |
        |    200 F21    |                 |               |
        |-------------->|    200 F22      |               |
        |               |---------------->|    200 F23    |
        |               |                 |-------------->|
        |               |                 |               |
```

FIGURE 8.7 Ladder Diagram Including Proxies

Often, users are required to authenticate when they register to the network. The registration serves two purposes. The first is for admission control, where the user has to authenticate against the network using established credentials. Once the user has authenticated, the network, by way of a registration server, has information about where the user is located. When a call comes in, the registration server will know how to get the SIP messages to the correct IP address. So, the second reason for performing registrations is to provide a location or an address of record where the phone or user can be found. The listing below shows a REGISTER message. The information in the headers provides the contact. The To: field in the message is the location of the user, including the username. You can see that it makes use of a familiar e-mail style with user@location syntax that makes it easy to understand.

```
REGISTER sip:ss2.biloxi.example.com SIP/2.0
  Via: SIP/2.0/TLS
client.biloxi.example.com:5061;branch=z9hG4bKnashd92
  Max-Forwards: 70
  From: Bob <sip:bob@biloxi.example.com>;tag=JueHGuidj28dfga
```

```
    To: Bob <sip:bob@biloxi.example.com>
    Call-ID: 1j9FpLxk3uxtm8tn@biloxi.example.com
  CSeq: 2 REGISTER
    Contact: <sip:bob@client.biloxi.example.com>
    Authorization: Digest username="bob", realm="atlanta.example.
com",
    nonce="f1cec4341ae6ca9c8e88df84be55a359", opaque="",
  uri="sip:ss2.biloxi.example.com",
  response="61f8470ceb87d7ebf508220214ed438b"
    Content-Length: 0
```

Network address translation

The problem with this is when the user sits behind a network address translation (NAT) device, like a firewall. All of the information in the SIP headers is set in the application and maybe it can pick up the local IP address from the system to send in the headers. The problem with the local system is it has no idea whether it's behind a device that's going to make changes to the IP address and the port information. If a hard phone or a soft phone is behind a NAT, there is no way to get to that device with the address of the local network the phone is on. When a call comes in and has to go to that user, the messages will be sent to an address and port that may simply not be routable on the Internet. Another problem is that when the network address gets changed, it gets changed in the network headers but not in the application headers since the NAT device doesn't know anything about higher layer protocols like SIP. So, the message gets sent through the NAT device with a different IP address in the source field and an unreachable address in the application headers.

As a result of this, we need a way for the different layers to get reconciled. This is usually done with a NAT traversal device like an application layer gateway. The application layer gateway will capture the SIP message and keep track of the source IP address in the network headers as well as the source port. It maps this set of information to the username in the SIP headers so it knows how to get back in touch with the user in case a call comes in. If we just had to respond to messages coming in from the user device, that would be easy. That gets done all day long with Web and mail and other types of network servers. The problem is that we need to get messages back to the user when the user hasn't originated any communication so the firewall would block the incoming messages. In order to make this work, we need to keep a way to get communication into the user open. If we force the user's device to REGISTER on a regular basis with a very short interval, we can make sure the path through the firewall is open and we can be sure what the IP address and port is because that binding would be held for some period of time in the firewall.

Using NAT traversal, we can place calls to users who may be behind firewalls or NAT devices. There are a number of ways of handling NAT traversal, including using the application layer gateway already mentioned. There are a few protocols that were designed to handle this task because it's a very common problem. You might use Simple Traversal of UDP NATs, Traversal Using Relays around NAT, or

Interactive Connectivity Establishment in order to handle the NAT traversal. All of these solutions require additional systems in your network infrastructure, and the only purpose for the devices is to handle NAT traversal. Later on, when we talk about security considerations, we will talk about a session border controller that can offer NAT traversal features as well as offering other security services.

Unified communications

One of the advantages to using digital communications like VoIP is that the end-points generally have to register so they can be located on the network. Dialing a phone number isn't helpful if the phone infrastructure doesn't know where on the data network the phone belonging to that number is located. Registration not only serves the purpose of making sure only the right people get access to your infrastructure, but also ensures that the phone network knows how to get to the user as well as knowing when the user is available to be reached. Knowing when the user is online and what their current status is, including on a call or maybe doing something where they don't want to be disturbed. All of this information is provided with a feature called presence—knowing what the status of any user is.

You may not only want to place calls to someone, whether that call is voice or video. You may also want to send an instant message to them. As noted previously, SIP is capable of handling a number of types of sessions. Unified communications (UC) is a way of tying everything together into one package. With a UC solution, you get a number of ways to interact with your coworkers or even with your customers or vendors in a deeper, more meaningful way. This sounds like a sales pitch. The fact is that UC solutions can combine voice, video, presence, and instant messaging together in a single platform and application. On top of that, you may be able to add online whiteboard interaction or possibly even desktop sharing to the mix.

A couple of years ago, I worked with a mid-sized regional bank that was in the process of rolling out a UC solution to interact with their customers. Rather than making a call to a call center, the customer could place a call through a piece of software and get connected to someone who was online. This is where the presence part of the UC solution is so important. Before trying to connect with someone, you can be sure they are around and available to talk. If they aren't, you might choose to simply send them an instant message and they could get back in touch with you either by phone or by instant message. Again, all through the same application.

Along with UC comes unified messaging, which is an attempt to pull different types of messaging into the same platform. Your voice mail messages would be in with your e-mail messages. You may find this in different voice mail systems. HulloMail, available on mobile platforms like Android or the iPhone, provides not only voice mail but also a setting that allows you to have the audio sent to your e-mail so you don't have to call into your voice mail in order to listen to your messages. You can just listen to the WAV or MP3 file that gets sent to you. Google also has a unified messaging platform that they got when they acquired the company

GrandCentral. Since its launch, it's been rebranded as Google Voice. You get a phone number from Google, and you can provide additional numbers where you can be reached. Google will attempt to forward calls onto you at your other numbers. If it can't reach you, it falls back to voice mail. The message will show up in your e-mail in the Gmail account that's associated with your Google Voice account. On top of that, Google will transcribe the message into text so you don't even need to listen to the message. You can just read it.

UC solutions often try to provide additional features that wouldn't normally be part of a traditional phone experience. Google, for example, uses a follow-me feature as mentioned above. You call the one phone number that belongs to your Google account, and Google will fork the call off to as many endpoints as you have provided, hoping to find you at one of them. Other vendors provide similar functionality. You may also have the ability to react differently to individual callers in your contact list. HulloMail, for example, allows me to record different messages for people in my contact list. This way, I can have a more personalized experience for people who may regularly call me and get my voice mail. SIP has provided a lot of capability to offer these enhanced features and programmatic access to our communications experience.

VoIP in the cloud

The first VoIP in the cloud was probably Skype. Skype started as a protocol and peer-to-peer network allowing for communication between people across the Internet. The idea behind Skype was not to have to rely on a centralized infrastructure as was common with not only the phone network but also other VoIP networks. Skype eventually began offering connections to the PSTN so you could use Skype to place calls to someone who just had a traditional landline. You might be on your computer, while they were on their phone but you could be talking, and Skype would provide the bridge between the two different networks. Skype was acquired by eBay and then later sold to Microsoft but it continues to offer much the same service has it has from the beginning. Figure 8.8 has a capture of the startup screen from Skype on my system. One of the big differences between what you can do today and what you could do a decade or more ago when Skype was still young is the inclusion of connecting to Facebook to get contact information.

Other companies have gotten in on the VoIP model using a cloud delivery mechanism. What this really means is that you can get access to a softswitch or other voice infrastructure over the Internet itself. Microsoft, for example, offers access to their UC solution over the Internet. Other companies like ShoreTel also have a hosted PBX model where you can get access to a Private Branch eXchange (PBX) over the Internet. In addition to simply offering access to a PBX is an attempt to offer calling services through a Web interface. This is done using a standard called Web Real-Time Communication (WebRTC). The idea behind WebRTC is to offer

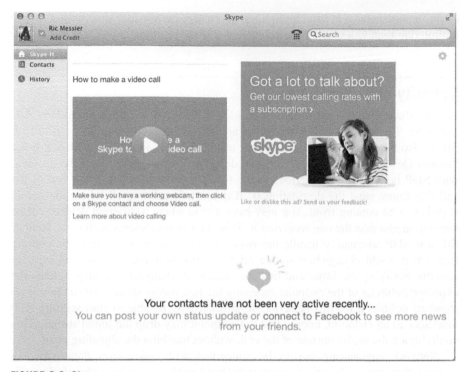

FIGURE 8.8 Skype

an application programming interface to allow voice and video calls through a Web browser without requiring a plugin. This could make interaction with customers considerably easier. Rather than having to get a phone number off a Web site and then placing a call, the user could just place the call directly through the Web interface itself and reach a customer service representative, for example.

While WebRTC is one way to get voice calls over an Internet connection and it has a promising future to create a complete experience, businesses have other needs. A business that wants to have a telephony solution that can travel and be flexible may want to investigate Unified Communications as a Service (UCaaS). With a UCaaS provider, you get not only telephony that can be accessed anywhere your people are but also presence services and messaging all from the same platform. This might typically cost a lot of money to get installed as infrastructure but again, as with other cloud services, you can take advantage of the investment made by other businesses, namely the service provider. You'll get the benefit of the solution without the outlay to buy the infrastructure yourself. Plus, you outsource all of the maintenance and troubleshooting, and a service provider may have a higher uptime rate than you would have yourself as a small business.

Security considerations

We've talked about some security considerations when it comes to VoIP or UC solutions. The fact that SIP registrations are easily cracked is definitely a problem. SIP is also a fragmented set of protocols, much like H.323 is. Along with SIP is the Session Description Protocol (SDP) that describes the media session. The problem with SDP is that it only describes where to send media to so the other end of the call can know what the destination is. It doesn't describe at all where the media is going to be coming from. You may have a case where a different device will be sending media than the one receiving it. This can cause problems with trust. Neither SIP nor SDP adequately handle the issue of where media is going to be coming from. You could change the source address of your media in mid-call without actually notifying the other end that the address is changing. Nothing defines the expected behavior of the endpoint receiving the new media stream. Since there is no standard definition for this behavior, an attacker may be able to start sending RTP messages to an endpoint, hoping that the endpoint may drop the initial stream. This could hijack the media portion of the call, without touching the signaling at all.

Network engineering has to be concerned with voice over data networks because they need to be able to support the bandwidth of support codecs for a sufficient number of calls, based on expected use of the VoIP infrastructure. A malicious user may be able to get RTP messages that are too large to be sent into a network and if enough of them are sent, you may be able to flood the network. This could be a problem without something that can perform bandwidth policing to ensure that the codec that was chosen is the one being used and the bandwidth used by the actual RTP stream is right for the codec that was chosen.

SIP messages make use of Multipart Internet Mail Extensions (MIME) in order to send other protocols, like the SDP component. This MIME body part might also be used to send malware into the voice network. This is also a threat to users if the malware can get all the way to the user's system and that system is a soft client running on the desktop computer rather than simply a hard phone.

All of these challenges come with implementing a VoIP or UC network but that doesn't mean that there aren't solutions. First, SIP does support the use of SSL/TLS encryption to protect the messages as they are sent. Encryption should always be used where possible to provide protection of the messages, including and especially the authentication messages since it's so trivial to crack SIP passwords if you have access to the right messages that include the challenge and the response. Encryption can also protect the call itself since RTP transmitted in the clear can be easily captured and played back later as audio. If you make sensitive calls on a regular basis, you may want to ensure you are using encryption of not only the signaling but also the media.

When it comes to NAT traversal, bandwidth policing, and protection against malware, you may want to look into making use of a session border controller (SBC). The SBC is really an application layer gateway that understands VoIP. It can provide all of the functionality mentioned in addition to protecting your internal infrastructure against attack by blocking messages that don't look right. These malformed messages may cause problems with your SIP proxies or with the softswitch at the core of your network. The SBC could also protect against floods of traffic, designed to take down the internal voice infrastructure.

Since the SBC might function as a type of proxy server called a back-to-back user agent (B2BUA), you can further protect your voice infrastructure. This is done by terminating one SIP dialog on the inside of the SBC while reoriginating the dialog on the outside of the SBC. In doing this, you can swap out all of the internal addresses in the original SIP header, and all someone on the outside of the network would be able to see would be the addresses on the SBC. If they don't know where the internal network infrastructure is, attackers will find it much harder to attack. The best they could do would be to try to attack the SBC, which should be far more resilient and hardened against attack than the internal infrastructure.

CONCLUSION

When it comes to collaboration, communication is essential and VoIP or UC make that possible. There are many benefits to making use of a UC solution, including reduced cost because you are making use of infrastructure you already have in place with your data network. You also get cost benefits by carrying phone calls to separate locations over a data network you are already paying for rather than paying phone charges to carry the calls from one office to another. You can also often get SIP trunks from a VoIP network provider that cost less over time than paying the phone company for those calls. In addition to lower cost, you get all the benefits of a UC solution like presence and having a single platform for communication, whether it's instant messaging or voice or video.

There is no question, though, that there are challenges when it comes to VoIP installations. These are complicated protocols, and some of the call flows in use can be complicated as well. Because of this complexity, you can have problems with security. The instance of the bank I mentioned above was using a vendor solution where the vendor just wanted a block of thousands of UDP ports opened up through the firewall so there would be no problem when you tried to set up a call through the firewall. This sort of mentality can leave an enterprise exposed to attack or compromise. Fortunately, there are solutions in place that can offer the enterprise protection. One of these solutions is a session border controller, and there are a number of vendors that sell these solutions. They have become fairly commonplace additions to a VoIP installation because they offer so many benefits to companies who are trying to make use of the collaboration and communication possibilities of a US solution.

Summary

Some ideas to consider from this chapter:

- Telephony solutions are critical to business communication.
- VoIP solutions have been around for several years. H.323 is nearly 20 years old and SIP is over 15 years old.
- SIP is enabling a lot of newer styles of communication.
- UCaaS can provide a way for businesses to get full-featured telephony solutions without a lot of outlay on equipment and software.
- There are security risks that come with telephony services over data.
- Application layer or VoIP-aware firewalls are important security features to protect businesses from attacks against any VoIP infrastructure including clients.
- Some voice mail services will also transcribe messages and send them to your e-mail or text message them to you, meaning you can more easily check your voice mail messages.

Remote Workers

INTRODUCTION

The world has certainly become a smaller place. With the continued adoption of Internet-based technologies and certainly the various technologies we've been discussing so far, it's much easier to stay in almost constant touch with coworkers, friends, and family. Whether it's cell phone, constant access to e-mail with a smartphone, or social networking, staying on constant communication is not only easy and commonplace but also just expected. It's hard to imagine doing something as mundane as shopping with your significant other and separating for individual tasks while still be able to meet up or just find one another again.

When it comes to business, having constant access to these communication mechanisms is not only considered a good thing, but it's also often simply expected, particularly as you climb higher up the organizational ladder. Also, there is a class of employees, who really do need constant access to both communication as well as a way of getting remote access to the business network. Your IT staff is generally expected to be constantly available in case of outage since the service level agreements between IT and the business are probably fairly high, whether it's an implicit or an explicit expectation. If the IT staff didn't have the ability to get access to the network remotely, you could have much longer outages of critical infrastructure while you wait for someone to drive into the office.

Fortunately, there are a number of ways of handling this problem and it's also fortunate that what works for a small number of people who have either an actual need to be constantly in touch or even just a perceived need will also work for a larger workforce. Once you give someone the ability to get access to e-mail

155

and other services remotely, it opens the door to providing them work flexibility. Additionally, you get more productivity because they don't need to call in sick or take time off for a number of events like a child who is sick or an appointment for services that require you to be at home. Beyond these sporadic needs to get remote access to the network, there are some workers who, by the nature of what they do, need access remotely on a more regular basis.

Remote workers

There are a number of situations that can create remote workers for a business. One of the easiest ones to imagine is what is typically called the road warrior. The road warrior lives life from a hotel room, bouncing from city to city. This might be someone in sales, constantly on the road visiting clients, or it might be someone in marketing going from one conference or show to another. No matter what the situation, a road warrior is always somewhere new with potentially uncertain Internet connection who still needs to have access to information from the office, including scheduling and communication about strategies, and products.

In the old world, the road warrior may have been armed with a briefcase of information, relying on phone calls back to the office wherever a phone was available to check in on progress and get any additional updates or tasking. The advent of laptops allowed them to carry information digitally and also opened the door to allowing for an easier time of remote access. It did require dialing into the business network over a phone line. This was slow and often had a number of other problems. Once upon a time, nearly 20 years ago, I administered a network for a small business and it included a modem pool for our road warriors to dial into. The modems could be flaky and the access gateway (a Shiva) could be difficult to manage, especially at a time where it preferred Novell networking protocols and we were beginning to use TCP/IP as our primary and later our only networking protocol.

It could be frustrating getting access from the road in such circumstances. Cell phones were starting to gain some traction but they weren't always reliable in terms of getting a signal to be able to make or receive phone calls. On top of that, they could be pricey, especially when you factored in roaming across multiple networks in the days before the large nationwide carriers we have today. A road warrior was stuck out on the road; sometimes unable to get the critical information they needed to get a sale or have the latest information for the show or conference they were at. In addition, having modems exposed the business to dial-up attacks. Anyone with a modem and a war-dialing program could locate all of the numbers within a particular telephone exchange that had modems on the other end. Once an attacker had the number of a modem, they could proceed with something like a brute force attack on usernames and passwords. They may also have been able to take advantage of weak default usernames and passwords to gain access to equipment.

Eventually, of course, Internet access from the road became more ubiquitous and that led to the use of virtual private networks (VPNs). This required a new set of infrastructure that was now accessible to anyone on the Internet. If done right, it could be very secure. IPSec could require certificate-based authentication as well as username and password authentication. However, IPSec VPNs can be complicated to set up and get working correctly. Certificates themselves can require a lot of work getting the right infrastructure in place to issue, revoke and renew the certificates issued to employees. For large organizations, this can be a lot of work. You could also purchase certificates from a certificate authority for your people and simply make use of those, but then you may have more problems maintaining the list of users whose certificates are allowed to connect.

Once you had the infrastructure in place, support of remote workers fell primarily to the IT staff and it could be a lot of work troubleshooting issues over the phone, trying to determine what was going wrong with a system that may have out-of-date software or may have had additional software installed that was breaking access to critical business systems. This could be a substantial burden for smaller businesses and it can definitely be a hindrance to productivity of the remote worker. There are solutions for these problems, of course, but they can cost money and resources in terms of the infrastructure required as well as the people required to implement and manage the infrastructure. Windows servers, for example, offer a lot of capabilities in terms of managing users and their systems that have continued to improve over time. Windows servers and someone with the right set of skills to implement a solid Group Policy Object that could be managed across remote users cost money.

The remote access for your road warriors that were hopefully making you money provided the ability for other users to similarly be somewhere other than their primary office location when they were working. In addition to your road warriors who are almost always remote, you can also have telecommuters. Telecommuting is a term that was coined in the 1970s and it indicates the use of telecommunication mechanisms to get to work. With the ability to gain access to corporate infrastructure, telecommuting becomes an option for a lot of people and it's an option that a pretty significant number of people in the United States take advantage of. While it's not clear exactly what percentage of workers are taking advantage of telecommuting options available to them, it does seem clear that the ability to telecommute is increasing.

According to Global Workplace Analytics and the Telework Research Network, working remotely has increased to 80% between 2005 and 2012. The largest growth has taken place in the ranks of the federal government and while a big part of that growth took place in the spans 2005–2006 and 2007–2008, the trajectory of the growth has been upward. This is in spite of an overall loss of jobs in the economy in the same time period. One of the reasons it's so hard to pin an exact number down on the number of people who are telecommuting or working from home is the varied number of definitions for what we are talking about when we talk about telecommuting or working from home. The US census asks about telecommuting in the context of working from home for most of the week before the question was asked. This is a fairly limited perspective on telecommuting. A remote worker may only be part-time remote on an as-needed basis. If you don't work primarily at home doesn't mean you don't telecommute. It just means you don't have a telecommuting job.

Certainly there is some percentage of people who work from home either full time or at least primarily, but there are also a good number of workers in the United States who work from home on an as-needed basis. This can be for a number of reasons that may be personal in nature. In some cases, it may also be a result of a desire for fewer distractions for longer periods of time. In an office environment, there are a number of distractions including the noise of your coworkers as well as people stopping by your desk or calling on the phone. There might be distractions at home, as well, of course, but there is also a possibility of there being fewer distractions around in many cases. In my own case, if I needed to write a report or do some other documentation, I often worked from home to get it done because it was harder to complete it in the office. At home, I had my dogs to be taken care of, but they weren't that much of a distraction. Not as much as being surrounded by people talking, working, and moving around.

There is evidence that working from home can be very productive. A study done by researchers at Stanford University suggests that there is a significant improvement in productivity from people who work from home. Not only do they accomplish more, but they also work longer hours. Without the need to commute or even take the time to dress in office attire, people are more inclined to start their day earlier than they would if they were in the office and also end later.

This particular study was focused on a call center company and they found that employees not only took less sick time if they had the ability to work from home, but they also took fewer breaks and as a result, fielded more calls. This does bring up a type of worker who would seem to be perfect for working from home. Anyone who works in a call center has the ability to work from home since there isn't as much of a need for them to directly interact with their fellow employees (more on interaction later on). There are a number of other employees who, similarly, may not need to directly interact with their fellow employees and they would make good targets for working from home.

JetBlue has been employing people to do customer service for them and placing them directly in their home. They have been doing this from very early on in the company's history. Numbers of course change but at one point in the last couple of years, JetBlue was placing 1800 of their 2100 customer service employees at home. They are not the only ones. There are Web sites like FlexJobs.com that are geared toward finding flexible working situations like work-from-home jobs. In many cases, it can provide a lot of benefits to the company.

Executives are another source of remote workers. In fact, in my experience, executive management can often be a first adopter of technology, particularly in small- or medium-sized businesses. That was my experience with the Blackberry, where suddenly management wanted to have their Blackberry and IT organizations had to figure out how to provide the backend functionality to support it. The same was true of the iPad particularly, though I suspect it was also true of the iPhone, though I didn't witness it myself. On top of wanting constant, remote access to their e-mail and phone, management also often wants to have the ability to get access to other information, no matter where they are. You may have top management who travels a lot to help close deals or to negotiate business development agreements with other companies.

While they aren't direct workers, outsourcing brings a lot of the same sorts of challenges that remote workers bring since the people who work at the outsourcing company need to gain at least limited access to corporate resources if not outright getting into their network. Sometimes, this can be controlled, depending on the task being outsourced. In other cases, it's a lot harder to limit the access you provide to the employees of the outsourcing company. Later on, we'll discuss risk management but what this really comes down to is an issue of determining where the risks are that you are most concerned about and making business decisions, like that to outsource, appropriately.

Pros and cons of telecommuting

Telecommuting can bring a lot of positives for organizations that want to embrace it, including the potential for cost savings. There is no question, however, that there are also concerns. These concerns exist not only for the company and its management but also for the worker. While the business has to be concerned about doing what's best for them, it's also helpful to keep in mind the health and well-being of their employees if they expect them to continue to be productive.

Management concerns and productivity

When you talk about telecommuting, one of the concerns is that management doesn't have any visibility into what the remote worker is doing. They fear that their people are sitting at home playing MineCraft, Halo, or Grand Theft Auto. The feeling is that if the employee is within the friendly confines of the offices of their employer, management can be more effective at managing. However, many companies have locations all over the country or the world and people work together on projects that cross those geographic boundaries. In this case, the team members may not be all in the same facility, but there aren't concerns about whether the job will get done over and above the usual concerns around deadlines and finishing tasks on time.

In reality, management isn't looking over the shoulder of the people who are in the office so the same techniques for ensuring work gets done can be used for in-office workers as those for remote workers. In reality, though, remote workers can end up being more productive. In part, this is simply because if they can work from home, they don't have to take sick days or vacation days to deal with simple personal issues. This may be taking a trip to the Department of Motor Vehicles (DMV), the town office for property issues, or a doctor or dentist appointment. It may also be waiting for a package or someone who is coming to your house to perform some work. There are endless possibilities for why someone may need to be away from the office for a period of time that may be unpredictable and why it may be more convenient to use home as the base of operations. Without the ability to work remotely, someone might be forced to take time off. If they take time off, they don't get any work done.

Additionally, a little time at home to take care of personal items can lead to better health. You don't have the stress of worrying about a lot of different factors that sit in the back of your head, cluttering up mindshare, because you are getting the issues taken care of. Not having to deal with the stress of a commute or being home sooner for dinner with your family can be beneficial for your health and well-being. The flexibility to take care of yourself without having to be in the office to get your job done might be enough to keep someone healthy so they don't have to take time off because they are sick.

In reality, a busy office can be antiproductive for a lot of jobs, particularly those that require quiet or creativity. Offices are great for extroverts who desire a lot of personal interaction. Businesses may find that they save costs in the short run with densely packed offices and prairie dog farms, but there is a significant cost to productivity. Many workers who are knowledge-based like engineers or software developers often require a quieter environment that can allow them to focus and reflect on what they are doing in order to perform their job better. The distractions of a modern office building can lead to work taking longer and maybe being of a lesser quality. There are more and more studies taking place that strongly suggest this to be the case. Having the ability to work from home can provide that quiet and reflection that can allow engineers, software developers, and others who require a degree of quiet, reflection, and creative energy to function well.

Antisocial behaviors

There is a very brief series of Dilbert cartoons that spring to mind when I think about this particular concern. Dilbert gets the ability to work from home and over the span of a couple of days, he gives up all attempts at hygiene or putting on anything resembling appropriate dress. He also has no social interaction of any kind. In Dilbert's case, it becomes amusing but as with so much of what we read in Dilbert, there is more than a kernel of truth. This is perhaps particularly the case if you work in an IT or development organization. Many have been the time over the years where I was sure Scott Adams was sitting in meetings I had sat in the week or so before. This situation is no different from the stories about the ignorant pointy-haired boss.

People who work regularly from home may have a tendency to forego basic hygiene since they aren't coming into contact with other people on a regular basis. This is particularly true for younger workers who live alone. At least if you are in a relationship, you have a shot of being in contact with someone outside of working hours and that can provide the societal pressure to ensure you take care of yourself and your health and hygiene. When your work routine consists of rolling out of bed and making your way to either the couch or your desk, wherever that happens to be, there isn't a lot driving you to get dressed or even brush your teeth or comb your hair. This may sound like a cliché but in fact, during the process of preparing for this chapter, I polled friends on Facebook to get some sense about people who worked from home and one of my friends said that he worked from home a lot over a period of time and he did end up giving up on a lot of basic hygiene. On the other hand, he said his laundry was always done.

Another challenge with working from home on a regular basis, particularly if you aren't in a relationship, is that you don't get a lot of interaction with other humans. There are potential consequences when it comes to mental health if you get too isolated and don't talk or interact with other people. Perhaps it's not obvious that people suffering from mental health disorders may eventually become less productive. Working from home can lead to social isolation which may be a symptom of depression, though it may also be a source of depression if it is brought on by simply not seeing a lot of people because you work from home and don't have many social activities.

It may be a cliché or a stereotype but my experience is that a lot of people who are in computer-related fields like IT or development are introverts. Introverts are less likely to have a lot of social activity or structure outside of work and if their work takes place primarily at home, they are at risk of falling into a depression, which can have an impact on their work. This is certainly not an argument against introverts working from home since introverts are more likely to be productive in a quiet environment like that of their home, away from the bustle and noise of the office. It's worth keeping an eye on them, though, to ensure their mental health remains intact.

Cost savings

There are personal and business aspects to cost savings. If someone doesn't have to commute to work, they save on gas as well as on upkeep on their vehicle. If they commute using public transit, they will save the cost of the bus or subway to get to and from the office. This can end up being a significant savings over time for the employee. On a related note, the environment benefits when there are fewer cars on the road generating carbon dioxide, not to mention using up gasoline. There is less wear and tear on vehicles that can save money as well.

From a business perspective, the cost savings are perhaps less tangible in some cases. If it's just offering the ability to work remotely as opposed to work remotely full time, a business may not see as many cost-saving benefits but when it comes to full-time remote workers, there are a number of benefits. A full-time remote worker doesn't require network resources or office space. They don't require lights or power and while this may be a negligible savings if the business is already supporting physical infrastructure, migrating enough workers to a remote model can offer cost savings to a business.

The study mentioned earlier that was done by researchers at Stanford demonstrated fairly significant cost savings per employee, in addition to the productivity improvements for employees who work from home. The study was focused on call center workers where productivity is easy to be measured in terms of call volume and customer satisfaction. Additionally, these are relatively low-wage workers when compared to engineers or software developers, as examples. It's hard to say from one study, but the cost savings from making use of remote workers likely varies based on other resources required to support the employee like office space and computing infrastructure.

Communication challenges

When you have a remote worker, you have a lot of communication challenges, both real and virtual. While a lot of work may be done in a disconnected sort of way, you probably want to be able to send e-mail to them. This can be addressed by way of a cloud e-mail service, as we've previously mentioned. There are also services that will host telephony for you, including Google Voice that sprang out of another company called Grand Central. Google Voice offers a single telephone number that makes use of a find-me feature. When someone calls that single number, the call will go out to any of the numbers you have configured with them. You can see the dialog box for configuring numbers in Figure 9.1. When you pick up on any of the lines that are called, the others stop ringing and the call is transferred to you. If you don't pick up, the call goes to voice mail. Google Voice will do a speech to text conversion and put the text of the message into your mailbox so you can read it if you don't have the ability to access voice mail immediately.

There are other companies that will do a full hosting or a private branch exchange (PBX) for your business and you can also get integration with Microsoft Lync through the Microsoft Office 365 service if you chose that way to go with your hosted e-mail. But at the end of the day, if you are an established business and aren't moving into the cloud for your voice infrastructure, you will have other problems. Using a standard Time Division Multiplexing (TDM)-based PBX will mean it's harder to be able to have remote workers and make it appear as though your worker isn't remote. Using VoIP/

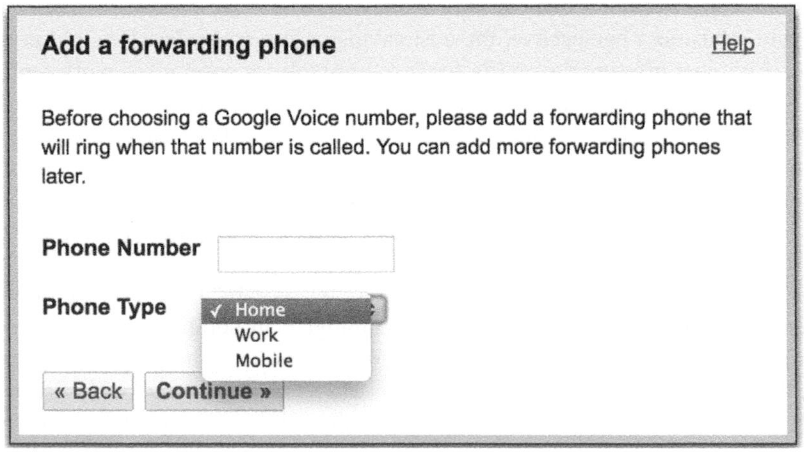

FIGURE 9.1 Forwarding from a Google Voice Number

UC, you can have workers connect from a remote location, but it also means that you will have to support the ability to offer that remote connection.

UC solutions can offer a lot when it comes to allowing remote users to connect just as though they were really sitting at a desk in a corporate office. It does, though, require a way to get access from the outside to the inside. There may be several ways of accomplishing this. One way is to simply open up your firewall to the ports that are required for the remote phones and soft clients to connect to the soft switch or PBX on the inside of the network. This wouldn't be the best approach to solve this particular problem because it exposes the network to a lot of potential attacks, even if you could lock the ports down to specific IP addresses from the remote phones.

You might also allow for your phones to VPN into your network. This may work well if you already have VPN infrastructure. However, it would require your phones to support a VPN connection before connecting to the PBX and not all VoIP phones have VPN support and even if they do, you have to make sure that they support the particular type of VPN you have. You may also use your existing VPN and use a soft client. This actually works well, particularly for those on the road. You don't have to spend the money to get a hard phone, which can be expensive if you are using a full-featured phone from your PBX vendor and the phone is always available as long as the user is on their computer and connected to your network.

Another solution that may be something of a hybrid is not using a VPN at all but instead using cloud solutions for e-mail and other applications while your PBX infrastructure remains in place. Instead of just opening up your firewall to anyone who wants to connect, you could employ a session border controller that would handle all of the registrations from your Session Initiation Protocol (SIP) or H.323 phone, protecting your internal infrastructure as well as the user and their phone. The border controller has a number of uses with regard to the security of your VoIP infrastructure and this is a very useful application that would eliminate your need to have a VPN just to support phones if you are going to more of a cloud-based scenario for your other applications. Your remote workers would never have to touch your internal network directly. Their phones, whether soft or hard, would connect through the border controller and everything having to do with the phone would terminate there, never directly touching the inside of the network.

Human resources and remote hires

I took a lot of time in and out of school before I eventually finished my bachelor's degree and when I did, it was online in spite of the fact that I didn't live too far from the university where I got the degree. It was more convenient to take online courses. Now, I teach part time in a master's program at Brandeis University. I teach online and have students who are primarily located in the Boston area, not too far from Brandeis, but I do have some students who are located in completely different parts of the country including one in Colorado and another in Washington. They are taking classes online because it's more convenient for their lifestyle or because they prefer the degree program at Brandeis and there isn't a comparable one closer to where they live.

Colleges can become breeding grounds for industry as graduates end up developing roots in the area where their college is. Additionally, college professors might develop ideas that eventually become businesses that could employ graduates or even pull more people into the area, continuing to develop human and intellectual capital. However, online education is becoming more popular. This means that people stay where they are in order to get their education and don't continue to collect around large colleges and universities. Cambridge, MA, and Palo Alto, CA, are two great examples of business incubator locations. So, what does this have to do with remote workers? The hiring pool is becoming more diverse geographically. In some ways, this is beneficial because it can lead to economic benefits to smaller communities, but in others it means that the best talent may not be near your business location. If you are willing to take on remote workers, you can remove the restrictions on just those who are nearby. In some cases, companies have been willing to pay relocation bonuses to get better talent but sometimes that bonus isn't really enough to cover all of the expenses involved in moving to take on a new job.

When you are talking about a purely remote hire, you could expand the boundaries of your hiring pool entirely outside of the country you are in. There may be a number of benefits from opening your hiring pool much wider. This may be especially true in the case of customer service personnel since you can offer a broader range of availability for customer service by using a model where you have people in a wide variety of time zones. Customer service people may not need to be located directly in a facility and being a remote worker may be a good fit for people in those roles. JetBlue and other companies are using the work from home for their customer service personnel.

Some countries in the world, though, have highly educated and skilled workers that don't have the same requirements for benefits or salary. I'd hate to advocate moving jobs out of the United States, but the reality is that the workforce is becoming global and if you have to extend your search outside of the geographical bounds that would allow someone to make a reasonable commute to your facility and if you were willing to allow remote workers, why not investigate talent around the world? This might raise HR challenges, of course, but in a cloud model, you could also crowd source any HR challenges that might come up from globalizing your workforce.

Asynchronous versus synchronous

A friend of mine I work with sometimes has a tendency to grab the phone anytime he wants to communicate. If there is a voice mail, he picks up the phone. Me, I send an instant message or e-mail. Sometimes, I send a text message. My friend prefers synchronous communication while I generally lean toward asynchronous. Of course, it all depends on how critical the issue I'm looking to communicate is. One of the advantages to many of the technologies we have been talking about is allowing people to accomplish their work wherever they are which also means whenever it is most appropriate for them.

Many of the communications advances, since we began networking systems together in the 1960s, have been of an asynchronous nature, allowing people to communicate when it's most convenient for them—instant messaging, text messaging, e-mail, social media, voice mail, and so on. All of these technologies have been asynchronous in nature, pushing us further and further from the need to be in direct communication in order to make progress working with someone. You can communicate with someone, as briefly or in as much depth as you want, and allow them to receive that communication in a time that makes the most sense for them, when they are most able to fully receive and understand the communication.

Certainly, these different communications mechanisms have also opened the door to far more informal and frivolous types of communications. When I see a friend available on instant messaging, I might send a quick hey to them just to see if they respond. If they don't, it didn't take me long to send it. If they do respond, we might be able to catch up quickly or chat about something that has come up. It may not be very important and may never come up in a more formal communication, but if it takes a second or two to say it and get a response, it may be worth tossing out. Text messaging and social media have brought their own challenges with regard to communications, particularly when it comes to understanding what is being said, considering the length limitations of SMS or Twitter messages.

Technology has also brought us better ways of communicating in a synchronous manner, meaning in real time. Unified communications have given us the ability to keep track of whether someone is available to talk or not. This presence capability can be very important if you really need to talk to someone. It's convenient if you know whether someone is actually available for a phone call before you pick up the phone to call if you need to actually talk to the person rather than just leave a voice mail. This makes synchronous communication far more efficient.

Cloud technologies offer a lot of ways to make asynchronous communication and collaboration more efficient, particularly for remote workers. As the workforce becomes more and more global with outsourcing and partners spread around the globe, asynchronous communication is very important. When your workers and partners are halfway around the world, it can be difficult expecting to do real-time, live communication on a regular basis. This isn't to say that you can't, but it's harder when people are roughly half a day off from your time.

Security considerations

Remote workers need portable devices, typically. This not only includes mobile devices like cell phones but also laptops. The easiest thing to say here is Veteran's Administration (VA). The VA has had problems with losing laptops and personal information along with them. This is one of the most significant challenges with any mobile devices and the mobile workforce that uses those mobile devices. People lose or misplace things. Laptops get stolen if the owner doesn't keep a close eye on them and sometimes even if they do. It may not be just personal information of clients or customers, as in the case of the VA, which would be bad. Someone may also be carrying documents that could be closely held intellectual property of the company. Intellectual property may have a lot of value and could make a work laptop highly desirable.

The best way to protect against the loss of equipment is encrypting it. We have talked about encryption previously because it's really a baseline security strategy. Mobile devices like laptops and smartphones have developed better capability to support encryption of the device contents without having a crippling impact on the performance of the device. Some devices, like iOS-based devices, have encryption enabled by default. If you have a device that isn't encrypted by default and you expect that device to be out of the office at some point, the device should be encrypted. Laptops running operating systems like Windows or even Mac OS X can support whole drive encryption (WDE) using either BitLocker or FileVault, both built into the operating system. BitLocker will also allow you to store recovery keys within your enterprise Active Directory.

Mobile devices may also give the ability to locate the device if it gets lost. You could use a cloud service to pinpoint where your laptop or mobile phone is. This may help in the case where the device has been misplaced or stolen. Mobile devices, as mentioned previously, also have the ability to be wiped remotely, which can protect the information stored on the device. While there is some capability to support remote wipe on a laptop using third-party solutions, I'd expect that capability to be built into the operating system over time as functionality from mobile devices like smartphones move into the laptop space and vice versa.

Other security concerns to keep in mind when you consider remote workers are those we have previously discussed like providing access into the inside of the enterprise network. Things we haven't talked about so far, though, are policies to support protection like antivirus. If you are taking your laptop to foreign networks, you run the risk of picking up malware that exists on those networks, even if the network is your own at home. Remote workers may also not have an easy ability to use an internally vetted update server for software updates so you have to take into consideration the software that is in use on the laptop and whether it is resilient enough to support automatic updates since those updates will provide better protection for the user and operating system.

You might also consider a data loss prevention solution. When laptops leave the enterprise, they get connected to unknown and completely unprotected networks. Unsuspecting users may not do the right thing when it comes to file shares or clicking the right protection to enable on a particular network, if they have that capability. While malware is a concern, there is also the concern that someone may attempt to break into a laptop while the user is sitting in a coffee shop or in an airport terminal. On top of using the network to gain access, a lot of laptops are coming with Bluetooth and that can be used to get access to files on a system if it's configured to allow it. This is also a concern. Ideally, you might just disable the Bluetooth functionality, except that if someone is using a softphone, they may want to use a

Bluetooth headset in order to not have to always be doing a speakerphone with the laptop or using a wired connection, like a USB headset.

CONCLUSION

There are a lot of reasons to consider remote workers because there are a lot of advantages to using them. There are a lot of things to consider when it comes to remote workers to ensure that the enterprise is safe while taking advantage of the benefits of them. Cloud services can help with the support of remote workers. One of the best reasons for this is simply because you aren't having to open your enterprise up to remote connections, even if they are funneled through a VPN concentrator. Instead, your remote workers are connecting to a shared infrastructure that is designed to isolate users from one another. Taking advantage of someone else's work to isolate one user from another can give you the benefit of these remote users without having to worry as much yourself about how you are having to protect yourself.

Summary

Here are some ideas to take away from this chapter:

- Road warriors are common in businesses.
- VPNs are common ways of providing remote workers access to corporate resources.
- Making use of cloud services can limit the amount of access to the corporate network required.
- Making use of cloud services can open the door to making use of talent outside of your local area.
- Cloud storage might reduce the amount of data loss from stolen laptops since data doesn't have to be local.
- Cloud services can also be used for telephony, also ensuring that users can get access to their communications needs wherever they are.
- Newer asynchronous communications mechanisms like instant messaging and e-mail can free people up to be more productive.

Further reading

Matthews, H.S., Williams, E., 2005. Telework adoption and energy use in building and transport sectors in the United States and Japan. J. Infrastruct. Syst. (11.1 21. Print)

How Many People Telecommute? 2013. Global Workplace Analytics. Retrieved November 17, 2013, from <http://www.globalworkplaceanalytics.com/resources/people-telecommute>.

Bloom, N., Liang, J., Roberts, J., Ying, Z., 2013, February 22. Does Working from Home Work? Stanford University. Retrieved November 17, 2013, from <http://www.stanford.edu/~nbloom/WFH.pdf>.

Risk Management and Policy Considerations

INFORMATION INCLUDED IN THIS CHAPTER

- Risk management
- Policy overview

INTRODUCTION

We are hardwired as a species to perform risk management and we aren't the only ones. As a result, you might think that it's just something we are natively capable of and shouldn't require a lot of introduction for everyone to be good at it. After all, we do risk management without thinking about it in our own lives. Whether to push through a yellow light at the very last second, whether to drink the milk that is just a bit past the sell by date and has been in the refrigerator for more than a week. There are a lot of little decisions that we make all day long that are based on understanding risk, even if it's not a full-out risk assessment leading to those decisions. However, when it comes to making decisions related to your business data and resources and how best to manage them, you can take a seat of your pants, gut-based decision, but it probably makes more sense to follow a better documented approach to make decisions based on provable data.

One of the challenges associated with risk is that perception plays a big role and perception isn't always accurate. I remember after the events on 9/11/2001, several people I knew became worried about flying on a plane. The reality is that the risk of such attacks had always been there, it's just that suddenly these people became aware of the risk. The idea of planes being hijacked had never occurred to them. The reality, in fact, is that flying shortly after 9/11 probably was much less risky than before because of the heightened awareness and increased security but also because the people who were mostly likely to attack had just launched an enormous planned attack and it was unlikely they had another one planned so quickly afterward and that sort of attack took a lot of time and planning to pull off so it wasn't a spur of the moment thing.

Risk management is such a large topic that there are entire courses built around it, not to mention entire books written about it. As a result, this will really just be skimming the surface of risk management, but it's worth talking about some basic principles to provide a framework for analyzing your own situation. This is really helpful if your business is entering into unfamiliar territory. You need to be able to analyze the risk associated with a move to a cloud-computing infrastructure before you hand over critical or sensitive data to something outside of your control. There can be a lot of advantages to it and it may actually end up improving your risk position, but you need to go through the exercise of evaluating where you are so you can make that determination.

Risk management

There are a number of ways to approach risk management and, as with many other things, there are advantages and disadvantages to the different approaches. One of the biggest challenges you'll run into is a difficulty in assigning actual numbers to some of the factors we put into our analysis. I want to cover that right up front. We'll be talking about probability and value and some other factors and sometimes those are really difficult to assign actual values to. What is the probability of an attack taking down your whole site? How many of those can you expect to see annually? Unless your site has been attacked several times over a period of years, it can be difficult to come up with real numbers there. However, even in the face of solid and accurate numbers, you still need to put something together to be able to make decisions from.

How do you go about making those decisions? There are a number of data points that you can use that require a little bit of math. Before we get into the math, though, it's worth talking about a little bit of vocabulary that you should understand so we can talk about the math formulas and have them make some sense. The first thing we need to talk about is an asset. An asset is a resource that has some value associated with it. It doesn't matter what the resource is or even what the value is. If you can assign any value to a particular object, whether it's a system or a piece of data, or intellectual property, you have an asset. We will be talking about assets as they are one of the fundamentals of risk management. Your risk management strategy will be all about protecting your assets, no matter what they are.

It's also worth noting that risk management is a process and it's not one that stops after a single iteration. You will constantly go through iteration after iteration. New threats arise on a regular basis. You may introduce new systems. There are a number of ways that the risk to your organization may change. This is certainly true if you are planning to make a move from traditional IT systems to cloud based. You have to periodically review threats and what it may take to mitigate those threats so you can make some determinations as to whether it's worth taking the steps necessary to protect yourself. It's probably worth repeating but risk management, like any good security program, is a process and one that should constantly be revisited for changes.

Figure 10.1 is a diagram of one risk management process. There isn't one and only one risk management process. You can do a quick search of the Web and turn

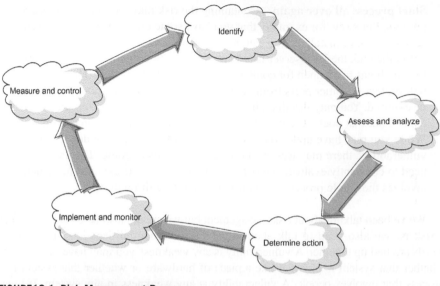

FIGURE10.1 Risk Management Process

up a few, but the one that is presented here is a pretty common one and it's also pretty straightforward. We'll revisit various aspects of this process through the rest of the chapter, but it's worth discussing the general framework now.

- **Identify the risk**—The first thing you need to do is to identify the risk. When it comes to information technology, there are a large number of risks. When it comes to making use of a cloud service provider, there may be a number of risks that need to be investigated, including the risk of placing sensitive business information with a third-party provider.
- **Assess and analyze**—Assessing and analyzing means taking into account stakeholders, identifying all positives and negatives, and performing a quantitative analysis using strategies like cost–benefit analysis (CBA).
- **Determine action**—Once you have performed the analysis, you can determine what you want to do. You might choose to limit the risk, remove it or just accept it. You can make this determination based on the analysis performed in the step above.
- **Implement and monitor**—Once you have an action, you can implement it. In the process of implementing, you will want to monitor the implementation to ensure that it was done correctly and that it did what it was supposed to do. Monitoring is an important part of this process.
- **Measure and control**—This requires that you know enough about the risk to be able to determine what could be measured and monitored in order to further evaluate the continued risk. Once you have determined what you need to be watching out for, you can implement controls to measure and contain the risk.

- **Start process all over again**—Containing the risk may well be a temporary process. Let's say, for example, that you have some concerns about the Web server you have installed. You can install firewalls to help protect your system but in the end, the Web server is always going to be vulnerable through port 80 which has to be open for content to be served up through it. The firewall will protect the other ports from being exploited but that one port will always be exposed. You may install an intrusion detection system as a monitoring control but that doesn't remove the risk. It just helps you keep an eye on it. While you may have updated the Web server software shutting down a current vulnerability, there may well be more vulnerabilities to come. This is why you need to constantly evaluate the risks that your business is exposed to, which involves the whole process and constantly iterating through it.

We've been talking about risk management but we should also be clear about what a risk is. We also need to talk about threats and vulnerabilities since all of these words are tied up together. A vulnerability is any weakness you may have in a system, whether that system is physical like a piece of hardware or whether that system is a process that involves people. A vulnerability is any weakness in any system. If I can take advantage of that weakness and compromise your system, I have exploited the vulnerability. An exploit is an action that takes advantage of a vulnerability. You will see a lot of talk about vulnerabilities and exploits, particularly with all of the transparency around fixes and system updates. Just because you have a vulnerability, by the way, is not a guarantee that it can or will be exploited. Even if there is a known exploit for a vulnerability doesn't mean that the exploit is guaranteed to work. There are a lot of factors that go into that and we will talk about some of those factors later on.

I have my asset that has a value. I have the potential for something bad to happen to that asset through vulnerabilities and exploits. Where does risk fit into all of this? Risk is an exposure to a potential for loss or an adverse situation. If there is a possibility of something bad happening, you have a risk. One of the big components to this, though, is the probability or chance of something happening that would cause loss. While you may be able to calculate the probability of being hit when you cross the street in front of your house and compare it to the probability of getting hit if you step off the curb on 7th Avenue and 42nd Street in New York City against the light, it can be a lot harder to calculate the probability of your system being compromised or attacked.

While there are a lot of attacks taking place all over the Internet all the time, there may not be attacks against every server on the Internet all the time. Most attacks are more targeted than that. It depends a lot on who you are, what you may have, and most importantly what services you have exposed to the Internet. You may have done a lot of work hardening up your operating system, shutting off all ports and introducing a firewall out in front of your systems to ensure that only traffic destined for the ports you want is allowed into your network. When you do this, you are mitigating the risk to your systems. When you mitigate risk, you are trying to lessen it so it isn't as great. Ideally, you take the risk as close to zero as you can though that's not always possible.

Once you have done what work you can mitigating the risk, you are left with what is called residual risk. You have some options when it comes to the residual risk that are pretty similar to the options available to you before you mitigate the risk. The first choice you have is to simply accept the risk. This requires full understanding what the risk actually is and deciding that doing anything else about the risk would cost more than it would save. You may also simply say that you don't believe the risk is real, meaning that you don't believe it would ever manifest so there wouldn't be any value in doing anything to remove the risk. If the service under evaluation is simply mission critical and/or core to your business, you may simply have to accept a lot of risk associated with it. As you can see, there may be a number of reasons you would just accept risk.

Accepting risk is actually something we do on a regular basis so it may not be as wild an idea as it may seem when simply written boldly, as above. When you board a plane to see your family on the other side of the country, you accept the risk that the plane may experience a problem in the air, forcing it to the ground. In reality, though, there is far more risk in getting behind the wheel of your car each day. You may not be aware of the risk that's associated with driving on public roadways or you may be aware and recognize that in order to get around, say from home to supermarket or home to work, you have to just deal with the risk.

Others may not agree with this, but I don't believe you can accept a risk without being fully aware of it. In the case of driving, you may not be aware of it. In a business sense, you may not be aware or you may not have been given the complete story with respect to the potential impact a risk may involve. If there is money associated with the deployment of a system that has risk associated, the impact or probability may be downplayed. Based on a less than complete picture of the risk, it's hard to say you have accepted the risk since what you may have accepted isn't the actual risk but some subset of the risk.

What you may choose to do is mitigate the risk. Even if you have mitigated the risk already, you may choose to continue to mitigate it. After all, until it's completely gone, you can always mitigate further. There may be a number of reasons not to further mitigate your risk, including the cost. Going back to our driving example, when you drive you presumably put your seat belt on and that act can help mitigate the risk associated with being out on a busy road with a lot of other drivers with varying degrees of attention and experience. You may further mitigate your driving risk by ensuring the car you drive has air bags. Of course, this may help and protect you but it won't do much to help your car survive an accident. You could mitigate that risk and the costs associated with it by investing in a car that is more rugged and built to be sturdier, of stronger materials.

Quantitative analysis

This brings up some interesting things to talk about and they are really important to analyze and assess step. The first is something we've touched on previously and that's the asset—the thing you are trying to protect. In this case, primarily it's you. However, there are also costs associated with keeping you alive and healthy but causing damage to the car. First, there are out of pocket costs associated with repairing or replacing a damaged or totaled vehicle. However, there is another cost to consider that's harder to put a dollar value on and this is something that you will run into a lot when you do a risk analysis. There is cost associated with the annoyance of being without a vehicle. If you have to replace your car, there is time associated with going car shopping. Your time costs money and you can factor into that cost other things you aren't doing because you are having to shop for a car or run around to repair shops getting yours repaired. Your auto insurance may pay for a rental, but there is also the time associated with getting your rental and returning it, not to mention the associated challenges of what you may be allowed to do with the rental, based on the cost your insurance company might be willing to pay. Given the cost, you may be limited in the number of miles you can drive. In many cases this may not be a problem but if you have a long commute, that can be a challenge.

In short, there is more to costs than just the monetary value of the particular asset you are talking about. There can be a lot of soft costs as well that may get overlooked and are sometimes hard to quantify. We talked about the costs of rentals and there are certainly costs associated with replacing your totaled car, but there are also the costs associated with your time to run around and get estimates. When it comes to some of the calculations associated with risk, it's helpful to consider the bigger picture and think about what might go into repairing or restoration of an asset if something bad were to happen.

There is a good reason for that and not just because it's a good idea to know what value your assets and resources have. When you want to apply a quantitative analysis of your risk, you need accurate numbers. There are a handful of calculations that go into a quantitative analysis. One of them is the annualized loss expectancy. The annualized loss expectancy requires not only an understanding of how much an asset is valued at but also a probability calculation around whether something is going to happen or not and how frequently it happens. When you calculate the annualized loss expectancy by taking the single loss expectancy, which is the value it would cost if a risk were to actually materialize against the asset, and multiplying it by the annual rate of occurrence which is effectively a number based in probability. As mentioned earlier, if you have a long track record in business, you may have a good idea how often events are likely to happen.

As an example, when you own a retail business, you can probably predict how much you are going to lose in theft or damage after you've owned the business for a while. While there are statistics across retail as a whole, it takes an understanding of your particular store which includes what you sell as well as where you are located since some areas are more prone to crime and theft in particular than others are. Other businesses are harder to predict the occurrence of loss for. That's really what you are doing, though, when you calculate the annual rate of recurrence. You are placing a number on an expectation of an event happening and how often it is likely to happen. Maybe you expect a risk to materialize once every 3 years and the asset is worth $60,000 when you total everything in. In order to get the annualized loss expectancy, you would multiple 3 times $60,000 and you can expect to lose $20,000 from that asset each year.

You may be wondering why we would go through this particular mathematical exercise. The reason is so you can quantify values of your assets that are exposed to risk. Once you have done that, you can make informed decisions about which assets are most at risk, not based on a perceived level of risk but based on the cost to come back from a risk if it was realized against that asset or resource. You can order the assets and risks based on how much you expect to lose if a risk were to be realized.

Return on investment

As part of this exercise, you may want to consider thinking about a return on investment. Just because one asset might be very costly to recover if it is damaged as part of an attack or incident. A return on investment calculation can make generating an ordered list of projects geared toward protecting assets much easier. However, it may not be the easiest calculation considering that what we are probably talking about in light of the subject matter of this book is information technology infrastructure and a return on investment suggests that there will be a monetary gain to come from the investment. If, for example, you were a farmer in my home state of Vermont. You would produce milk more than likely because Vermont has a lot of milk farmers. Growing much in the way of other crops is challenging because of the terrain and the large quantity of rock.

When you buy a cow, you might expect that cow to product something over 2500 gallons of milk per year. The farmer gets paid something around $1.50 for each gallon of milk the cow produces. Let's imagine Speedwell Farms is looking to increase its herd and let's say a cow costs $1500. Without factoring in any other costs like feed and the cost of upkeep on the farm—equipment, electricity, maintenance, any help that may be required to sustain the farm—we can do a quick calculation on the return on investment. In 1 year, an average cow might generate $3750 in milk. If you figure the cow cost $1500, you could say that the farmer had generated $2250 in profit on that cow on a cost of $1500. The return on investment could be calculated as 2250/1500. That gives me 1.5. If I multiply that by 100, I will get a percentage of 150%. The farmer's return on investment is 150% in just that first year, right?

The problem with that calculation is it doesn't take into account any of the costs associated with keeping the cows. Return on investment is typically calculated as a net gain and not the gross gain that we calculated above. Some of the costs, though, might be difficult to calculate or put a number to. For example, the farmer may actually own a lot of land that he hays in order to get food for his cows. If he owes a bank for that land, he may factor the cost of his mortgage into the overall cost to operate his farm. If his land is paid for, the cost of haying is the maintenance costs of the tractors and other equipment necessary to hay and bundle as well as any fertilizer or irrigation costs if there are any. However, this doesn't take into account the time of the farmer and haying can be a very time-consuming operation. How does the farmer, who doesn't get a salary, calculate his time to factor into the cost of maintaining his cows?

We run into the same sorts of challenges in the information technology world. Yes, we can calculate the equipment cost, not to mention the electricity and Heating, Ventilation and Air Conditioning (HVAC) costs. What is the cost of a system being down, though, as a result of an incident? You may be able to calculate the cost of the man-hours it takes to restore the service, but these are people you are already paying so the costs there are a little squishy. It may simply be easiest to do the man-hour calculation because if you start factoring in costs of other projects being delayed and not completed on time as a result of people being pulled off to work on the restoral, calculations start to get far more difficult.

In order to calculate the return on investment of many IT-related projects and certainly security projects, you have to calculate how much you are going to save by implementing the project as opposed to how much you are going to make since IT and security projects don't actually make money. They can help the money making process by automating sales or even providing a mechanism for customers to purchase goods and services online, but in general, it's not nearly as direct a correlation between these sorts of projects and, say, buying a cow.

Social return on investment

One factor that often comes into play, particularly in recent years, is the cost from a social or reputation perspective. When you have an outage resulting from an attack or an incident, your customers are impacted. Overall, you may not end up losing any money directly, depending on the severity or the duration of the incident because customers may try again later as opposed to simply giving up. If, as an example, I wanted a book or some other product from Amazon and I found myself unable to get to Amazon's Web site, I would likely try again later rather than just not buying it or trying to find another source for the book or other product I was looking to buy.

However, if the duration is long enough, I may start to wonder whether the company I was looking to do business with was stable enough that I would want to keep doing business with them. Rather than picking on Amazon any longer, especially considering their infrastructure and track record, let's talk about an attack that did actually happen. Sony's PlayStation Network and Qriocity services experienced an extended outage over the course of 24 days in 2011. In addition to this, roughly 77 million user accounts were compromised. While this may not have had a direct impact from a revenue standpoint, since these were customers who had already paid for the service, it may have impacted new subscribers.

In most cases, an outage of 24 days would have had a significant consequence on a business' reputation that may have prevented customers from either continuing with the service or adding any new members. In Sony's case, they were fortunate to have a more or less captive audience. Anyone with a PlayStation had to use the PlayStation Network in order to interact with other users from their PlayStation. There were no competing services or networks for PlayStation users. Some users may have gone looking for another gaming console, though that seems unlikely in the majority of cases because people get attached to their consoles if only because they have a set of games that only work on that one console and not any others.

However, Sony did put together a "Welcome Back" package providing users with incentives for returning to the PlayStation Network when it came back online. They offered free games and other incentives to users in order to restore goodwill for the service and get users back with their subscriptions. In addition to the identity theft program they introduced in the wake of the breach, the cost of the "Welcome Back" package and all the other costs of the recovery totaled $171 million according to their year-end financial statements. It's hard to say what the cost to Sony in terms of reputation was.

In recent years, a new measurement has been used to calculate some of the softer costs associated with reputation and other social factors that could impact the bottom line of a business. Social return on investment (SROI) is an attempt to put numbers to a number of factors that don't traditionally have monetary values associated with them. While the SROI is intended to factor in things like environmental and social impacts in a positive way, the strategies associated with it could easily be used to take into consideration the negative social impact of not protecting systems, assets, and resources and having those systems, assets, and resources become impacted by an incident. If the negative cost to consumers and reputation had been factored in while making decisions about protecting Sony's network and systems, would any decisions have changed? Perhaps not, but it's worth considering the potential threat to your business if something were to happen to your assets that are used to service customers.

Cost–benefit analysis

At the end of the day, what we are really talking about is all of the numbers that you would take into consideration when performing a CBA. A CBA is a facts and numbers-based strategy for making business decisions. It can be very well defined and systematic and can help the decision-making process. Businesses have limited financial resources and have to find ways of deciding where to place their investment dollars. A CBA can help with that. A CBA really has two purposes that will be helpful to us. The first is to help make good business decisions based on a defensible justification. The second is perhaps more important and that's to provide a basis for comparing multiple projects.

Ultimately, when you are going through a risk management exercise, you need to do a risk assessment as discussed above but when it comes time to jump into project work, you want a prioritized ordering of projects. After all, once you know how much each project is going to cost you and what you will get out of it, you can make objective decisions. You'll be comparing apples to apples, so to speak, because the advantage of a CBA is getting everything into the same language by putting costs to things and ensuring that there is a time value associated. There is a timing consideration, of course. Costs accrue over a period of time, particularly when you are talking about projects and associated business operations, and values of resources change over time as well. The timing of all of this has to be factored in when you come up with your final figures.

In the process of performing a CBA, you need to identify the stakeholders. This would be anyone who would be affected by a change in the resource in question, whether a positive or negative change. This can be an extremely beneficial task in itself, actually. Sometimes you don't know who is likely to be most impacted by the loss of an asset or resource until that asset or resource is actually gone. In the case of a customer-facing resource like the systems in a Web application, you can't very well have the customers themselves involved in the process but you would have the line of business to represent the users and their needs. The line of business should be one of the stakeholders representing your customers. You may also consider executive management, information technology workers, as well as financial management, who would be able to provide information about associated costs. Operations staff are also important to take into consideration since they are the ones who have to manage either the systems or the customers or maybe both.

Financial professionals will also be important to bring to the table for a couple of other reasons. The first is because you may need help coming up with a common currency to define everything in. You need to assign dollar values to damage, hours and various other elements that you will need to factor into your CBA. Without that common currency, you will have a lot of numbers that can't be compared because they don't mean anything in relationship to one another. Another reason why financial professionals are important is because they will understand the calculation of things like depreciation, as an example. You can't simply apply the value you purchased an asset at when you start calculating value over time. Assets generally are worth less over time so you have to apply a reasonable rate of depreciation to them. This needs to be calculated into the cost and the benefit to get a true picture of what has been lost, if the risk were to materialize.

Once you have applied all of the numbers to all of your options, you can then compare them. One thing you don't take into consideration as easily with a CBA is the criticality of one resource over another. If you are deciding to move forward with project A because you get better bang for your buck than with project B without taking into consideration how important the resources involved with project B are, you may end up not fixing a more significant problem. While this should have been factored into all of the costs and benefits, there are challenges at times when it comes to determining critical or sensitive resources and assets.

Qualitative assessment

Quantitative assessments are based on facts and associated data. As mentioned above, it may not take into consideration the real sensitivity of one of your systems. Or when it comes down to ensuring that the criticality is factored into your calculations, it might be difficult. This is where a qualitative assessment comes in. A qualitative assessment takes into consideration less tangible factors and is based more on gut reaction than on hard facts and data. This isn't to say that your gut reaction can't be based on numbers you are aware of, but if there are factors that are difficult to quantify, you may rely on a feeling or instinct that will help you make a decision as to where you want to apply your limited resources to better protect the enterprise.

When it comes to making decisions about what projects you take on, you may at the end of the day make your decision based on intangibles rather than on something you could easily put your fingers on. As an example, let's say you had a Web application that your customers make use of. It's based on some open source content management system. You have a certain amount of sensitive information in the database that the Web application uses for persistent storage. Your IT people are recommending an expensive Web application firewall installation along with load balancers. You have a limited budget for projects and you are weighing that one against replacing an aging payroll system that is running on an older operating system because of the support requirements. While there is a good case for protecting your customer-facing infrastructure, it somehow feels right to make sure your payroll system keeps running so spending the money to upgrade there may make more sense.

Obviously, when it comes to a qualitative assessment process, there are no rules. It comes down to your instincts and preferences for risk. There may be some areas you just feel more comfortable accepting risk in than others, regardless of what the numbers say. Another thing to keep in mind is that when it comes to quantitative assessments, some of the numbers are going to be based on qualitative assessments anyway, especially when it comes to the probability side. When it comes to things like hardware failures, you can use the statistics that are available for each piece of hardware and be reasonably comfortable with the number of failures you are going to see. When it comes to security incidents, it gets to be harder. It can also be hard to put actual numbers on the cost of an incident, especially when you have never had one at your business.

Some businesses are more natural targets than others, but that doesn't mean that you won't be a target just because you aren't in a high value market—you don't have a lot of intellectual property or information. There are also targets of opportunity and you could easily be used as a launching pad for other attacks if you are exposed enough. You should always factor being complicit in other attacks into your decisions and not just on what you want to protect. Saying you don't have anything of value may be fine for you but it could make finding the real attacker harder in a compromise at another site.

Security policies

A security policy is a statement from the management of an organization as to what is important to them and how they expect people to behave when it comes to information systems. They will involve a lot of definitions in order to be very clear what the expectation is. A policy is also specific to a particular area and your organization will likely have a number of security policies including an Acceptable

Use policy outlining appropriate uses of a computer system or network. You may also have an Ethics policy, a Remote Access policy as well as a Wireless policy, a Mobile Device policy, and maybe a Bluetooth policy. Each of those would cover the specific requirements for that area of computing usage.

Once you have a set of policies, those will cascade down to the creation of standards that are a bit more specific than a policy in that they may be based on specific systems. As an example, you may have a Bluetooth policy that would then have standards that were geared toward the implementation of the policy on Windows, Mac OS, and maybe Linux if you had those operating systems within your organization. A standard is something that has to be followed and may have specific procedures for how you would comply with a policy. If you were looking at the standard for Windows that talked about implementing the Bluetooth policy, you may have a specific set of procedures for disabling Bluetooth on your system. On a Windows system, for instance, your standard may indicate that you should disable the Bluetooth service as indicated in Figure 10.2.

In addition to policies and standards, you may have guidelines. While guidelines have system-specific information and procedures, they differ from standards in that

FIGURE 10.2 Disabling Bluetooth Service on Microsoft Windows

they are not required. They are strongly recommended but they are not requirements. They are a set of details that may outline a best practice. If they were required, though, they would have been outlined in a standard, rather than a guideline. This doesn't mean, though, that you wouldn't hope that guidelines were followed as well.

As far as policies go, though, your policy should have a purpose and a scope to start off with. This outlines the expectations of the outcomes from the document. It sets the parameters for what will be covered in the policy. The meat of the document, though, is set out in a series of requirements. As an example, an information sensitivity policy would include the different data classifications as well as the requirements for each classification. Additionally, the information sensitivity policy would detail how you would handle the documents—where they could be stored, who could access them, how they might be transmitted, and so on.

Finally, the policy should also include a section on enforcement. The policy not only outlines the expectations but also what could happen if someone violates the requirements outlined in the policy. This may often just indicate that someone found to be in violation would be subject to disciplinary action. Depending on the policy and the importance of it, that disciplinary action may go all the way to termination.

Legal and regulatory requirements

In addition to the requirements of your own organization, you will have to take into account any legal and regulatory requirements that your business may be required. There are a number of requirements that you may have to incorporate into your security policies, including the Payment Card Industry Data Security Standard (PCI-DSS), the Health Insurance Portability and Accountability Act (HIPAA), and the Federal Information Security Management Act (FISMA). Some states may also have breach notification laws where you would have to provide public notice if your business has been breached. Different states will have different thresholds before those laws kick in.

In addition to US laws and regulations, different countries also have their own laws and you may fall under those laws if you do business in those countries. Additionally, when you are considering cloud services, if your cloud provider has facilities in other countries, they would fall under those laws and regulations as well. It's worth knowing where your data is actually being stored and what sort of laws are regulating the storage and handling of it. As an example, Germany passed a law in 2007 that made illegal the disabling or circumventing by an unauthorized user any measure that is put into place to provide computer security. This also includes the manufacture or installation of any software whose primary purpose is to disable or circumvent computer security.

On the surface, this sounds like a fine idea. The problem with it is that many businesses make use of such software to ferret out any holes in their own security infrastructure. Any vulnerability scanner like Nessus or exploit framework like Metasploit couldn't be used in Germany or on any system in Germany or it would be a violation of this law. This could have an impact to the safety and security of any data that is stored with a German company since the law has made it much more difficult to ensure that the security programs they have in place are adequate for protecting their systems and any information stored on them.

Controls

Policies themselves are only pieces of paper and no matter how many threats about termination of employment may be mentioned in those policies, all you have to do is drive down any street to see how good people are at following rules, even when there is a stiff penalty attached. As a result, just as with traffic laws, you want to make sure you have some enforcement in place. This is what we call controls. When it comes to policy enforcement, you need a way of monitoring and measuring whether they are being followed. For example, you have a policy of only using authorized and approved wireless networks and access points. This helps to keep down the use of unauthorized systems on the network as well as cutting down the risk of access to your internal network from outside the building. You need a way of determining whether anyone in the building is running a rogue access point.

This is not necessarily a difficult problem. Periodically, you scan your physical location for any wireless networks. This can be done easily using any computer and, often, just the wireless network drivers installed with your wireless interface. The operating system will generally very happily locate all security set identifiers (SSIDs) in the area. If you want something more than that, there is a lot of software that will provide a lot of detail on the strength of the signal and the details of the access point that is broadcasting. When you write down a procedure for doing these periodic scans and then taking action as a result of the findings, you have created a control.

If you struggle with coming up with a set of controls to go with your policies, you could look at a control framework. Fortunately, there are a number of places that have frameworks in place where you can go and get a start on your security policies, standards, and controls. The National Institute of Standards and Technology (NIST) has special publication SP 800-53 that outlines 18 areas for security policies. The Department of Defense (DoD) has specified 8 Information Assurance areas and controls in DoD Instruction 8500.2.

ISO27001 is an information security standard defined by the International Organization for Standardization (ISO). ISO27001 was updated in 2013 and includes specifications for 114 controls in 14 groups. The 14 groups that the controls are organized into are as follows:

1. Information security policies
2. How information security is organized
3. Human resources security
4. Asset management
5. Access controls and managing user access
6. Cryptographic technology
7. Physical security

8. Operational security
9. Secure communications and data transfer
10. Secure acquisition
11. Security for suppliers and third parties
12. Incident management
13. Business continuity/disaster recovery
14. Compliance

The 2013 update includes more controls than the previous version. In 2005, the last version of the standard had 11 groups and 133 controls. While the number of controls has decreased, the number of groups has increased. The changes were made to have ISO27001 fit better alongside standards like ISO9000 and ISO20000. The newest standard also includes sections to cover the reality that a lot of organizations outsource some of their IT functions.

CONCLUSION

The fact that standard frameworks come with a large number of areas where policies and controls fit in might be an indicator just how important it is to have your paperwork in place. Paperwork, meaning policies, isn't enough, of course, but pulling your policies together will provide you a way to organize your thoughts and priorities when it comes to your security strategy. Risk management and security policies go hand in hand. In part because risk management will inform your security policy and a security policy may mandate what a risk management process will look like.

The most important thing to keep in mind is that no matter what road you take from a risk management perspective, whether it's quantitative or qualitative or somewhere in between, it's a cyclical thing. You will be constantly going through the process of assessing your risk and then deciding what to do about it, whether it's accepting it or remediating it or simply removing it.

Summary

Some key points to take away from this chapter are:

- Risk management is a process that you will keep going through.
- CBA is a way to put some structure around your analysis using a consistent currency in order to compare projects head to head.
- Quantitative analysis takes facts and data into consideration.
- Qualitative analysis is sometimes necessary in order to make decisions where you can't use facts and data or where facts and data are not sufficient.
- Controls are used to monitor and measure your environment to determine violations of security policy.

Here are some ideas to come away from this chapter with:

- Risk management is a process and one that should never end.
- Different people may handle risk in different ways.
- Quantitative assessments use data to help make decisions about risk and projects.
- Qualitative assessments use subjective information to help make decision about risk and projects.
- There is an SROI that could be taken into account—this could be goodwill or word of mouth.
- Understanding how to perform a CBA is an important part of doing a risk assessment.
- There are a lot of legal and regulatory requirements to take into consideration that may help guide decisions when it comes to risk analysis.

Further reading

PlayStation Hack to Cost Sony $171M; Quake Costs Far Higher, 2013. PCMAG. Retrieved December 16, 2013, from <http://www.pcmag.com/article2/0,2817,238>.

Future Technology

INFORMATION INCLUDED IN THIS CHAPTER

- Wearable computing
- Challenges to moving forward
- Your data wherever you are

INTRODUCTION

It's hard to write a chapter title called "Future Technology" without chuckling and imagining the opening to The Jetsons TV show where everyone lived in high rise buildings so far up that there was no ground in sight and in fact, all travel appeared to take place in the air with little bubble cars that emitted small clouds of exhaust. Clearly, nearly 50 years since that show was on the air, we haven't seen the types of technological breakthroughs that were envisioned, including humanistic robots that could function as maids. While it's not the year 2062 that the show depicts, we're roughly halfway there and while there have been enormous technological advances in that time in some regards, there are others where we haven't progressed nearly as far as had been dreamed. Since they were so far off, it's difficult to expect that any chapter I write titled as this one is will be on the mark with respect to where we are headed with regard to how we interact with computing infrastructure for the purposes of business and collaboration.

It is clear some of what's in the near future, however, and we can spend some time investigating some of those capabilities as well as speculate about some other areas where there may be advances in terms of how we interact with one another and the enormous volumes of data we produce and consume. Some of this is a question of businesses making decisions for us but we also have choices to make for ourselves.

Pushing into the cloud

As I sit here and write this, more and more data is being pushed up into a cloud storage solution. The reason I say this is that after upgrading to the latest version of Mac

FIGURE 11.1 Opening SkyDrive Documents

Used with permission from Microsoft.

OS, I noticed several programs I use from time to time started to default to storing and retrieving data to an iCloud account. Apple is clearly driving users to store data with them with their most recent operating system releases. It's actually more convenient in some regards since it can be so difficult to get data to and from your mobile Apple device, whether it's an iPhone or an iPad. It's not nearly as easy to create a document on your iPad and then drop it over to your desktop. What will make the document sharing process much easier between a mobile device and a desk or lap bound device is to have a place of common storage. Since you can't add external storage to your iPad or iPhone and probably wouldn't want to keep plugging and unplugging it just to move a document over, the most convenient place is using cloud storage. In the case of Apple, where they provide their own applications that work on both their mobile and their desktop platforms, they can provide the capability for those applications to just push you to using Apple's cloud storage. Many of Apple's applications are starting to offer ways of storing documents remotely. Making this a default for many applications is a way of pushing people to think about data not being local. This subtle change would commonly encourage an average user to just accept iCloud as the place to store data.

Apple and Microsoft are more traditional application development companies moving to the cloud but they are not the only ones. Google, after all, stores everything in the cloud including the application. The difference here is that cloud storage is no longer an add-on or a Web visit. It's built directly into the operating system. You can continue to fight it, of course, and, like me, insist on storing all of your documents locally, but the trend is clearly toward storing everything with cloud storage providers. Of course, in my case, too many years of not having Internet access everywhere I was leaves me with a bias toward having my data with me so I can sit on a train and write this chapter, as I'm doing now. This bias will hopefully disappear especially since, in this particular instance, I also have Internet access on the Amtrak train I'm sitting on.

Microsoft also has cloud storage features built into applications. Figure 11.1 shows a dialog box offering options for where to get a document from within

Microsoft Word. You can see in the middle pane where SkyDrive is where I would get access to files that are stored with Microsoft's cloud storage platform. In this case, I haven't signed myself into my SkyDrive account and, worse than that, Word doesn't think I have an Internet connection, because I am running Word inside a virtual machine and while my host operating system has a network connection, I have to go through the process of authenticating to the wireless network on this train in my guest OS. This does highlight a problem with cloud storage, though. If I go through a place where I don't have Internet access, like on a plane, for example, and the document I want isn't cached locally, I won't be able to get access to it. One of the problems we have is a lack of ubiquitous Internet access, particularly in less populated areas, which is really the vast majority of the geographical area of the country.

Ubiquitous broadband

It's amazing to think of how far we have come in what is really a remarkably short amount of time, considering the forerunner of the Internet, a small four-node network commissioned by the Advanced Research Projects Agency (ARPA) and built by a company that hadn't long been in the computer business, Bolt, Beranek & Newman (BBN), was turned on just about 45 years ago. Considering how fast everything seems to move in the network space that seems like forever ago but consider that PCs didn't exist for another 10 years and they didn't become so affordable that a majority of people could have one in their home for probably another 25 beyond that. The life of the Internet when it comes to average people having access to it is really just a teenager.

While the various networks that eventually grew together to become what we call the Internet had a long, slow ramp, the last several years have seen explosive growth. The major carriers have enormous capability to transport data. The problem is where we get to what telecommunication folks call the last mile. This is the connection to your house or maybe even the mobile device you are using to get access to the network. This last mile access, particularly to a physical location like a house or apartment, is commonly called broadband. Broadband has become a very generic term but it was originally used to reference communication that used a higher set of frequencies. Communication mechanisms that used lower frequencies, like phone lines in a plain old telephone service (POTS) system, were called baseband.

Originally, broadband was meant to designate transmission speeds higher than what was primary rate, or T1 speed, which is 1.544 Mbps. This was defined by the International Telephony Union in the late 1980s. Since that time, of course, marketing groups from various Internet access providers have gotten their hands on the word and it began to mean anything that was faster and more permanent than dial-up Internet access. This access may reach your house by way of Digital Subscriber Line (DSL), cable, satellite, or it may be a wireless signal originating from a tower in the area. The last is not a cellular signal, like your phone is, and it's commonly a line of sight signal, meaning that you have to be able to see the tower in order to get a signal from it and get Internet access from that service.

Unlike other countries, our utilities have commonly been commercial endeavors but they have often been protected in one way or another by natural monopoly status. Without that status, we may have ended up with a lot more phone lines because with a lot of different phone companies, as an example, each phone company would have needed a way to get their lines from their central office to their subscribers. In the early days of the phone company, there were some competing phone companies and it was a mess as lines were run all over. Eventually, we ended up with the Bell Telephone System that lasted about 100 years and operated as the single phone company. Given the monopoly over the phone system, Bell could do what made the most sense for Bell and didn't have to worry about interoperability. They could also invest in infrastructure, sure that they had a pretty steady stream of profits coming in. Without that guarantee, they may have been less likely to invest in building the network out.

In the 1980s, Ma Bell was required to separate into a lot of smaller companies and allow for competitors. The problem with that scenario is, in order to keep infrastructure from consuming our telephone poles alongside our roadways, each competitor was required to make use of the existing infrastructure and the various regional Bell companies were required to allow competitors to use their infrastructure at a reasonable price. Eventually, Internet access becomes a service that customers were looking for and the phone companies were very slow off the mark in getting it to their customers. While they could have offered DSL services to their customers easily beginning in the mid-1990s, they often didn't view it as a viable long-term business and essentially yielded to the cable companies who were offering Internet access service across their infrastructure.

The argument that led to breaking the Bell system up into various component pieces was that competition would lead to lower costs and better services to end users. The same argument should also hold true when it comes to providing Internet access. In reality, however, the cable companies and perhaps one most especially have been immune to competition, which has led to high prices, poor reach, and low speeds to consumers. In the days of the Bell system, the densely populated areas were able to compensate for the lower populated areas so Bell was required to serve everyone as part of the natural monopoly status they had. Laws that have been past in the past couple of decades removed a lot of hurdles to communications companies. The Bell companies have been slowly divesting themselves of the local, last mile access that was becoming onerous to them since locations with lower population densities didn't make them as much money. At the same time, they have been collecting back up into large companies again like AT&T and CenturyLink, offering a variety of services that no longer cater to local subscribers. Without this requirement to service all households, these companies don't have the interest in building higher level services like Internet access through DSL and the smaller companies that now own the households don't have the resources to build out large networks that can fully support their customers with high-speed Internet access.

Meanwhile, the cable companies, without meaningful competition, have been able to offer Internet access services at prices and speeds that most benefit them and their bottom lines. Currently, the United States is far back in the pack when it comes to affordable high-speed Internet access, which seems shameful since the very first building block of what is today's Internet was built here about 45 years ago.

The reason this is important is because as more work for high paying, knowledge-based workers becomes remote, wherever the person happens to be, the people who are going to get those jobs are those who have fast and reliable Internet access and at the moment, that's not the United States. Countries that have a lot of real competition in the way of Internet service are able to ensure their citizens have access to reliable and fast network access and those people will have the ability to compete for high paying jobs in a global, networked marketplace. People who are remote and have no access to the Internet will continue to get more remote as money moves to where the network access.

The big companies who may be able to provide some competition to the choke-hold the cable company has on the marketplace are looking at the wireless space for where they are going to provide their services. The problem with that is that wireless will not guarantee fast, reliable, or cheap. Wireless services continue to get more and more expensive and again, they are not keeping pace with the networks available in other countries in terms of speed, price, or quality of service. The United States is a large, geographically diverse place. The terrain is always a problem when it comes to offering reliable Internet service. I currently live in Vermont and cell signals are spotty all over the state. I can't reliably make a call in the state capitol if I am in my car. The terrain and lack of adequate tower coverage because of environmental concerns means there are a lot of places where there is just no cellular signal. If I am relying on this service for my Internet as well, I don't have Internet.

Without a push to close gaps in Internet coverage around the United States, we will have a lot of potential workers who could be providing enormous benefit to companies who are unable to do so because they can't move to the location where the company is and they don't have Internet access where they are. This situation isn't beneficial for either businesses or for people and it should be resolved. If it isn't, it will continue to keep progress slowed.

Wearable computing

At some point, you've probably seen some form of wearable communication device whether it's the wrist radio that Dick Tracy used or the shoe phone of Maxwell Smart. Over the years, creative people from film to television to books have envisioned a time when we would wear various communications devices. That time really arrived when the first Bluetooth headset was placed in someone's ear as they walked through an airport terminal. It was a wireless communication device that was being worn. We've moved well past the idea of wearable communication devices and jumped into wearable computing devices. You may have seen one of these by this point, whether it's Google Glass or one of the smart watches like the Pebble or the Galaxy Gear.

So far, these devices are in their infancy when it comes to what they can do. The watches advertise the ability to change the watch face or perhaps read social media updates or text messages from your wrist. In the case of the Galaxy Gear, we really have entered the era where Dick Tracy (a cartoon strip that originated in the 1930s that introduced a two-way wrist radio in the 1940s) might be able to wear a full-fledged communication device on his wrist. In fact, the first smart watch came out in 2000 and ran a version of Linux but obviously it didn't really catch on.

One of problems with that early smart watch that continues today is that of the battery. A wearable computer that does much useful will require a lot of battery and if you look at your wrist, you'll see there just isn't a lot of space there to put computing power plus the battery that is capable of powering it for a long period of time. At the moment, it appears that the time a smart watch can run on a single charge may be measured in hours rather than days. This could become a stumbling block to them really taking off. Another challenge is going to be the types of applications that can be written for them and whether those applications turn the watch into something more than a toy. It's hard to know for sure how important or useful these devices will be since it is going to take work to resolve the issues with the battery as well as a useful programming interface to create killer applications. If the best we'll get out of a smart watch is the ability to make phone calls from our wrist or the ability to see texts or a social media status, the smart watch will likely become a niche product that never really achieves the dominance that a device like a smartphone has achieved. Smartphones have become something of a must have item, even for people who could likely get along with a phone that was far less smart.

Mobile computing has become something of an addiction. When you have the ability to be in constant communication, it becomes difficult to get away from constantly checking to see if there is something you need to react to. How often do you see someone with a smartphone who is just sitting somewhere quietly without either checking their phone every minute or so or have it on and just flipping through it without doing much of anything in particular. I think we might have a bit of a biological need for the glow of a display.

In the process of writing this, I picked up a Galaxy Gear smartphone to do a little testing with this wearable computing and it does have some potential. One of the challenges I've always had with cell phones, that frankly get harder as the phone size starts to increase again, is figuring out where to carry it. I put it in my front pocket, typically, but unless I'm standing up, it's hard to pull the phone out particularly if I am trying to get to it to pick up a phone call. It used to be easy when belt-mounted holsters were readily available for phones, even if they do look a little dorky. It was far less about the look and more about the ease of access to the phone if I wanted to look at an incoming text message or check a phone call. You can see the Galaxy Gear in Figure 11.2 and on the day the picture was taken, it was 13° outside and sunny. The weather gets updated on a regular basis.

With the Galaxy Gear, I have a watch, which I would typically wear anyway, and when I get a text message, all I have to do is turn my wrist and touch the face

FIGURE 11.2 Galaxy Gear Smart Watch

where the alert is and I can see the text message. I can then reply by speaking my message into the Gear. So far, while it can be very convenient to have a lot of information on my wrist within easy access, it's not exactly a must have item, though I can certainly see the advantages of having a device like this with all of the additional functions it provides. However, it does require you to have your phone with you for it to do a lot of functions. It cannot work like a phone, send text messages, or perform some other functions without making use of your phone and although it uses Bluetooth to communicate with the phone, you do have to have a compatible phone to make use of it. Eventually, it's possible that these devices will be less proprietary but in the meantime, they are locking us into a single vendor for your phone and watch. While Samsung maybe the first really big name to market with a device like this, others are not very far behind. Apple has been acquiring and patenting in order to get an iDevice out to market, presumably.

One of the features that does seem to be interesting, in a way, is the fact that it takes pretty good pictures. In the first couple days of having it, I took several photos, including playing with taking pictures of Thanksgiving dinner. The watch transfers the photos to my phone and I was able to upload the photo to Facebook from there. Looking at the pictures later on a larger device, it was a little surprising how good the pictures look. If you already have a smartphone, you have a camera so why one more, especially one with lower resolution? A camera on your wrist can be more convenient than trying to dig your phone out from wherever you are storing it unless, like some people I've seen, you have it in your hand constantly because you are constantly texting or on social media. A wrist camera can still be much quicker than getting your camera into place and the camera app opened up. Additionally, and this is where the whole spy watch thing comes in, you can point your wrist band at someone or something a lot more surreptitiously than you can with a phone or camera where it's probably clear you are taking a picture since most people hold the phone out away from them as they look at the display to line their photo up.

FIGURE 11.3 Picture Taken from Smart Watch

Used with permission from Kathleen Nichols.

In the case of the watch, I can cross my arms and appear to be looking at my watch or just down at my hand while I line the shot up. Then I just tap my phone. The giveaway is the shutter sound the watch makes when it takes the photo. In a noisy area, this may be unintelligible, though obviously it could be a giveaway if you were more up close to your subject. I was able to take a test shot of some diners at the restaurant in New York City where we were having Thanksgiving dinner without them noticing a thing. It would be wrong to post that image since I'd have to explain what I did to them in order to get permission to print the photo so Figure 11.3 shows a photo I took of my family across the aisle on the train. Until the shutter sound, they had no idea what I was doing.

In addition to watches, Google has developed another piece of retro futurism with Glass. Google Glass is a computer that you wear like a pair of glasses. It includes a camera as well as the ability to display directly to your eye. You interface with Glass using your voice, speaking commands to it. Glass will be able to offer something that has been tried previously, without a lot of success. There have been attempts at augmented reality applications previously, including an app I tried a few years ago called Layar. The problem with those apps is they required you to hold your phone out in front of you while it made use the camera and then placed additional information on top of the camera image. Layar, as an example, could then overlay the locations of businesses and other features of interest to you. Using Layar, you could determine where something was in relation to where you were and you could do it visually. Layar currently supports interactive print where you can take something like a book that would typically be static content and get digital content available for that book.

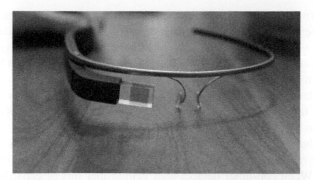

FIGURE 11.4 Google Glass

The source of this image is Tedeytan.

Google Glass removes the phone from the equation and gives you the ability to get all of that digital content without ever touching a device. You might look at a QR code while you were wearing Google Glass and it would display a Web page of information for you. You may also look at a UPC code and check for prices from competitors while you are standing in a store. You can already do this very easily with a smartphone but Google Glass provides you the ability to do it without needing to dig up your phone and trying to line up the QR code in a viewer so you can get a reliable image and look up the information. Google Glass could free up your hands to do other things.

You can see Google Glass in Figure 11.4. One of the challenges it will have, since it looks like a set of glasses without the glass, is how it would work with people who do have prescription lenses or maybe want to wear it outside and how it would work with sunglasses. These are not insurmountable obstacles, though, and Google is already working with companies that make prescription glasses to integrate Glass. There may also be challenges when it comes to wearing these devices while driving and some locations have already indicated an intent to ban their use while driving, although it could be argued that there could be enormous benefit while driving by providing something like a heads-up display providing useful information like traffic status or weather conditions ahead.

Interfaces

When I first got an Xbox with Kinect, I couldn't help but think about the movie *Iron Man* and the way Tony Stark interacted with Jarvis, his computer. First, it was primarily by voice. Kinect allows me to speak to the Xbox and have it carry out commands that I say. This itself isn't particularly new or even very interesting since voice recognition has been around for a while and it generally works well. With Kinect, though, we finally have the ability to interact with a computer system kinetically, meaning we can gesture in the air and the computer will recognize these gestures and be able to do something with them. It does have some limitations, not the least of which is making sure you are within view of the camera and reasonably well-lit. However, researchers have been able to take the Xbox Kinect and using the system, they were able to perform tasks like drawing in the air and having the drawing get replicated on the TV screen. This is merely a step away from being able to use gestures to manipulate images on a computer screen that's similar in nature to what Tony Stark was doing. The new Xbox One has improved the visual technology, pushing the capabilities of the Kinect even further. Where the Kinect liked to have light, the Xbox One can see in the dark.

Lately, I have been seeing televisions that offer voice commands and gestures. You can use your hand to do things like changing the channel or turning up or down the volume. When consumer devices start getting this sort of capability, the computer companies that develop software and operating systems like Microsoft and Apple must be making note of it. Especially since Microsoft pioneered the capability with their gaming system. Prior to that, of course, Microsoft was pioneering touch devices. Many years ago, Microsoft had a very large table that they were using as a demonstration of touch technology. You could interact with the table, which was a very large computer display, using your hands. It was very much like a 2D version of the *Iron Man* capability. At the time it came out, Microsoft was calling it Surface but that name has since gone on to be used for a different, though related, product and currently the large format touch interface is called PixelSense.

It's hard to imagine that these different ways of interacting with computers won't affect the way we make use of systems in the coming years and, as a result, collaborate with one another. Take Google Glass as another example. With Google Glass, and other wearable computing devices, we may be able to be constantly available when it comes to work-related tasks. We will also be interacting with Google Glass in a very different way than we have with other computing devices.

HTML5

We have been using HTML for more than a couple of decades and it's gone through a number of revisions. The current revision is a very significant one, however, and makes significant changes to the previous version of HTML, including features that have been in use for a while but that required the support of additional specifications. Over the last several years, Web developers have continued to find ways to extend the functionality of HTML by including a variety of new features including the <div> and <span> tags that provided, along with the Document Object Model (DOM), ways to programmatically interact with the page.

One of the challenges has long been that HTML is a markup language and not a programming language and as a result, you end up with static content if you write in HTML. In order to create things like dropdown menus or other interactive content, you need a programming language. JavaScript has long been that programming language, for the most part, but in order to make content on the page change without refreshing the page after a visit to the server, the JavaScript functions needed ways to find the sections of the page that needed to be rewritten in a dynamic fashion.

If you used the DOM and the right tags with labels, you could write the page in a way that specific sections could be updated based on actions of the user that didn't involve clicking links, which would create a call to the server for additional content.

Asynchronous JavaScript and XML (AJAX) has been used to pull new content into pages, again using the DOM to update specific sections of the page. You can see this if you go to a lot of pages with content that doesn't lie lifeless in your browser but the easiest places to see it are the social networking sites like Facebook and Twitter where new updates are loaded into your page without you clicking anything so you get a running ticker of everything your friends are doing or saying. AJAX, though, was created without any real specification being written as to how it would work in a standardized fashion. In addition to AJAX, several sites use Adobe's Flash for their programmatic interface. These different ways of accomplishing similar goals has led to browsers being required to support a lot of working code that doesn't have standards associated as well as a lot of standards that have long since been outdated or obsoleted.

HTML5 attempts to unify all of the work that has been done in the field with a set of standards that not only allow for better interaction with page content but also a way of embedding multimedia content since that previously required plug-ins to the browser in order to function correctly and didn't work simply with the HTML standard as it was. Now, using HTML5, you can embed video or audio into the page and the browser will know what to do with it without requiring an additional plug-in to be able to support the tag. This isn't to say that there won't be codec issues, based on how the video or audio is stored. The browser isn't expected to be able to render all content without any helpers so you will still need support for the right codecs to play the audio or video.

In the early 2000s, there was a move to try to go to a more extensible version of HTML that was called XHTML, introducing elements from XML into the HTML. While both were descendants of the Structured Generic Markup Language (SGML), XML is more extensible than HTML since HTML is well defined and XML allows the developer to create descriptions of the content as necessary using XML tags. XML is also less forgiving than most HTML parsers have been since XML is expected to be full well formed, meaning that tags need to be opened as well as closed not left half-open as is often the case with a lot of HTML that's out there on the Web. HTML5 includes an updated XHTML specification rather than leaving the XHTML specification separate and requiring browsers to implement a separate specification. In addition to other features, XHTML also provided the ability to have a mobile profile to support browsers on mobile devices where the functionality or the screen real estate may be less than a desktop counterpart.

HTML5 not only cleans up a lot of what has commonly been in use up until this point but it also introduces a lot of new content. However, it still ends up looking a lot like the HTML you have grown used to. Figure 11.5 shows the start of an HTML5 document. One of the first things that is apparent is the doctype looks quite a bit cleaner here than it has previously where there were references to transitional. Now, it's simply a document type of HTML without any additional explanation. HTML5 introduces application programming interfaces (APIs) that haven't existed previously, including

```
<!DOCTYPE html>
<!--[if IE 8]><html class="no-js lt-ie9" lang="en" ><![endif]-->
<!--[if gt IE 8]><!-->
<html class="no-js" lang="en" >
<!--<![endif]-->
        <head>
                <meta charset="utf-8" />
                <meta name="viewport" content="width=device-width" />
                <title>HTML5 Notifications</title>
                <link rel="stylesheet" href="css/normalize.css" />
                <link rel="stylesheet" href="css/foundation.min.css" />
                <link rel="stylesheet" href="css/codemirror.css" />
                <link rel="stylesheet" href="css/app.css" />
```

FIGURE 11.5 HTML5 Document

support for drag and drop, document editing, browser history management, and Web storage. The Web storage is similar to what we are used to with cookies today. All of these APIs can be accessed through JavaScript, meaning that there are finally standards within HTML itself for the way pages have been built. It also means the door is open for a lot of highly interactive content being delivered through a browser.

Since mobile is increasing and HTML5 is moving toward adoption, we can certainly expect to see more Web-based content that is geared toward mobile devices. Additionally, HTML5 moves away from the static content basis that HTML was formed on, since it was created primarily as a way to display scientific papers and share them with colleagues quickly and easily. With HTML5, the standard will be for rich content including multimedia. This brings us back around to the concerns over bandwidth for all discussed above. As content becomes larger and more based around highly interactive, multimedia, we need the bandwidth to be able to have these sites without the same complaints from 15 years ago where Web developers were putting large images on their pages because they could and it was causing rendering times to be very slow to the point of nearly unusable for people who only had dial-up connections or simply very slow broadband.

Consumers as producers

One thing also seems clear as we move forward and that is that the Web is maturing into a completely collaborative space. To date, the consumer-based Internet has been designed in such a way that it sees everyone in the last mile as a consumer of content. Think about the asymmetric access lines you have coming into your house. That asymmetry assumes that you will be consuming a lot of content but not producing any yourself. There is nothing technically different about the way you deliver these access modes to an end user. Many years ago I worked at a small ISP and we were delivering DSL to customers before the regional Bell Company decided they could get into the game. We were delivering synchronous DSL, meaning the customer could upload at the same rate they could download. As far as the network infrastructure was concerned, we required a single copper pair to the customer and we took care of everything else. Essentially, we were ordering wires from the central office without any power or circuit switched connection coming down them, just as a fire alarm line would be ordered.

The difference between offering the same bandwidth for upload and download and having different speeds depending on the direction has to do with the money on the provider's end. If your provider is primarily providing eyes to content networks, they can connect to those content networks for just the cost of a connection and if it's a local handoff, it's not much. Once your provider starts actually sending data back up to other networks, there are peering arrangements that have to be made that might mean your provider would have to pay for you to send content into the network. If you are just a pair of eyeballs, you can get a free ride because the content networks are essentially paying for you with advertising. If you expect to be a producer of content, you need to have a way to pay for yourself.

Certainly the bar is being raised here as everyone is recognizing that the people who were formerly consumers are now every bit the producer as well by way of YouTube and Vines as well as Facebook, Twitter, LinkedIn, and so on. The speeds for upload are increasing to allow you to upload all of that content to those sites, primarily because it's good business to do that. Without your content, those sites aren't as valuable, meaning fewer people come to visit them because there isn't as much content available on them.

This is actually a very good thing when it comes to business-related collaboration since at some point you will want to upload documents to Web-based storage and not all of those documents are going to be small. The faster they upload, the quicker you can move on to more important things. Also, you may want to be able to audio or videoconference while you are doing this uploading of data and that also requires bandwidth. The more bandwidth you have, the more productive you can be in a data rich, not to mention data hungry world.

CONCLUSION

Not entirely coincidentally, I've been rereading a book on the creation of the ARPANET that is the forerunner of everything we have today. Without it, we may not have the Internet and World Wide Web that we have come to rely on for personal as well as business reasons. One thing that struck me while reading it again is that they talked about all of the resource sharing and collaboration that they not only envisioned but also ended up taking place. More than that, though, it wasn't long before the ARPANET's primary source of traffic was simply communicating with other people at other sites. E-mail, such as it was in the early 1970s, consumed the vast majority of the limited communication links that were in place at the time.

In some ways, we have come a very long way since the first ARPANET link in 1969 but in others, we are still looking to work with other people and have a connection that revolves around working and communicating with other people. That is still here today and as we move forward, no matter how we end up interfacing with our computers, we will continue to be working with and communicating with one another and looking for more ways to do that. This includes finding better ways to collaborate with one another in the business arena, regardless of where we happen to be. The vision of the founders of the ARPANET was that it shouldn't matter where you were located if you had the skills and ability to contribute something interesting because you could connect to resources around the world.

It's also very clear that small, mobile, and agile is better and that we continue to look for ways to provide better interaction in our interfaces with computers. The primary driver of traffic around the Internet is that coming through Web pages and Web sites. We continue to look for ways to get more content in that way as well as content that is more feature and media rich and it's unlikely that trajectory will be changing anytime in the near future. HTML5 is bringing us more abilities to create feature and content rich pages that will also support mobile devices as well. More and more business functions are being driven to the Web and HTML5 will allow those to be done without requiring a lot of additional technology other than just your browser and the infrastructure on the server side.

Summary

Some ideas to take away from this chapter:

- Newer technologies are requiring a lot of bandwidth in order to store data and services in the cloud.
- Users are beginning to produce content, which also requires a lot of bandwidth.
- Touch screens and 3D interfaces are changing the way we interface with systems.
- HTML5 has changed the interface language, allowing for more multimedia content without requiring additional plug-ins.
- Wearable computing like Google Glass and smart watches like the Samsung Galaxy Gear along with smart phones are making information nearly constantly accessible.
- More apps and functionality will be available via wearable computing, again changing our system interface.

Further reading

Hafner, K., Lyon, M., 1998. Where Wizards Stay Up Late: The Origins of the Internet. Touchstone, New York, NY.

Levy, J., 2012. Hey America! We're Ranked #16 in Broadband! The Huffington Post. Retrieved November 30, 2013, from <http://www.huffingtonpost.com/josh-levy/broadband-rankings-worldwide_b_1400630.html>.

Pulling It All Together

INFORMATION INCLUDED IN THIS CHAPTER

- Straw man for building a business on cloud technologies
- Security considerations
- Building requirements

INTRODUCTION

It's time to pull it all together now. While you are surely in a different position, what we're going to do now is imagine a small business that is just getting started. Rather than making use of typical infrastructure that can take a lot of capital to get up and running with and also potentially hamper the growth of the company, we're going to have this business make use of cloud services. While we haven't gone over this before, there is a challenge for small businesses. At some point after you found the company, you have to have computers for people as well as phone systems and networked resources. After all, you can't have a printer on every desk and you also need to take care of other shared resources like file shares. The best way to handle this is to use a Windows server that can centralize your account management as well as resource sharing but the hardware and software, not to mention the maintenance can be pricey.

This is something I've been through before, actually. I worked for a small software company in the late 1990s. When I started, everyone was on Windows for Workgroups and there was one system that was acting as a "server" that was actually just a standard Windows for Workgroups system that had a file share as well as a tape drive. This allowed the developers to store all the source code on a central system that could then be backed up to tape with the backups stored offsite. The problem is that the company started to grow and eventually, there was a need for a centralized server system for not only file services but also account management and eventually mail and calendar services.

Everything had been done ad hoc with user accounts on each system and shares all over the place. By the time we were talking about going to a server-based system, everyone was on NT-based systems meaning that they were logged into local accounts so switching them over to domain-based accounts meant a lot of moving of profiles and data and back in the mid-1990s, the problems associated with moving profiles around weren't as well understood and there weren't a lot of tools to handle it. I recall several cases where Windows would simply report that it couldn't copy the profile as well as other, similar errors. This meant that the users had to essentially recreate all of their settings. With the amount of possible customizations, not to mention other data stored in a user's profile, losing that profile could be more than a simple annoyance.

In short, starting with ad hoc and moving to a more structured approach can be expensive and challenging. At a minimum, it can be inconvenient for the very people who make the company go. This brings up a dilemma. The dilemma is whether to take the monetary and staffing hit up front to get the infrastructure in place to support your business correctly as it grows or whether to go ad hoc and deal with the technical organization down the road when it becomes necessary. Fortunately, we may be able to handle this by providing the right top-down approach and organization of technical resources with user and data management. I say top-down because it means that the business owners and managers get to make decisions about who gets access to what and when users are created and removed.

If we make use of cloud services, we can take advantage of the work the providers have done to pull together infrastructure without involving a lot of capital. Before we can make any decisions about what services to go with, we need a set of requirements based on the business and what it needs. The requirements will help us decide what providers to go with.

Background

First, we need a company so let's create one out of thin air. Hopefully, this will have just enough of the messiness of the start of a new company that you may be able to relate to it. Five friends from college who had an idea for a piece of software started the company we are talking about. Three of them remained in the area around the college they attended while two more returned to their home but all are working for the fledgling company. One of the locals is a software developer along with the two who are remote. The other two who are local are handling business management (including sales) and marketing. They have registered the domain name cloudroy.com that they expect to use for business purposes. They are currently in alpha stage with their software with intent to provide mobile versions as well but they are very limited on cash while they look for venture capital to really get them off the ground. They have set up an office but want to be able to start using business-related services so they look more like a going concern.

While they have offices, the two responsible for marketing and business are often on the road. This means that in addition to the remote developers, the business people also have a need to gain access to business and corporate resources from wherever they are. While they could do everything in-house, as we've previously discussed, that could be problematic. One of the developers could take on the function of a system administrator, but it takes away from their role as a software developer getting the product ready for shipment. Taking on additional roles ends up causing potential delays to getting to a point where they can generate revenue for the company.

Requirements

As with any modern business, and certainly one associated with computers, there are electronic communication requirements. When you are talking about a business where people are in multiple locations, facilitating communication is critical. The business also has needs for storing contact information about customers, getting human resources support, and project management capabilities. Additionally, there are document/revision control needs and also the standard need for document creation. This may be word processing, spreadsheets, or presentations. Having said all that, here are the requirements we have for this company.

- **Messaging**—This should be a rich messaging platform including e-mail and instant messaging. This should also include the possibility of having presence notifications so everyone can know when colleagues are available since they can't often walk by an office to see if they are in or occupied.
- **Human resources**—This includes payroll and benefits management as well as records management for all employees.
- **Telephony**—The company needs to have a way of getting access to one another by telephone. This will include voice mail services, which may be the most important component when it comes to telephony.
- **Project management**—The software being developed has a lot of moving pieces so they have a need for project management to keep track of who is working on what. Also, there may be business-related projects like acquiring customers and market segments. This effort and the efforts of the marketing group may also require project management to keep track of activity and progress.
- **Storage**—Since some employees are located outside of the physical building where the headquarters is located, they will need to be able to remotely access critical business documents. This may include features lists for the developers and it may include business strategy documents for the business people.
- **Source control**—With a number of employees and partners working on developing the software, they need a way to check out and check in the source when they go to make changes. This prevents inadvertent clobbering of work someone else is doing. Where this would normally be handled within the confines of the facilities, they have developers located remotely and it would be more convenient to use a cloud provider to handle this.
- **Customer management**—As the company is starting to develop business relationships and acquiring customers, they need to store their contacts and the

activity that the business engages in with those partners and customers. This will help as they bring on more sales people. It will also help to ensure the right paperwork is communicated to the customer or business partner and keep track of the status of any documents and contracts that are being exchanged.

Messaging

There are a number of options for messaging, particularly if we limit our focus to e-mail. There are a large number of providers that will provide e-mail services for you. E-mail is one of those services where the protocols have long been standardized and while there are newer access methods using Web services, there are well-established protocols for communicating with e-mail servers for sending and receiving messages. As a result, we don't have to worry about interoperability requirements.

When it comes down to it, while there are a number of providers that can do e-mail, we also want to factor in instant messaging as well. We could have the employees join a specified public service like AOL Instant Messaging, Y!, MSN, or any Jabber-based service including Google's messaging service. Public services may be useful but if we are already in the market for an e-mail provider, we may be able to make use of the instant messaging that comes along with some of the e-mail providers.

Without getting too far ahead, there are really a couple of providers that make the most sense considering the other requirements. The first one is Google. With a Google account, we would not only get access to e-mail but the collection of apps that Google offers as well. We would be able to make use of the domain we acquired for our e-mail addresses. We would also get calendaring. This can be particularly helpful in the case where employees are located in a number of locations. In order to ensure that you are connecting regularly with your coworkers, you may want to schedule meetings with them. Google offers large mailboxes to store a lot of messages and Google also has the search capabilities they are well known for in order to locate messages that may have accumulated. At the time of this writing, Google is offering 30 GB of storage for e-mail and support for offline access. Google also has messaging capabilities with Google Hangouts, formerly Google Talk. With Google, you also have social networking capabilities because you are automatically enrolled in Google+ . This may be useful for a new business. It's also a useful way of seeing what colleagues are doing. You can see the request to enable circles on one of my Google accounts in Figure 12.1. Adding circles to join hangouts gives you another way to communicate with people, whether individually or in groups.

The other option that would meet our requirements of large storage space, the ability to use our domain address and secure remote access in addition to messaging and calendaring is Microsoft Office 365. Office 365 provides a lot of benefits including meeting all of the requirements listed above. Additionally, we get access to Microsoft Lync for messaging. Lync is the latest generation of Microsoft's communication software, following NetMeeting and Communicator. Lync provides

FIGURE 12.1 Google Hangouts

Google and the Google logo are registered trademarks of Google Inc., used with permission.

both instant messaging and voice and video communication that will run on both computers and mobile devices. This would be used to communicate between colleagues within the organization but could also be used to communicate with people in other organizations who are also using the Lync platform.

With Microsoft, we also get another communication platform. You can see in Figure 12.2 that Office 365 subscribers not only get e-mail but also get collaboration capabilities and a public Web site. Additionally, if you are an Office 365 subscriber, you get access to SkyDrive, which is Microsoft's cloud storage platform, and their online Office applications. You also get their regular office suite for desktop use for some number of users that would be based on the number of users in your enterprise.

Sharepoint is underneath a substantial portion of what isn't the e-mail portion of Office 365. Sharepoint provides a way for the enterprise to share data, much like a wiki would have the ability to store data through pages and files. On top of that structured approach, Sharepoint also provides a platform to host Web logs (blogs). There is also a social network component, similar to Google+. You can see that aspect of it in Figure 12.3. You can follow other users and see what they post, just as with other social networking platforms like Google+ or Facebook. Microsoft calls it a Newsfeed. You can also quickly pull together team sites and public sites that use Sharepoint as a platform with a simple Web development platform. The public site can even use your domain name so we would be able to use www.cloudroy.com if we were to go with Microsoft.

While Microsoft offers a lot of advantages, Google is more cross-platform because of its Web-based nature. While Microsoft also offers Web-based solutions, they are more geared toward devices that have Microsoft operating systems underneath, though they are certainly branching out more. Microsoft generally supports Apple devices, including Lync for devices like the iPad or the iPhone. There is less support for Android devices. The company isn't prepared at this point to provide mobile devices and also isn't in a position as yet to dictate a specific platform for

FIGURE 12.2 Microsoft Office 365 Communication Options

Used with permission from Microsoft.

FIGURE 12.3 Microsoft Sharepoint Communication

Used with permission from Microsoft.

its users. As a result, the decisions that get made should be as inclusive as possible, while still offering what is necessary to the company in a secure manner.

There are also several additional benefits that Google offers us that we don't get with Microsoft. The first is that we can use our Google account across multiple services using OpenID/OAuth. In addition, using our OpenID and Google Marketplace, we can add applications to our account that have been developed by third-party developers. Since they have developed these apps for the Google Marketplace, you don't have to go through the process of creating an account with them, you just use your Google account that we created. We can also protect our reputation by using Sender Policy Framework (SPF) and DomainKeys Identified Mail (DKIM) to prove that mail from our domain is really from our domain. Google supports both SPF and DKIM. Mail servers that support those should verify that messages from our domain have the correct information before accepting the message. If it doesn't, it's likely a spoofed message and might be malicious in nature.

The company used register.com in order to register the domain name cloudroy. com and then went through the signup process at Google. Google would also have registered the domain for us at an additional charge on top of the monthly or annual

Google Apps

Products

Accounting & Finance

Admin Tools

Calendar & Scheduling

Customer Management

Document Management

Productivity

Project Management

Sales & Marketing

Security & Compliance

Workflow

EDU

Professional Services

Archiving & Discovery
Implementation

Custom Application
Development

Google Analytics

Medium-Large Business
Implementation

Small Business
Implementation

Support & Managed Services

Training & Change
Management

EDU Specialists

FIGURE 12.4 Google App Marketplace

Google and the Google logo are registered trademarks of Google Inc., used with permission.

charge for the service. I should say that the charge for the service is a per user charge. Google helpfully walked through the process of setting all of the correct Domain Name System (DNS) records, including a text (TXT) record indicating to Google that I did own the domain name I indicated that I did. In the process of setting up the corporate account, Google provides pointers to additional apps that can be added to the account. As noted above, once you have your Google account, you can use it to authenticate to the Google partners offering applications providing a lot of different functionality. You can see a list of the categories in Figure 12.4.

Not everyone is created entirely equally. Just because there is an app that Google offers to a business doesn't mean the business wants users to be able to make use of it. Every app can be disabled across the business account by the administrator. Additionally, each app may have a number of other settings restricting access. One good example of that is Google Drive that can be used to store information. There are a lot of reasons why you may want to restrict what someone may be able to do with the files stored in their Google Drive and the account administrator can configure settings within Google Drive to prevent someone from sharing information outside of the organization. This can be used to prevent corporate espionage or the accidental loss of other sensitive information. Of course, I say accidental but that's really just to be sensitive. In actuality, as we've discussed previously, these cloud storage accounts can be used to exfiltrate a lot of data from an organization. You can see the different settings available for Google Drive in Figure 12.5.

While we've talked about the different settings available for Google Drive, all of the Google Apps available have similar settings. Calendar has sharing settings, including whether information can be shared with outsiders. Calendar also allows you to define resources that can be shared like conference rooms and projectors. Once you have these resources created, users can make use of them in their calendar appointments. Gmail, similarly, has a number of settings including the ability to allow users to set their own themes. These themes would be used in the Web interface. You can also allow users to set delegates. Gmail also has an extensive set of options for protecting your users and your organization from malicious e-mail, including spam. One of the problems with spam filtering is that there are regularly good e-mail messages that end up caught in spam filters. The administrator of the company account has the ability to make adjustments to the spam filters as well as a number of other security options.

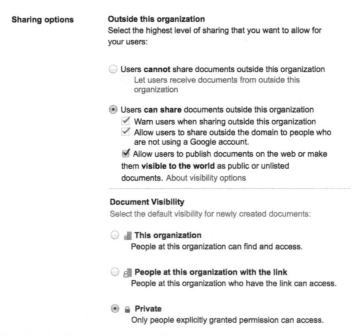

FIGURE 12.5 Sharing Options with Google Drive

Google and the Google logo are registered trademarks of Google Inc., used with permission.

Gmail also has one security function that's very useful and, while it's becoming more popular, still hasn't been implemented nearly as often as it should be. Google has the ability to perform two-factor authentication and a Google admin can allow or disallow two-factor authentication on accounts. In Google's case, your mobile phone would be used as the second factor. Text messages with an authentication code would be sent to your phone that would be further proof, above the password, that you were who you said you were. Gmail admins can also force the use of encryption when connecting to Google servers to get mail.

Often, e-mail is accessed from a mobile device. When people are on the road or anywhere away from their desk, they may be inclined to access their e-mail from their phone just to keep in touch. Google has very solid capabilities for remotely managing capabilities for phones. This is similar to Microsoft's ActiveSync technology. Mobile devices can be forced to use passwords and encrypt storage, along with a number of other settings, some of which can be seen in Figure 12.6.

One thing to be aware of when signing up for Google Apps, though, is that one way Google keeps prices low for their services is by using its users to sell to its primary customers—advertisers. Google makes the majority of its money selling targeted ads to businesses. Anyone using e-mail, storage, or other services provides information to Google about what they like and are interested in so ads that are interesting to that user can be targeted to them. When your users make use of Google's e-mail, they could be served up ads or at least targeted references to other

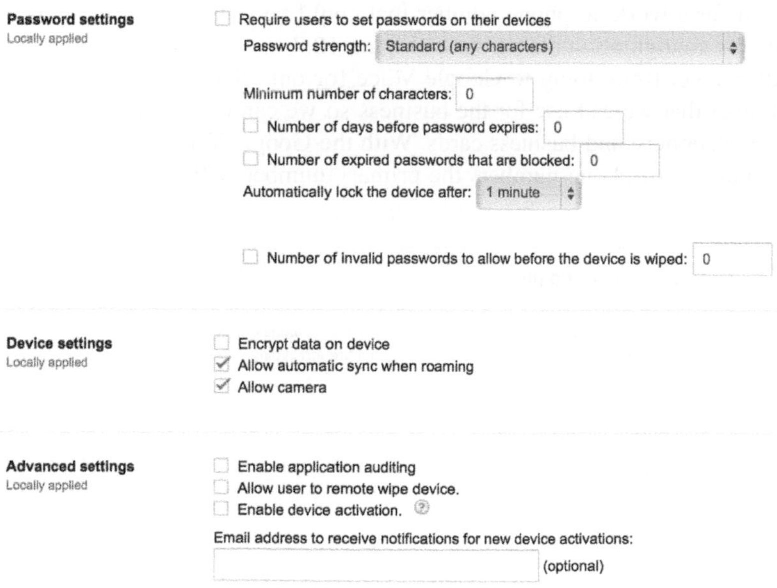

Password settings
Locally applied

☐ Require users to set passwords on their devices
Password strength: Standard (any characters) ⬍

Minimum number of characters: 0
☐ Number of days before password expires: 0
☐ Number of expired passwords that are blocked: 0
Automatically lock the device after: 1 minute ⬍

☐ Number of invalid passwords to allow before the device is wiped: 0

Device settings
Locally applied

☐ Encrypt data on device
☑ Allow automatic sync when roaming
☑ Allow camera

Advanced settings
Locally applied

☐ Enable application auditing
☐ Allow user to remote wipe device.
☐ Enable device activation. ②
Email address to receive notifications for new device activations:

(optional)

FIGURE 12.6 Google Settings for Mobile Device Access

Google and the Google logo are registered trademarks of Google Inc., used with permission.

services. Using the Google business e-mail hasn't shown me ads as yet through several days, it does show Google+ pages for related businesses. Google does currently say that Google Apps for Business is ad free, though that's no guarantee that they will remain ad free.

Telephony

We've talked about telephony. More specifically, we've talked about mobile phones. Everyone has one. We are going to assume that everyone in the business initially has their own mobile phone. Since everyone has their own phone, it may not make much sense for people to also have desk phones with an additional phone number, especially considering the percentage of the people who may be on the road. There are a number of ways of providing remote access to people who are not located at the corporate headquarters where a private branch exchange (PBX) may be located.

A PBX, though, can cost a lot of money and while there are low-cost options for a PBX, those can take a lot of maintenance. Again, we are back to the issue of either having to hire an administrator for these sorts of issues or taking away from the primary job function of another employee. Fortunately, there is a better idea. Again, we are going to turn to Google for a solution. In 2007, Google acquired a company called GrandCentral. The reason for the acquisition was to provide some additional voice services for Google. In 2009, Google launched Google Voice. Google Voice offered a way to get one phone number that could follow you no matter where you went. When you enroll for a new number with Google Voice, you will be asked for a working phone number that could be used to forward calls to. You can see the configuration dialog box in Figure 12.7.

What do we get from going to Google Voice for our telephony needs? We get a single number that we can use for the business so we can post it on the Web site as well as on stationery and business cards. With the Google Voice number, we can configure a number of phone numbers the primary number will attempt to ring to.

Add a forwarding phone   Help

Before choosing a Google Voice number, please add a forwarding phone that will ring when that number is called. You can add more forwarding phones later.

Phone Number   8026580001

Phone Type   Mobile

« Back   Continue »

FIGURE 12.7 Adding Forwarding Number to Google Voice

We could easily rotate the recipients of calls to the primary number through the employees so no one would have to take the responsibility full time and if the calls were routed to cell phones, the primary number could be answered no matter where the person was located. We could also have a backup callee just to ensure calls get routed correctly.

If no one is able to answer the phone, it will roll to voice mail hosted with Google. This voice mail can be accessed through the Web easily since calls get placed in a Google Voice mailbox. Even better, though, the voice mail will get transcribed and the resulting message will get sent to an e-mail address. Unlike a traditional phone number on the Public Switched Telephone Network (PSTN), the Google Voice number can also receive text messages and those text messages can be forwarded to e-mail addresses as well.

We do have a problem, however. If the Google Voice number is forwarded to the cell phones of employees, how would the employee know when to answer the phone as themselves and when to answer as though it were a business call? You can see in Figure 12.8 that Google has an answer for that. When a call comes into your Google Voice number, you can have Google leave the initiating caller information intact so the originating number shows up in your caller ID or you can have Google change the caller ID information to look as though the call is coming from your Google Voice number. If the call is coming from the Google Voice number, you know it's a call to the company phone number and you should answer it as such by indicating to the caller that they have reached the company that owns the phone number.

We may be able to get a few numbers that could be routed to the correct department like technical support or sales. You can also see from Figure 12.8 that calls

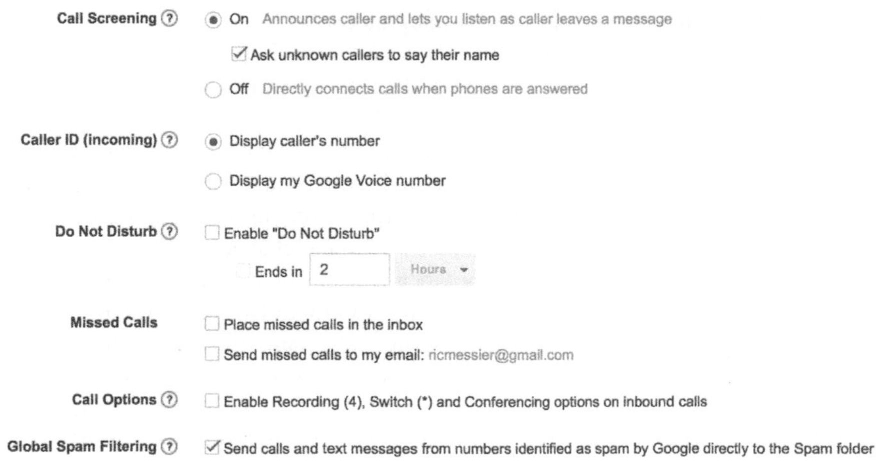
Call Screening
On Announces caller and lets you listen as caller leaves a message
Ask unknown callers to say their name
Off Directly connects calls when phones are answered
Caller ID (incoming)
Display caller's number
Display my Google Voice number
Do Not Disturb
Enable "Do Not Disturb"
Ends in 2
Hours
Missed Calls
Place missed calls in the inbox
Send missed calls to my email: ricmessier@gmail.com
Call Options
Enable Recording (4), Switch (*) and Conferencing options on inbound calls
Global Spam Filtering
Send calls and text messages from numbers identified as spam by Google directly to the Spam folder

FIGURE 12.8 Call Handling Options with Google Voice

Google and the Google logo are registered trademarks of Google Inc., used with permission.

coming in from Google Voice can be recorded. This could be helpful in the case of a support call. You know the drill from calling any customer support line, whether it's technical support or your bank or credit card company or a number of other businesses. They tell you that calls may be monitored for quality control. You may not want to record them solely for quality control in the sense of reviewing calls to ensure customers are handled appropriately, though it's a good reason for recording them. You may also want to record them to ensure all of the information has been taken down correctly. It may be difficult to listen fast enough to keep up with the information a caller is providing, especially if you are trying to take notes on a technical support issue.

Storage

This issue becomes much easier in light of what we've implemented above. While we may have to make use of some other solutions depending on who we are working with for partners and vendors, our primary storage solution is going to be Google Drive. In Google's case, Drive is tied strongly to their office suite of applications. Any document that is created using one of the office applications is automatically stored in Google Drive. Once it's in Google Drive, we have a lot of options when it comes to collaboration. There was a time when the de facto way of sharing files was by sending them in e-mail. What you ended up with was a lot of copies of one file taking up storage space when storage space was probably at a bit of a premium. On top of that, you ended up with version control problems. Everyone had a copy of the document and anyone could make changes to it and then redistribute. In the meantime, they have probably changed the file name to indicate they have made some changes. Along with the version control, you have no way of knowing what changes have been integrated.

A solution for this is to use an online document repository, preferably where the repository itself can handle synchronizing changes live when multiple people are in the document. There have been companies that have tried to go after the document repository market with some amount of success but unless you are in the market for that sort of thing, those companies and their products may not be familiar to you. Google Drive, together with Google Apps, ends up being an online document repository where the most efficient way to make changes is live, in real time because the document is designed to be opened with the online Docs, Slides, and Sheets applications provided by Google. With a Google Doc, for example, if two people were trying to edit the same document at the same time, everything would happen in real time and be indicated by a unique cursor with that user's initials. It's possible to overwrite something someone else is doing while they are doing it, but it would almost have to be deliberate because you'd see two cursors in the same place at the same time.

This does, though, require people to be online all the time, which may not always be convenient. You may be traveling and not have a network connection, whether it's in an airplane, a cab, or a train. You may just be somewhere that doesn't have particularly reliable Internet like your parent's house over holidays. No matter what the circumstance, there are just times when you can't be online, but you may want to make changes to a document. You can do this with any document you store on Google Drive, including the Google Apps documents. In order to enable offline access to documents, you would need to install the Google Drive app on your computer and also have your offline document access enabled for your account. Once that's done, you can make changes and when you get back online, your changes are re-synced back to your Google Drive. You can see some of the settings for Google Drive in Figure 12.9, where you can enable offline access to users in your company.

Another advantage to using Google Drive is the ability to audit a Google Doc. When you enable auditing, you get a record of who has looked at a document and also who has made changes to it. This may be very helpful for a number of reasons. One immediate thought is if a document becomes altered in a way that wasn't wanted or expected, you could track down who made the changes. What you do with them once you have tracked them down is of course another matter. However, it can be useful to know whether they were making the changes to fulfill an expectation or if they made the changes accidentally.

With Google Drive and Google Apps, we lose the versioning problem. It also seems like we fix the issue of transmitting and protecting documents. Our Google admin has the ability to determine with whom documents can be shared. We might

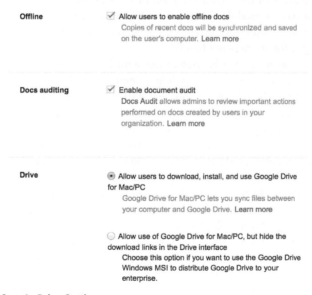

FIGURE 12.9 Google Drive Settings

Google and the Google logo are registered trademarks of Google Inc., used with permission.

set our account up so that no one can share outside of our own organization to keep our data loss to a minimum. After all, everything is stored in a repository that we have control over. It is still possible to print documents in hard copy and it's also possible to print or save to PDF. Beyond that, we can store everything in our Google Drive on our local system as well. However, the Google admin at our company has the ability to either allow or deny users from installing the software onto their PC that would allow for data to be mirrored and synced between the cloud storage and the local storage. Again, though, this may be an illusion that you are protecting information since there is no reason someone couldn't keep a copy of the same information in a different format. This can be another case where having auditing enabled could be useful since you'll get an audit trail of who accessed the documents in the Drive and when they accessed them. While it may not prevent data theft, it can at least provide some information about who was looking at a particular document and when.

Human resources

When it comes to human resources (HR), you want a place to store critical and sensitive information about your employees. In our scenario, there aren't a lot of people and the majority of them early on are partners. This doesn't mean, though, that you don't need to keep track of dates of hire and any salary information as well as keeping a record of benefits. There is a lot of data that would be kept about employees. You also need a way to write checks for employees and keep track of payroll. While accounting software for small business will often take care of payroll or at least have a module for it, you will also want to keep a record of things like paystubs and a variety of other information related to employment and pay that the accounting software may not handle.

Eventually, you may also be concerned with keeping track of attendance and also keep a record of time cards for hourly employees like interns or temporary workers. In order to handle all of this, we will want a vendor for our HR needs. Kronos started in the late 1970s by a Massachusetts Institute of Technology graduate, who was looking for a way to keep track of employee time transactions. Currently, Kronos offers a wide range of HR-related applications in addition to the time management they started with. While they don't currently have a Google app that could be attached to your Google business account, as is the case for other needs we have, they do have a cloud-based solution that may be quite a bit more cost-effective than bringing in a more cumbersome implementation to run locally. Kronos also has apps for mobile devices.

When it comes to HR information, you want to be very careful about the vendor you choose. This is one reason I ended up selecting Kronos. In addition to their history and reputation, they make a point of explaining all of the security measures they use to ensure your data is protected. While no one can be absolutely assured of avoiding a breach of their security, the fact that Kronos takes it seriously enough to explain it to potential customers is a step in the right direction.

Project management

Earlier in the book, I mentioned a software as a service (SaaS) provider called SmartSheet. SmartSheet will provide you the ability to do project management and resource management in the cloud. This will help when you have your resources scattered all over the place geographically. When you are in multiple time zones or regularly on the road, it's far easier to check a Web site than it is to load up your project management software and through the Virtual Private Network (VPN) either check in with a project management server or, worse, pull the latest file from a shared server. Using SaaS also keeps you from having to clutter your system with additional software, not to mention keeping track of licenses.

While today's desktop computing systems are very powerful and generally come with a large amount of memory, developers still generally like to have all of their computing resources at hand for things like compiles or maybe needing to run emulators of mobile devices if they are developing apps for Android or iPhone/iPad, as examples. Having to keep project management software running in order to stay up to date with the latest project plan and update status can take away resources. Typically someone would have a browser open anyway so another tab or window open to a project management site wouldn't be nearly as big an issue, though it will still take memory resources to keep that tab open.

Looking at Figure 12.10, you can see just how feature rich the application is. In addition to the standard Gantt charts you would expect in project management software, you can also see tabs for discussions and collaboration available in the application. You could use these tabs and features to facilitate communication outside

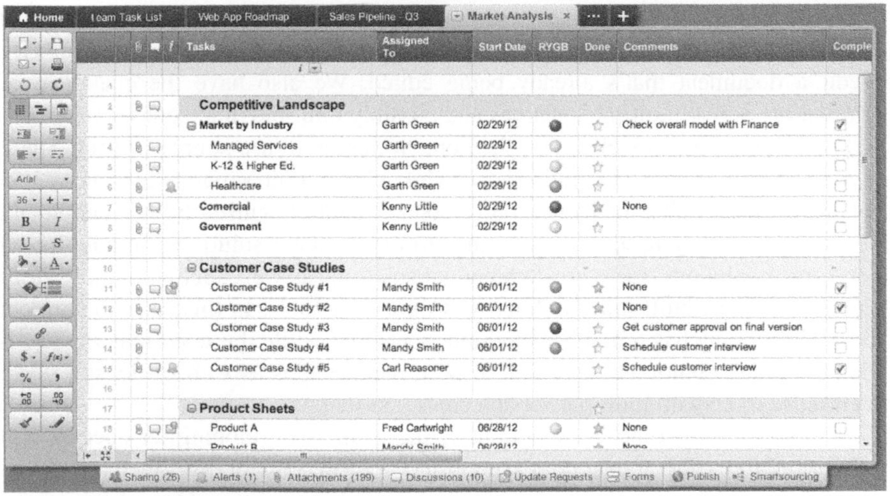

FIGURE 12.10 SmartSheet.com Gantt Chart

Used with permission from SmartSheet.com.

of regular project meetings and, using asynchronous, shared communication like a discussion on a Web page, you may be able to keep your project management meetings moving faster, getting developers back to work faster which generally keeps them happier from my experience.

We talked earlier about making use of Google and adding apps from the Google Marketplace to your Google account so they are more immediately available for you. SmartSheet is also available as an app from the Google Marketplace. Signing up for it will give you a 30-day free trial so you can see how well it works for your business before starting to pay. Even if you don't add the app to your Google account so it's available as a link on your Google pages, you can still make use of your Google account to register with SmartSheet.com. They will authenticate you using your Google account and pull your information in as necessary to make registering even easier. While it's not quite single sign-on, it can be convenient and as long as you trust Google to keep your account information safe, it's probably better than creating a lot of accounts at a lot of businesses that don't have the resources Google does when it comes to data security.

Source control

The moment you have more than one person on a software project, it's best to start thinking about adding in source control. This is the same problem as the versioning issue discussed earlier with documents. The biggest difference is that when we are talking about software developers, they may be in and out of source documents on a regular basis. In that case, one developer may be trying to edit the document while another developer is also trying to edit it. Sometimes, it's just to add a line or a library reference so it's a quick in and out, but that quick in and out can be enough to kill one of the edits. There are other ways of ensuring that someone doesn't try to edit a document that's already being edited. We also have the challenge of coordinating across multiple locations and possibly multiple time zones.

The solution, and a well-established one at that, is to use source control. There are a lot of source control solutions and while Concurrent Versions System (CVS) was previously a well-established source control solution, currently Subversion and Git are more widely used when it comes to open source solutions. In addition to open source solutions, there are commercial solutions as well, including those from Microsoft that are built into the Microsoft developer tools. In this case, the project we are developing has a number of components and while the team may be developing Windows solutions, there will also be mobile apps as well. It doesn't make much sense to go with multiple version control systems.

While there are some great options if the team is developing an open source application, like code google.com and Github or even SourceForge, there are fewer cross-platform solutions that are available for commercial use. One of the ones I found was CloudForge. CloudForge offers both Subversion and Git for version control systems, making them a good solution across tool sets. CloudForge also has very nice pricing options. If all you want is to have your project hosted, you don't pay anything. If you want to have access control and backups, you'll pay more. This means that smaller teams and projects can get started for nothing and as the team grows and its needs get more complex, you'll pay for the extra features.

Customer relations

Early on, customer relations will be very important and while our initial scenario suggests that only a couple of people will be touching customers, it's best to be prepared for others to be added to the mix. Earlier, we discussed Salesforce.com for a customer relationship management (CRM) solution and that is certainly a well-established solution. Just for a little perspective, however, let's take a look at another CRM solution. Sugar CRM is a solution that has a Community Edition that can be used for free on your own equipment. There are a number of options if you want support or if you want to have your data stored in the cloud.

In addition to cloud support with Sugar CRM, you also get an app in the Google App Marketplace that can be pulled into your Google business account for your users to use. While Salesforce.com doesn't have a similar app, there are a lot of apps you can get that will provide some level of integration between Google/Gmail and Salesforce.com. This may or may not be required, but integration with Google can be very helpful as a single portal to access all of your primary business applications. In the case of this scenario, we're going to go with Sugar CRM, in part because they have a community edition and it's nice to give back to the community.

CONCLUSION

Less than a year ago, I was looking for a solution for e-mail, calendar, and Web hosting. I had two out of the three already, but having a reliable calendar solution is so critical as I'm now spread across multiple devices and some sync solutions between desktops and mobile devices don't work so well. Using a cloud solution to synchronize with seemed like the best solution and Google didn't work well for what I wanted to use it for. I ended up going with Microsoft Office 365 because of the reliable calendar and also getting Office applications as well as Lync. At the time, I did some reading about Google's apps but I was so turned off by the Google office suite that I didn't want to be bound by that.

The mistake I made at the time was not to go for a trial of Google Apps for Business. Their marketing information available on the Web site doesn't do justice to the capabilities that Google offers. This is not to suggest that Microsoft is a bad solution but, as seems to be typical with Google, users of Google Apps get a lot of control and flexibility. When it comes to security features, particularly those associated with e-mail, Google has some additional capability that either isn't available with Microsoft or isn't as obvious.

Choosing a messaging provider is just a starting point, however. The business has a lot of needs and, again, in Google's case, we get integration with the account we have there. This may or may not be an important feature but it can certainly be handy to have one place to manage accounts for all of your employees. It's also helpful to have all of the control from an administrative perspective in one place. A single point of failure can be a problem and lots of providers have been breached in recent months and years but Google has a lot of resources they can put into protecting information, including your accounts. Also, Google's use of two-factor authentication is a very enticing option when it comes to protecting login accounts.

Summary

Here are some ideas you should take away from this chapter:

- Google has a lot of security options, including support for protecting e-mail as well as protecting your reputation from e-mail spoofing.
- Going with Google as our primary provider gives us not only messaging and Web hosting but also provides a single source for managing credentials.
- All of the major business applications you would need to get a business started have cloud-based providers.
- Most of your business application needs integrate with Google. This may just be using OpenID/Oauth with your Google account, but it may also be tight integration with Google where the app is available through the Google App Marketplace.

Index

Note: Page numbers followed by *"b", "f"* and *"t"* refer to boxes, figures and tables respectively.

Printed and bound by CPI Group (UK) Ltd, Croydon, CR0 4YY

03/10/2024

01040327-0011